Spaces for Criticism
Shifts in Contemporary Art Discourses

Thijs Lijster, Suzana Milevska, Pascal Gielen, Ruth Sonderegger (eds.)

Antennae
Valiz, Amsterdam

Spaces for Criticism

Shifts in Contemporary Art Discourses

Thijs Lijster, Suzana Milevska,
Pascal Gielen, Ruth Sonderegger
(eds.)

With contributions by

Luc Boltanski
Sabeth Buchmann
Robin Celikates
Hans D. Christ
Ingrid Commandeur
Katy Deepwell
Iris Dressler
Sonja Eismann
John Ellingsworth
Pascal Gielen
Daniel Givens
Max Jorge Hinderer Cruz
Christian Höller
Ines Kleesattel
Vida Knežević
Thijs Lijster
Ivana Marjanović
Suzana Milevska
Dan Perjovschi
Jorinde Seijdel
Ruth Sonderegger
Terre Thaemlitz
Niels Van Tomme

Contents

11 **Introduction**
A Topology of Criticism
Thijs Lijster, Suzana Milevska, Pascal Gielen, Ruth Sonderegger

Part 1
Spatio-Temporal Shifts

25 **Between Criticism and Critique**
Towards an 'Espacement' of Criticism
Pascal Gielen & Thijs Lijster

45 **Elsewhere**
Helicopters and Safe Places of Criticism
Max Jorge Hinderer Cruz

53 **Spaces of New Social and Art Criticism and Their Re-Conditioning**
A Few Theses from the Post-Yugoslav Context
Vida Knežević & Ivana Marjanović (Kontekst Collective)

77 **The Apparatus of the Mind**
John Ellingsworth

Part 2
Institutional and Professional Shifts

93 **'Un-Common Sense'**
Social Critique and the Struggle over Commonality
Christian Höller

111 **Criticism, Critique, and Capitalism**
Luc Boltanski in Conversation with Robin Celikates and Thijs Lijster

129 **Rethinking Institution and Critique**
Hans D. Christ & Iris Dressler

151 **Involvements in Art Criticism**
As We Experience It and as We Claim It
Sabeth Buchmann
Sonja Eismann
Ines Kleesattel
Ruth Sonderegger

Part 3
Media and Identity Shifts

171 **Feminist Critique**
Open and Critical Enquiry
A Conversation between Katy Deepwell and Suzana Milevska

193 **Information as a Site of Conflict and a Site of Critique**
Jorinde Seijdel

207 **Queerness in a Situational Sense**
Terre Thaemlitz in Conversation with Daniel Givens and Niels Van Tomme

231 **The Beautiful Risk of Criticality**
Ingrid Commandeur

251 **Contributors**

261 **Index**

267 **Colophon**

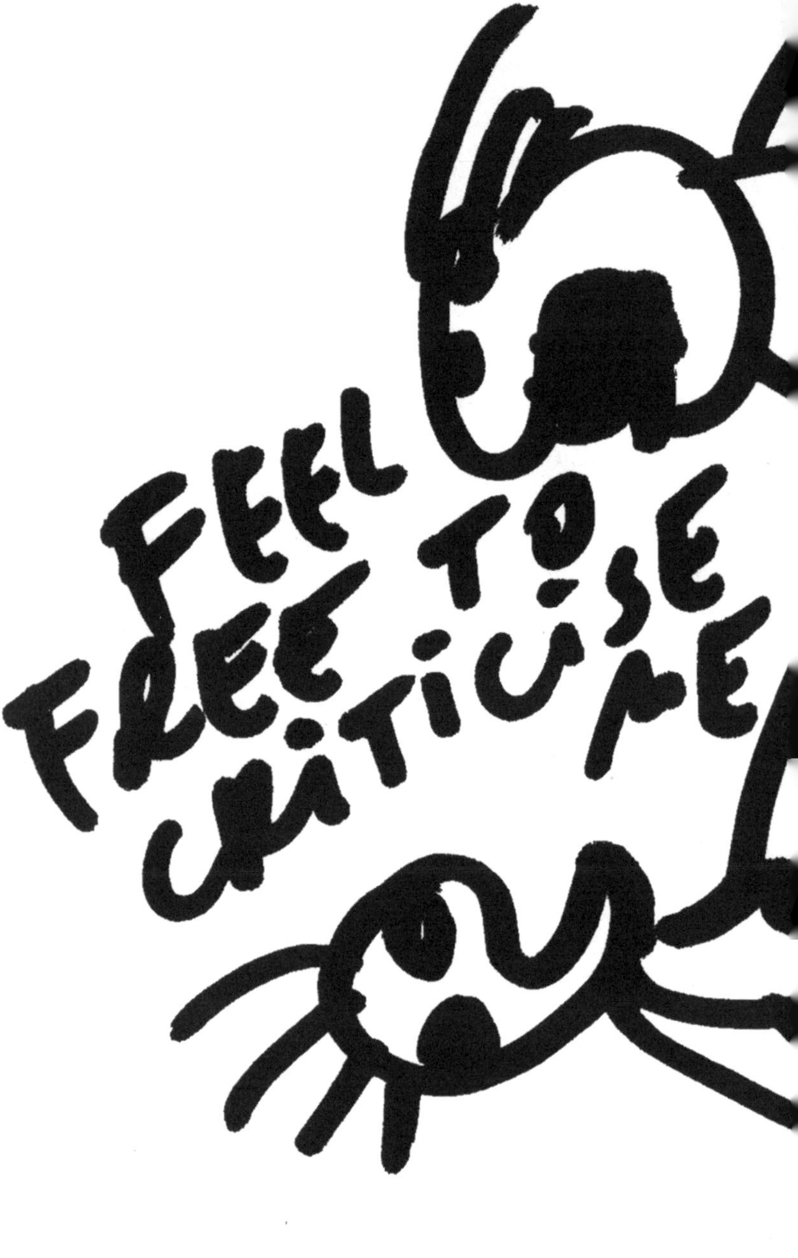
FEEL FREE TO CRITICISE ME

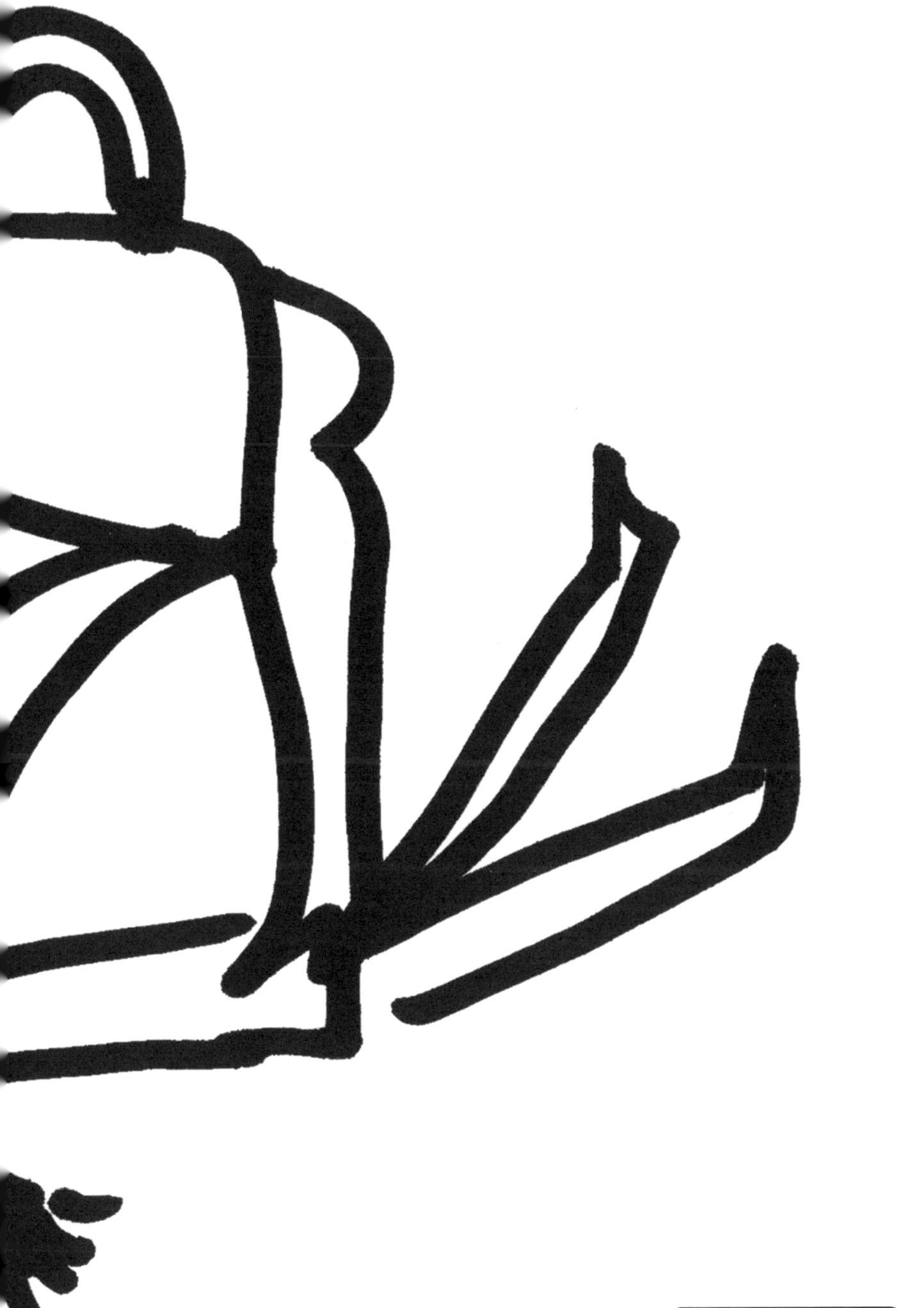

Dan Perjovschi

Introduction
A Topology of Criticism

Thijs Lijster
Suzana Milevska
Pascal Gielen
Ruth Sonderegger

> What, in the end, makes advertisements so superior to criticism? Not what the moving red neon sign says – but the fiery pool reflecting it in the asphalt.
> Walter Benjamin – *This Space for Rent*

In recent years, many critics, theorists and philosophers have argued that our time witnesses a 'crisis' of art criticism, or perhaps even the 'death' of the critic.[1] Critics seem to suffer from an identity crisis – since it is no longer evident whether criticism's primary task is evaluation, judgment, explanation or merely noticing – as well as from a sense of aimlessness, as traditional critical frameworks (Marxism, psychoanalysis, deconstruction) allegedly have dissolved into one big 'critical mess'. Moreover, the authority of the art critic has lost its self-evidence. Increasingly, the public either ignores or contests the 'professional' judgment of the critic and prefers to express and share its own opinions on websites and weblogs. At the same time, mainstream media has exchanged criticism for human-interest interviews with artists, and more promotional announcement of art events.

Contemporary art, however, hardly speaks for itself. On the contrary: never before has an understanding of art been more dependent on concepts, theoretical frameworks, art historical contexts, et cetera. One would expect, therefore, that the critic still has an important task as a translator and mediator between artist, art work and public. It seems unclear, however, how the critic might address this task, and how he or she might once again be recognized as a figure of authority. Today, the classic critic is overshadowed by curators and artists who have learned to reflect and theorize themselves.

Spaces for Criticism does not go along with the pessimism that has dominated the recent debates on art criticism. Instead of adding another swan song of criticism to the chorus, it wants to explore new ways in which, and especially new *spaces* where art critics might interact with the public, works of art, artists and scholars. The title of this book is inspired by an aphorism written by the German critic Walter Benjamin, 'This Space for Rent' (1928). In it, he argues that it is foolish to lament the decay of criticism. In Benjamin's view, the 'space' of the traditional critic was vacant, which means that we should reinvent the practice of criticism. This is precisely what *Spaces for Criticism* sets out to do: to point at new forms of, and new spaces for art criticism.

As the title indicates, the book is first and foremost a topology of criticism. Whereas most recent discussions have revolved around the question 'what is criticism?', this book wants to provide answers to the question: 'where is criticism?' While many have argued that criticism is losing ground, some more positive voices herald a 'golden age of criticism' with the rise of Internet criticism and art blogs.[2] Instead of the 'death' of criticism, we suggest that what we are witnessing is rather a 'displacement': criticism has moved on, and now takes place in different spaces and on different stages.[3] This is a displacement not only with regard to media (from journalism to blogs, catalogues, press releases, et cetera), but also a displacement in the geographical and institutional sense. The professional art world is global now, and even if many countries and classes do not have access to this 'global art scene', they still find themselves having to relate to it. Criticism today comes from many different directions and from diverse cultural and historical backgrounds. Closely related to this is the shift from institutional critique to a critique of criticism itself as an institution.[4] Institutionalized gender and racial borders within the practice of criticism in the professional art field are contested again and again. The walls that modernity raised between the life worlds we used to live in (and this 'we' is of course itself subject to contestation) are eroding, so that it becomes increasingly difficult to distinguish between private and public life, art and economy, aesthetics and politics, criticism and critique.

This raises all kinds of questions: do these new spaces for criticism demand new ways for critics to address their public, and how has this affected their practice? What is the responsibility of the critic towards his or her public, towards the artist, and towards the work of art? What about those art critical texts that are part and parcel of (the press releases of) exhibitions in public spaces and galleries? What does it mean that most art critics see their critical engagement as one of the many elements of a precarious life? But one can also ask the reverse question: is art criticism appropriate in all spaces, or are there places and spaces that criticism should stay away from? For instance, does the increasing focus on theory and criticism, including self-criticism, in the educational space run the risk of having a disciplining, if not normalizing, effect? And what to think of the place of the critic in the market and as an employee of art institutions, now that the critic becomes increasingly dependent on commissioned writing? Furthermore, many have pointed out that the traditional borders between critic and artist, curator, and dealer are fading.[5] Should this be welcomed or does this also bring risks with it? What about the critics' independence? Do they have to develop new strategies to keep their autonomy? Or, was that independency a myth to begin with?

For *Spaces for Criticism*, we invited critics and art theorists to reflect on their practices, their social function, and their place within society. Bringing together critics from several disciplines within the visual and performing arts, academic and non-academic, the book provides an overview of actual practices and possibilities. Moreover, *Spaces for Criticism* addresses often neglected issues such as the role of feminist art criticism, the availability and role of art criticism produced in marginalized cultures and languages, and the repercussions of postcolonial critique on the state of art criticism. Many contributions also 'perform' a shift in criticism, by opting for a text in the form of a conversation or collaboration, instead of assuming the authorial role of the solitary critic.

This book is aimed at critics, artists, researchers, students, and all those who are interested in the current state of art criticism or concerned about its future. Combining timely analyses of the contemporary 'state of the art criticism' and inspiring visions for what might lie ahead, *Spaces for Criticism* attempts to set the agenda for the debate on the function and value of a lively practice of art criticism.

The first part of the book is devoted to 'Spatio-temporal shifts', and opens with philosopher Thijs Lijster and sociologist Pascal Gielen, who relate contemporary developments in art criticism to the 'time-space compression' that characterizes modernity. The shift from modern to contemporary art in the 1980s comes with both a de-historicization and de-territorialization of criticism: the influence of the historian-as-critic is increasingly overshadowed by those of philosophers, sociologists and other theorists, while the internationalization of art discourses threatens to bury criticism under thick layers of woolly jargon. These shifts tend to push criticism to the border of the understandable, to an ephemeral murmuring that almost nobody understands. But although Lijster and Gielen consider this development critically, they also argue that these new theoretical sources might generate the discourse that allows us to step out of the expert field of traditional criticism, thus creating a new space for criticism. The challenge of the new intellectual consists in finding a bridging link between criticism and critique, and so, between art and society.

Max Jorge Hinderer Cruz's contribution 'Elsewhere. Helicopters and Safe Places of Criticism', starts out with a reflection on the ideologies and exclusion produced by what is called the globalized art world. In his view, this art world and its acclaimed globalization process is not facing a crisis of criticism at all, to the contrary. Hinderer Cruz rather diagnoses an overproduction of criticism. Moreover, he contends that the so-called crisis of criticism might be nothing but art criticism's own constant self-evaluation process with which it confirms and contributes to the larger neoliberal framework.

Vida Knežević and Ivana Marjanović's text stems out from their critical curatorial practice and is based on their constringent experiences as founders and members of the independent curatorial collective and gallery 'Kontekst' (based in Belgrade, Serbia). They argue for an art criticism that would embed postcolonial theory, art and activist practice, as well as a profound curatorial engagement, which in their view is the indispensable response to the specific cultural regional 'context'. In their text they discuss several related artistic and curatorial projects from South-Eastern Europe and the Balkans, calling for 'new criticism' that would encompass the complex socio-political and economic conditions in the post-socialist and post-traumatic context and would strategically change the work frames and perspectives via 'contra-hegemony relations of collaboration'.

In 'The Apparatus of the Mind', theatre critic John Ellingsworth describes his own quest and considerations to achieve a position as a critic. Ellingsworth writes about his 'hands-on' style, his experiences with making a magazine and his difficulties of making money from his job(s). Just as the position of many artists and other creative workers, the job of the critic is indeed a precarious one. Ellingsworth observes how critics often try to solve their financial problems by working together with presenters, and sometimes even the marketing department of festivals and theatres. This of course affects the critic's independence. But Ellingsworth also shows us more hopeful spaces where the critic can keep his independence, such as education and the work of documentation.

In analysing the situation of art criticism, it is advisable to draw inspiration from recent debates within the field of social theory and philosophy concerning the concept of (ideology) critique.[6] This is what happens in the second part of this book, 'Institutional and Professional Shifts'. This part opens with Christian Höller's contribution. His essay '"Un-Common Sense". Social Critique and the Struggle over Commonality' contextualizes the concerns of this volume within the ongoing recent debates in respect of commons and commoning in the context of neoliberal societies as an 'age of individualisation' (Jeremy Gilbert). More precisely, Höller offers a profound discussion regarding the complex relation between critique as a concept and the issues of 'commons', 'collective' and communities. Starting from Stuart Hall's and Alan O'Shea's quest for a meaningful relation between social critique and the realm of received ideas, popular 'doxa' and 'common sense', he positions his analysis in contrast to the overwhelming manipulation of 'common sense'. By recalling Antonio Gramsci's understanding of common sense as not 'critical and coherent but disjointed and episodic', and Zygmunt Bauman's pointing to the tension between the tendency of homogenization of 'common sense' from above and its fragmentation from below, Höller prompts a closer look at dissensus, competitive individualism, and other critical potentials of the newly emerged collectivities and commonalities.

Höller's text is followed by an interview with French sociologist Luc Boltanski, one of the most original voices in contemporary critical social theory. In his sociological work of the 1980s and 1990s, Boltanski famously abandoned the traditional 'bird's eye view' of the social or cultural critic and replaced it with the 'actor's perspective'. In his recent *On Critique*, however, he argues for a return to the 'sense of totality', which artists and scientists can provide in different ways. In the interview conducted for this volume he talks about the relation between critique and criticism, and investigates the question how 'critical' criticism still is today, now that the 'domestic' regime of criticism has been replaced by a regime dominated by the market. Contemporary art discourses, he argues, suffer from the increasing influence of the market, and the difficulty of adding (economic) value to the very object of their critique.

Being the current directors of the Württembergischer Kunstverein Stuttgart (Germany), Iris Dressler and Hans Christ write about contemporary challenges of establishing critical art institutions. They address current tendencies of commissioning (artistic) critique in order to just sell it or use it for the promotion and valorization of the respective art institution. Despite the fact that said dangers are ubiquitous and pressing in the current art field, there are, in our view, only few representatives of art institutions that do work with them as openly as Dressler and Christ do. Their aim is to develop a form of institutional critique that is willing to learn from artistic practices (of institutional critique) without co-opting them. The curatorial experiments about which they write go as far as letting 'their' institution be invaded and taken over by 'unexpected guests' from the field of political activism. The drawing by Dan Perjovschi that we included in *Spaces for Criticism* was part of Dressler and Christ's exhibition *The Art of Not Being Governed Like That* with which they made room in the Würthembergische Kunstverein for the protests against 'Stuttgart 21', a huge railway and urban development project.

Coming from different disciplines, institutional backgrounds and generations, Sabeth Buchmann, Sonja Eismann, Ines Kleesattel and Ruth Sonderegger see their conversation as an experiment with polyphonic forms of performing art criticism. In doing so, they aim at questioning the figure of the strong, solitary (male) critic. In spite of and in light of current attempts to criticize institutional critique and art criticism because of their complicity with what they criticize, the participants of the discussion defend forms of engaged critical practices and plead for an art criticism that self-critically addresses its contested criticality instead of giving up on criticism. Their basic assumption is that the imperative to be critical, however problematic and ubiquitous, has neither corrupted all forms of artistic institutional critique nor all variants of critically writing and talking about contemporary art.

The third part of *Spaces for Criticism* is about how contemporary criticism shifts between different media and different identities, and how these shifts interrelate. In a conversation, Katy Deepwell and Suzana Milevska reflect on the specificities of the feminist critical discourse and contest the power relations in art theory, history of art and art criticism in the context of publishing and critical curating. Their arguments are based on their own curatorial, teaching and editorial practices and determined by their different cultural backgrounds (Deepwell is a journal editor and professor of art history from UK and Milevska is a curator, art theorist and art historian from Macedonia). They claim that, depending on various socio-political, cultural and media contexts, feminist critique requires and needs to inhabit various public spaces and media in order to make the necessary shifts in representation and evaluation of art and to overcome the existing hierarchies and privileges, based on gender, sexuality or class. They propose that such shifts within feminist criticism also enable substantial changes in art criticism in general and thus push its limits.

In her contribution 'Information as a Site of Conflict and a Site of Critique', theoretician and editor in chief of the onine platform Open!, Jorinde Seijdel, asks what the position of criticism could be in a digital and globalized information culture where people are continuously 'liking' activities and each other. Public criticism is undermined by an affirmative culture with prefabricated instruments of criticisms. But criticism can be revitalized in this condition by making the information flow into a 'site of conflict', by generating an 'illegality of information', as Seijdel writes.

The interview of Niels Van Tomme and Daniel Givens with DJ Terre Thaemlitz questions the border between criticism and critique, and this also touches upon the outline and condition of production of *Spaces of Criticism* itself. Being a queer DJ, Thaemlitz conceives of her own artistic work as a medium to criticize the economic structures surrounding art production, including art criticism and the discursive production that *Spaces for Criticism* is part of. Is what Thaemlitz says and does a form of art criticism?, the interviewers ask themselves in their introduction. Probably, this struggle over the definition of criticism is symptomatic for a practice that is searching for a new space. In any case, we can say that in her quest Thaemlitz is navigating between criticism and critique, and between art and social mechanisms in general.

In 'The Beautiful Risk of Criticality', Ingrid Commandeur investigates several attempts to revive criticism in the last decade. She finds Irit Rogoff's notion of 'criticality' the most inspiring. Whereas traditional critique entails an analysis of already existing meanings, criticality refers to a process in which 'meaning takes place as events unfold', not in isolation but as the result of a cooperation of different participants (e.g., artists, critics, curators, public). Criticality, Commandeur argues, is more apt for an art world that becomes increasingly interdisciplinary and interactive. To illustrate this she looks at experimental exhibition models of the early 1990s, and the way Dutch art critics responded to them.

Criticism, so it appears from the contributions to this volume, is constantly on the move, heading in different directions, assuming different roles and functions, and taking on different shapes. But if that is so, is it then still possible to say anything about what criticism should be, become, or do? Maybe we should take another look at Benjamin's provocative statement on advertisement and criticism, which we chose as an epigraph for this introduction: 'What, in the end, makes advertisements so superior to criticism? Not what the moving red neon sign says – but the fiery pool reflecting it in the asphalt.'[7] What did he mean by it? What he did *not* mean, for sure, was that criticism should turn into a form of advertisement, which is essentially affirmative. But one thing one can say about advertisement is that it is 'in the street', among the people, and that it can hit you when you least expect it. Perhaps criticism should adopt this performative force of advertisement – its ability to appeal to and reach out towards ever-new publics, to occupy new spaces – and deploy it as a counterforce against the uncritical and unquestioning nature of advertisement. Criticism is and should be part of the public sphere, and like that public sphere it is always in flux. This is not the same, of course, as swimming with the tide. On the contrary, if there is one thing all authors in this volume agree upon, it is that criticism should be thoroughly *critical*. That may seem like a truism, but in an age in which the art world increasingly becomes entangled with city branding and financial speculation it certainly is not. This is precisely why it is important for criticism to explore and occupy new spaces, in order to be, to paraphrase Benjamin once more, never consistent but always radical.

Thijs Lijster, Suzana Milevska,
Pascal Gielen, Ruth Sonderegger
Groningen, Vienna, Antwerp, 2015

Notes

1 See for instance Berger 1998, Elkins 2003, Rubinstein 2006, Newman and Elkins 2008.
2 See for instance Martha Schwendener's article 'What Crisis? Some Promising Futures for Art Criticism.' In: *The Village Voice,* January 7, 2009. For other references see Wuggenig 2012.
3 For the notion of a 'displacement' of both critique and its object, see Boltanski and Chiapello (1999).
4 See also Raunig and Ray 2009.
5 Groys 2008, Elkins and Newman 2008.
6 Jaeggi and Wesche 2009; Boltanski 2011; Birkenstock, Hinderer Cruz, Kastner, and Sonderegger 2013
7 Benjamin 1999, p. 476.

Bibliography

- Adorno, T. W. (1983). *Prisms,* transl. by S. and S. Weber, Cambridge MA: MIT Press.
- Benjamin, W. (1999). *Selected Writings, Volume 1, 1913-1926,* ed. M. W. Jennings. Cambridge MA: The Belknap Press of Harvard University Press.
- Berger, M. (ed.) (1998). *The Crisis of Criticism,* New York: New Press.
- Birkenstock, E., M. Hinderer Cruz, J. Kastner, and R. Sonderegger (eds.) (2013). *Kunst und Ideologiekritik nach '89 / Art and the Critique of Ideology after '89,* Köln: Walther König.
- Boltanski, L. (2011). *On Critique. A Sociology of Emancipation,* London: Polity.
- Boltanski, L. and E. Chiapello (2005). *The New Spirit of Capitalism,* London: Verso.
- Elkins, J. (2003). *What Happened to Art Criticism?,* Chicago: Prickly Paradigm.
- Elkins, J. and M. Newman (eds.) (2008). *The State of Art Criticism,* New York and London: Routledge.
- Groys, B. (2008). *Art Power,* Cambridge MA: MIT Press.
- Jaeggi, R., and T. Wesche (eds.) (2009). *Was ist Kritik?,* Frankfurt am Main: Suhrkamp.
- Raunig, G. and G. Ray (eds.) (2009). *Art and Contemporary Critical Practice. Reinventing Institutional Critique,* London: Mayfly.
- Rubinstein, R. (ed.) (2006). *Critical Mess. Art Critics on the State of their Practice,* Lenox MA: Hard Press Editions.
- Wuggenig, U. (2012). 'Krise der Kunstkritik?' in: H. Munder and U. Wuggenig (eds.) *Das Kunstfeld. Eine Studie über Akteure und Institutionen der zeitgenössischen Kunst,* Zürich: JRP/Ringier.

Part 1

Spatio-Temporal Shifts

Between Criticism and Critique

Towards an 'Espacement' of Criticism

Pascal Gielen & Thijs Lijster

In his essay 'The Storyteller' (1936) Walter Benjamin describes the loss of the traditional story. The storyteller was someone with a certain authority, based on experience, and was able to communicate this experience to an audience. Benjamin distinguished two archetypical storytellers: the 'trading seaman' and the 'settled tiller' (Benjamin, 1936 [2002: 144]). Both based their authority on a *distance*, in space, and time, respectively: the former had travelled far and wide and seen strange things, the latter had known many local people and knew many regional stories he had heard during his long life. That this oral tradition had disappeared was, of course, according to Benjamin, first of all because of the invention of printing, but journalism was even more to blame. The value of the traditional story was not based on the information it contained, but on the experience that was communicated through it. In the age of journalism, however, everyone has, at any time, more information than they care to have; the feeling of distance that was essential to the traditional story has disappeared. The result, says Benjamin, is that we may be fully informed, but have nothing to tell to each other anymore.

Could the same diagnosis also be true of art criticism? After all, the classic art critic can be described as either a 'trading seaman' or a 'settled tiller'. On the one hand there are the travel accounts of writers such as Stendhal, Goethe, Mme de Staël or Huysmans, who share their intense experience of Italian or Dutch art masterpieces with the people back home. On the other hand men such as Baudelaire and Ruskin wrote essays in which they applied their knowledge of local traditions and of the history of painting to place the art of their time in a historical perspective. Art critics were men or women who either visited places where no one in their audience would go, saw extraordinary art there and attempted to communicate their aesthetic experience to that audience; or, they had a thorough knowledge of art history, which allowed them to interpret new art and to judge whether the newcomer measured up to his illustrious predecessors. Nowadays, the first type of art critic is challenged, first of all, by cheap air travel, making it possible for just about any art lover to go and see the art for themselves. Whereas the famous *tours d'Italie*, or *tours d'Europe* for Americans, used to be the privilege of a small elite, they are now within the reach of many. There is no need anymore to report from distant lands, except for the purpose of luring art tourists, in which case the critical note usually disappears from the message. The second type of art critic, the historian, seems to have lost much of his relevance since the transition of what we call modern art to contemporary art. We will discuss the reasons for that in more detail later.

Art criticism itself is of course a product of the advent of journalism, or, in a wider sense, of the 'public sphere', which Benjamin specifically accused of having dug the grave of the storyteller (Lijster, 2013). As Habermas has described, this public sphere consisted of salons, coffeehouses, clubs and periodicals where people could exchange arguments about the true, the good and the beautfiul on equal terms. Not one's pedigree was decisive, but the force of one's arguments (at least in Habermas' ideal-typical portrayal of the public sphere). At the same time, however, it is clear that art criticism is always about more than just information, facts or arguments: the main point is communicating or constructing an experience. This is why it can also be argued that art criticism is subject to the same forces as the story.

It is precisely the distance that was a requirement of both the story and art criticism that seems to be increasingly lacking. The modern era is characterized by what the anthropologist and geographer David Harvey, in line with Marshall McLuhan, has called 'time-space compression': briefly, the process by which distances in space and time are increasingly losing their meaning (Harvey, 1989). We wish to study what the consequences of this loss of meaning are for art, and, following that, for art criticism. As we said, just like the storyteller the art critic based his authority on a certain distance (created by either his travel experience or his knowledge of local history) and this distance and authority were given even more weight by his use of the written word: the pen and later the typewriter. 'Literacy', says McLuhan in *Understanding Media*, 'had, by extending the visual power to the uniform organization of time and space, psychically and socially, conferred the power of detachment and noninvolvement' (McLuhan, 1964: 365). However, the implosion of time and space through electronic media such as television and computers abruptly ended this both geographical and social distinction. The mediatized art lovers want to experience all these goodies directly and 'feel' them themselves. The iconography of television and Internet puts us in 'a tactual mode of perceiving' that is 'sudden but specialist' (McLuhan, 1964: 365). New media render the opinion of experts redundant and the experts themselves even rather helpless. Below, we wish to further explore what happens to art and art criticism when distances in space and time disappear. We will argue that what passes for the 'crisis' of criticism is in fact the result of this development.

As an aside, but no less important, let it be noted that we, no more than Benjamin, wish to speak of this development as a history of decay. In his essay – and these rules are often ignored – Benjamin writes this about the disappearance of the art of storytelling: 'Nothing would be more fatuous than to wish to see it as a mere "symptom of decay," let alone a "modern symptom." It is, rather, only a concomitant of the secular productive forces of history – a symptom that has quite gradually removed narrative from the realm of living speech and at the same time is making it possible to find a new beauty in what is vanishing.' (Benjamin, 1936 [2002: 146]). Like Benjamin, we are first and foremost interested in how art criticism develops, in where besides loss there are gains, and in where new spaces for criticism open up as a result of recent developments.

Anywhere in No-time

Much has been written about the effects of globalization and mediatization, in both scientific and popular literature. Marshall McLuhan already pointed out communication media and means of transport as the engines of progress and, following his lead, authors such as Virilio, Harvey, Bauman and Rosa have referred to *acceleration* and *compression* as basic characteristics of the modern era. In itself there is nothing new in this. In the age of the horse-drawn carriage and sailing, power meant the manipulation of time as well: to arrive at your destination quicker than your competitors. In the modern age, the law of speed rules, but when this process increases in speed exponentially, the quantitative development becomes a qualitative one: when any place can be reached in a fraction of a second, the notion of place as such becomes meaningless. Zygmunt Bauman describes this as the transition from 'heavy to light modernity', which he summarizes as follows:

> In the era of software, of light modernity, the effectiveness of time as a means of value-attainment tends to approach infinity, with the paradoxical effect of levelling up (or rather down) the value of all units in the field of potential

> objectives. The question mark has moved from the side of the means to that of the ends. If applied to the time-space relation, this means that since all parts of space can be reached in the same time-span (that is in 'no-time'), no part of space is privileged, none has 'special value.
> (Bauman, 2000: 118).

The consequences of this process are by no means unambiguous. On the one hand, Rem Koolhaas, for instance, speaks somewhat exaggeratedly of the 'generic city', the uniform urban space that looks the same everywhere in the world and is increasingly acquiring the character of a transit space or a 'non-place', in Augé's terms (Koolhaas and Mau, 1995). On the other hand, David Harvey stresses that the time-space compression necessitates capital to emphasize and exploit specific local differences: 'the less important the spatial barriers, the greater the sensitivity of capital to the variations of place within space, and the greater the incentive for places to be differentiated in ways attractive to capital' (Harvey, 1989: 295-96); this in turn explains the growing importance of the tourist industry in general and that of city marketing in particular.

What are the specific consequences for art? In quite general terms we may state that the local character of the arts, if not vanished at all, has at least become quite problematic. This of course was also true of modernism in art. If up till then one could still speak of an Italian or Dutch 'school', modernism in any case aspired to be an 'international style', which in fact was how modernism in architecture was referred to. Within modernism, however, this internationalism in the first place meant an open mind: a willingness to look beyond the borders of one's own tradition, to break with the tradition, to acknowledge its contingency and to be open to the influence of what was different (not just to what was different on the other side of the national borders but also to the 'otherness' of the subconscious, the primitive, the childlike, the insane – with all the problematic and stigmatizing aspects this included). Besides, this was still only internationalism and not globalism. National styles and art movements are still recognized and acknowledged as such in modernism, for instance Pop Art (primarily American), Arte Povera (Italian), Neue Wilde (German). This national identification has only begun to fade since the 1990s, which brought us labels such as 'International

Installation Art' at the start of the twenty-first century. This global art is the first in which a clear national identity becomes hard to discern.

What does lay in wait here we could call, paraphrasing Koolhaas, 'generic art': as soon as art becomes detached from its local embedding, place becomes irrelevant to its production and to its consumption as well, as it no longer matters where you look at art. Walk into any Museum for Contemporary Art and you will find it hard to tell whether you are in New York, Beijing, São Paulo or Dubai, if you only have the art works to go by. A specific genre of 'global art' has emerged that is by now the dominant art genre worldwide. Of course, local art styles and region-specific art practices still exist, but these are hardly taken seriously in the international art world, unjustified as this may be. This development is closely related to the boom in art biennials that we have witnessed since the start of the new millennium.[1] Although these are often popular instruments of city marketeers, one cannot help but notice that the art on display is mostly devoid of any *couleur locale*.

By mentioning the word 'contemporary' in the previous paragraph another problem is identified as well: nowadays art is not only lost in the generic space, but also in the generic time. The effect of the time-space compression on how we relate to time is not less complex or paradoxical than on how we relate to space. Following Adorno's famous statement that 'all reification is a forgetting', authors such as Jameson and Baudrillard conclude, on the one side, that there is a collective loss of memory: we live in an eternal 'present', without any awareness of history and therefore without direction or goal. In this respect too, modernism, which after all has its gaze fixed steadily on the future, has definitely had its day. On the other side, other authors state that the past is omnipresent and that we see a 'musealization' of reality, or even a commodification and 'spectacle-ization' of the past in the form of National Museums and the exploitation of heritage (Huyssen, 2001). Of course these are two sides of the same coin: media technology has burdened us with the problem that everything can be preserved and remembered, which inevitably makes remembrance practices rather arbitrary affairs. Also, the past is rather effortlessly injected into the present, thereby influencing again what is happening now and becoming contemporary in the process. Just about anything can potentially be reabsorbed in the here and now, as long as it is brought to our attention. The contemporary has no past and therefore no future. Only what is brought into our experiential world in the here and now counts.

In the world of art this is expressed by the fact that the term 'modern' is increasingly being replaced by the term 'contemporary'. Although these words may be treated as synonyms in everyday usage, they have quite different connotations in the discourse on art. People who are modern see a clean break between themselves and the past and place themselves in the vanguard of a new development; precisely because of this they need to be well informed about the past. Contemporary, on the other hand, means nothing more than just that: belonging to the present. This does not necessitate a clear notion of either the past or future. It is hardly surprising therefore that art historians have lost their authority as critics over the past few decades. When in the 1980s modern art became a page in history that had been turned, the role of the historian in the current art world was all but over. These historians-as-critics could only maintain some of their authority if they were able to withdraw once more behind the walls of the Academy or University where they had to defend their position by appealing to scientifically sound methods and other historical criticism of sources. Those who weren't that lucky got precarious positions in the art writing business among many, many others.

In any case, the contemporary art world didn't have much use for the linear history and traditional causal relations that art historians revealed. What to do with the outlook of this 'literary man', as McLuhan (1964) called him, so devoted to the historical perspective and so attached to a view of fixed places and regular timeframes of events? Art movement after art movement, from one nation to the next, from one place to another, this is how art historians have been taught to interpret and explain their study objects. In former writings there were references to this chronotopy as 'local time': time and place are neatly connected, sequence follows sequence in a just as neatly delineated space, just like museums for fine art were once constructed around a chronological path along which each new room introduced a next era (cf. Gielen, 2009). By contrast, the experiential economy of the contemporary art world rests on 'global time', in which only the law of immediacy in non-places counts. Aren't all international biennials interchangeable? They all show the same art works that do relate to each other – i.e. horizontally – but hardly to a previous history, i.e. vertically. Just like the illiterate tribe, lovers of contemporary art do not care about a perspective or historical accuracy. The new art crowd prefers magical words and especially magical images, the lure of immersive experiences as promised nowadays by both the internationally consecrated installation art and environmental art, including the all-in city trip to some biennial or other.

Again, the advent of biennials but also that of the so-called 'Kunsthallen' (art centres) are symptoms of this contemporary immediacy. As Boris Groys has argued on various platforms, the museum can be regarded as 'collection' and 'archive'. In his view the modernist orientation on the new and the preservation of tradition go hand in hand. It was only after the French Revolution that the art treasures of the *ancien régime* lost their context of use and were preserved as heritage, which then made it possible to relate to them in a historical sense. As Groys notes in *Über das Neue*: 'This makes innovation an act of negative adaptation to cultural tradition' (Groys, 1992: 19). Only in relation to the collection can it be established what is new; in that sense the modern always relates dialectically to tradition.

However, the biennial is not a collection, the *Kunsthalle* doesn't have a collection and neither are institutes in the traditional sense. They are rather post-institutes, as Deleuze has called them (Gielen, 2009). This also means that they lack the 'verticality' that museums traditionally had: the ability and authority to install hierarchies and differentiations in value, because they lack the foundation of the depot on which the museum based its authority. Nevertheless, or perhaps because of that, the biennials are pushing the museums off the international art stage. They are not only more popular among a wider audience because of their spectacle and event character, they are also more appreciated by new collectors and speculators in the art market, precisely because of their 'horizontality'. But when we lose sight of tradition because of this, it also becomes problematic to adopt a critical attitude to tradition. Instead of being modern one can at best be up-to-date, *en vogue*, which makes innovation in art aimless and directionless, running the risk of coinciding with the very thing it once rebelled against: fashion, once characterized by Walter Benjamin as 'the eternal recurrence of the new' (Benjamin, 1938–1940 [2003]: 179). In contemporaneity art loses its progressive and indeed very modern character. Contemporary relevant art is art that draws attention here and now, which is something quite different from art that has to compete with history.

International and Atemporal Criticism

Can criticism offer a way out of the problems caused by time-space compression? Initially this would seem improbable, as critics are children of modernity *par excellence*. As the ones who look across the borders of both time and space and constantly try to shift these frontiers, they are, in the words of Nicolas Bourriaud, 'agents of delocalization' (Bourriaud quoted in Munder and Wuggenig, 2012: 378). However, this delocalization – and, we should add, detemporalization – now appear to backfire on the critic. The same forces that produced him now make his position precarious. In what ways is criticism subjected to the forces of time-space compression?

Starting with space once again, we see how the internationalization of art criticism is a mixed blessing, to put it mildly. In an article that was published some years ago on the web platform Triple Canopy, Alix Rule and David Levine presented a shocking description and analysis of the jargon of art that was used in the international art world and which they dubbed International Art English (IAE). Following earlier formulations, IAE can be characterized as a 'generic art speak'. According to Rule and Levine it has its very own lexicon (aporia, radically, biopolitical, tension, transversal), regularly recurring prefixes (para, proto-, post, hyper-) and typical word transformations: 'Visual becomes visuality, global becomes globality, potential becomes potentiality, experience becomes... experienceability' (Rule and Levine). And, we add, with Irit Rogoff: 'criticism and critique become criticality' (Rogoff, 2003). IAE, the new *lingua franca* of the international art world, mostly resembles poorly translated French, according to these authors.

When criticism comes under attack, as in the article by Rule and Levine, this is often precisely because of the use of incomprehensible jargon that, instead of tempting the uninitiated to enter the world of art, rather scares them off. But what, we may wonder, is exactly wrong with jargon? After all, surgeons and plumbers also use jargon and nobody seems to take offence. There is, however, an important difference. As mentioned above, art criticism – and this is where it differs from the world of medicine or that of plumbing – takes place in public. In his

Strukturwandel der Öffentlichkeit (1962) [*The Structural Transformation of the Public Sphere* (transl. 1989)] Jürgen Habermas demonstrated how modern art criticism was born in the coffeehouses and salons of the eighteenth century, where people could freely discuss matters of public interest, such as politics and art. Although these locations were usually the preserve of exclusive groups, the assumption was that everyone, regardless of class and descent, was capable of discussing these matters. In practice, of course, this eighteenth-century public sphere was far more exclusive than today's art world, but its theoretical assumption that every being gifted with the power of reason could in principle participate in debates makes it clear what the danger of using jargon is: whereas art criticism's original aim was to open up the domain of good taste to everyone, jargon has an excluding effect. As soon as authority is no longer based on what someone says but on the words themselves, debate is no longer possible. Jargon demands unconditional confirmation, with no doubts allowed, which is fatal to a public debate about art.

However, for a critic, taking the step from the national or local public sphere to the world stage is not an easy task. As Habermas also noted in his later writings on Europe, as yet we lack a stable transnational public sphere. The world is more the stage of the consumer than that of the citizen and the jargon mentioned earlier is more used for the marketing and branding of art manifestations than that it really says something about the world. This of course has an effect on art criticism. That there is a relationship with the shift of authority from the museum to the art market and biennials mentioned earlier, was already established by the art critic Benjamin Buchloh. He said that the critic is being replaced by experts who provide certificates for investments in art (Buchloh in *October*, 2002). With the commodification of the international art world and the displacement of the salon and the museum by the stock market and the biennial, the traditional space for art critics also disappears.

This brings us once again to the temporal dimension: just like the museum, the critic was traditionally part of the historical conscience of art. The critic is capable of embedding a work of art in or contrasting it with the body of existing work. This is not to imply that this history is static; history rather develops along with the new, time and again.[2] It is precisely because critics have a historical awareness that they are capable of recognizing what is innovative and can argue why this is so. For a long time, knowledge of historical movements was the entrance ticket to the professional art world and those who were not knowledgeable enough soon faced exclusion, because 'if you don't even know that, there's no point in continuing this discussion'.

Ever since the 1960s, however, we see that traditional art-history-as-art-criticism is displaced by 'art theory', often of a strong *ad hoc* nature, which is produced by curators and artists themselves rather than by professional art critics. This 'art theory' makes much use of the jargon of philosophy and sociology or what is briefly called 'theory'. It is therefore not just the laymen who have problems with the currently used jargon as analysed by Rule and Levine, but art critics as well, who are faced with their displacement. *Their* jargon is becoming increasingly irrelevant, as it is simply exchanged for a different jargon – that of philosophers and sociologists. In short, Rule and Levine's analysis does not only concern the tension between laymen and experts but also the power struggle among experts themselves. Art historians often reproach philosophers and other theorists for not knowing or understanding anything about art. And, from a historical viewpoint they are not wrong about that. The art-historical knowledge of philosophers and certainly sociologists is often not far above that of the laymen mentioned before. Whether this fact makes them better suited to reach out to these laymen, is something we aim to explore further here.

Displacement and Espacement

Despite our promise at the start, we have so far mainly sketched the outlines of a history of decay. Nevertheless, we are convinced that it is especially art criticism that can and must give the answer to the problems introduced into the art world by time-space compression. As already mentioned in the introduction to this book, a one-sided focus on the alleged 'crisis' or even 'death' of criticism makes us blind to interesting developments that occur outside its beaten track. We could sooner speak of a 'displacement' than of a crisis of criticism. Having said that, it is hardly desirable – although often practised – to only sing the praises of a brave new world of nomadic, hybrid and amateur art criticism. Only too often a one-sided criticism of authority and institutions as such, combined with an uncritical praise of the 'network' has first and foremost stimulated commodification and neo-liberalization.

As Mark Fisher puts it: 'The time of de-institutionalization is past – now we must have the courage to invent new institutions, institutions that will have both the flexibility and the robustness to combat capital.' (Fisher, 2013: 114).

The question then is how to reintroduce some 'verticality' into art criticism. Here too we can learn from Walter Benjamin. Fundamentally, his narrative of the storyteller is not an elegy for a lost art, even though it is often thus interpreted. Benjamin was interested, in the first place, in the history and development of the transfer of experience and that is precisely the reason why, in later texts, his attention turned to new media such as film. To him, film had the potential to save certain elements of the art of storytelling: shared authorship, connection to and embedding in everyday life, dissolving the separation between artist and audience. But Benjamin's attitude towards the medium, *pace* Adorno, was far from uncritical; he was only too aware of the opportunities that film had to offer to both fascist propaganda and 'western film capital'. Like Benjamin, we should look for the new opportunities of criticism, without losing sight of the dangers that lie in wait.

To counterbalance the forces of time-space, it would seem obvious to explore the possibilities of a re-localization and re-temporalization of criticism. At first glance, this may seem a tall order: after all, art criticism was itself an 'agent of de-localization' (Bourriaud) and always directed its gaze beyond the borders of space and time. Still, its current problems force criticism to re-evaluate and rethink its natural inclination. What would such a re-localization entail? In the first place, the critic should reclaim the public sphere. The IAE mentioned earlier is a symptom of the crisis of that public sphere: it constitutes a barrier that prevents us from speaking about art from a common base, as it were. Practitioners of 'art theory' often hide their art-historical ignorance behind mysterious sounding claptrap that both laymen and art historians don't want to have anything to do with. Concepts such as 'radicality', 'altermodern' or 'criticality' are flung about carelessly indeed, lending a mystical aura to art that can only be understood by the initiated. Or, rather, by using this jargon these initiated isolate themselves thoroughly from the public debate.

The commodification of the art world and thus of the discourse about the arts is in fact an example of an 'enclosure of the commons': a domain that had been common property is claimed and appropriated by an elite. By this we not only mean the literal 'possession' of art works as commodities, but also possessing the authority to canonize: because of the growing influence of collectors, that authority as well comes to lie with the market. The importance ascribed nowadays to artists such as Jeff Koons and Damien Hirst can at least be partly laid at the door of those who speculate with the work of these artists (see, for instance, Ben Lewis' 2010 BBC documentary *The Contemporary Art Bubble*). The art history of the future is being written in the present and therefore writing and debating about art are too important to be left to the market, but also too important to be regarded as only amateurish hobbies. Art criticism should take itself seriously again as an institution, in the words of Fisher.

However, hardly anyone, apart from a shrinking minority, believes in the importance of art anymore. That is precisely the reason why art criticism needs a coup by philosophers, sociologists and other theorists mentioned earlier. By this we certainly do not mean an academization of art criticism through these disciplines. On the contrary, we believe that by breaking open the boundaries of these disciplines and letting their words 'pour over' into the art world, art critics can develop discourses that may resound in the public debate. Better than the art historian-expert, they can explain which practices matter in the art world and why these are relevant to politics, the economy and education or the juridical system alike. Through a discourse that can be understood by those who know little about art but are therefore not uneducated, they can 'translate' issues in art into issues outside art or wider social issues.

By no means we wish to imply that history should be cast aside. On the contrary, art criticism should again become a historicizing practice, but in a wider sense than traditional art history, and relate art to social, economic and cultural history. 'Always historicize', as Fredric Jameson said, who called it the only trans-historical imperative (Jameson, 1981: 9). Historicizing is important, precisely because it counters the appearance of obviousness and naturalness of the present. An historicizing art criticism is not, as in a Hegelian sense, out to prove an unavoidable tendency in history, but rather attempts to show the many possible outcomes of the historical process of which the present carries the potentials that are always only partially realized. In doing so, a historicizing art criticism actually breaks open the notion of the 'contemporary'; that notion recognizes no space outside the present. We might call this type of critic 'modern'. And although we consciously use this term in a polemic manner against the dominance of the 'contemporary', it is not our intention to return to the modern belief in progress. Rather, we use the term 'modern' like Foucault used it in his famous essay 'What is Enlightenment?', in which he characterizes 'modernity' not as an era but as an attitude (*ethos*). Referring to Baudelaire, he describes this attitude as a break with tradition in which the present is simultaneously made heroic and ironic: 'For the attitude of modernity, the high value of the present is indissociable from a desperate eagerness to imagine it, to imagine it otherwise than it is, and to transform it not by destroying it but by grasping it in what it is.' (Foucault, 1984: 41). In this manner, art criticism is part of what Foucault called an 'ontology of the present' that poses the questions who or what we are in the here and now.

In our view, the task of such an art criticism would first and foremost be to link the art work to the *experience* from which it came, even if this experience is, as Benjamin noted, the experience of a crisis of experience. For like Benjamin already asked, rhetorically: 'For what is the value of all culture if it is divorced from experience?' (Benjamin, 1927–1938 [1999: 732]). Do note that this does not refer to the experience of the individual artist – we certainly do not wish to argue in favour of biographical criticism – but rather to a wider sociohistorical experience from which the work came and in which the beholders may recognize themselves. To give a historical example: Baudelaire's famous essay on Constantin Guys, in which Guys is described as the seismograph of modern Parisian life; more recent examples are essays by critics such as Susan Sontag, John Berger or Fredric Jameson. With these critics art is never only about art; art tells us something about the world we live in and how we experience that world.

So we are not just presenting a conservative argument for the rehabilitation of the art critic here. It is precisely the link with the theorists that might create an interesting new space for criticism. The latter have proven to be increasingly socially involved, sometimes even as political activists. Together with the art historians/art critics of the past, these theorists therefore have better and also more possibilities to link and interpret the experience of art within the entire social experience we find ourselves immersed in today. After all, this so-called crisis of art criticism is in fact a crisis of modernity and therefore of all institutions that were built on the foundations of the modern age. Not just museums – and with them the autonomy of art – are under pressure, but also legal, political, medical and educational institutions that see the acquired modern values go up in smoke. Their – typically modern – autonomy is being questioned as well. It is remarkable, by the way, that this debate about other institutions takes place in particular in the art world of today. At a biennial, any debate worth its salt concerns a discourse that is much wider than the art world and its works, and currently valued artists are now relating to much more than just the issues of content or form of their own discipline. Both the artist and the critic concern themselves with the entire world and place their work in the context of a broader society. If we argue for a re-historicization of art criticism here, we certainly don't mean (re)narrowing it to its own discipline. On the contrary, this new historicization will be cultural-historical in nature and relate the histories of politics, economics and the history of mentalities or attitudes to each other.

But even if this operation were to succeed, it is crucially important to take this widened debate outside the walls of the art world. This means that the new-school art critics will have to make an appearance in places that are alien to art. They will have to actively look for crossroads of politics, economics, education and culture, together with civil society organizations. After all, the public sphere does not exist by and of itself but is continuously regenerated by the very acts of the critic. Within this context, a relevant reference is Michel de Certeau's distinction between place (*lieu*) and space (*espace*). Certeau defines 'place' as a geographical, stable location, whereas 'space' only exists as 'the effect produced by the operations that orient it, situate it, temporalize it, and make it function in a polyvalent unity of conflictual programs or contractual proximities' (De Certeau, 1984: 117). In short, space only exists as a practice and must be shaped by that practice time and again. Whether this occurs in a street, in a square, on the Internet or in the living room doesn't matter all that much. The public space is neither restricted to one place nor to a specific medium. What counts is the – dissonant – act that is performed and that generates new space or publicness.

To art and art criticism this means that there is no autonomous space for art as long as this space is not continuously conquered outside these walls and is reshaped in that process time and again; likewise, there are no ready-made spaces for criticism:

these spaces are only generated by the interaction between critics, artists and other players in the field of the arts. The 'displacement' of criticism will therefore have to go hand in hand with and be compensated by what we might call an 'espacement'.

Perhaps this is the main cause of the alleged crisis of art criticism: although it ventured to make more and more statements about *the* world in the past decade, the discourse was mostly kept within the safety of the walls of the professional art field. However, preaching to the converted, that is to those belonging to the art scene, does not exactly generate a public space. The common does not thrive on identical voices, but on dissonance or 'polyvalence', as De Certeau calls it. Perhaps art critics can take some cues from intervention artists in entering this unsafe territory. And perhaps the roles of artist, critic, curator, museum director, but also that of the academic or activist will become less defined in this exchange with the outside world. At least such roles will be regularly exchanged in a dynamics in which criticism and critique constantly take over from each other and sometimes even become completely interwoven. And yes – this probably comes as no surprise – only in this space will the traditional public intellectuals once again find their place. Not that this place will provide them with much quiet, but it is precisely this disquiet that will revive them and keep them lively.

Notes

1 See the special issue of *Open* magazine (2009, no. 16): *The Art Biennal as a Global Phenomenon. Strategies in Neo-Political Times*.

2 As T. S. Eliot phrased it in his essay 'Tradition and Individual Talent' (1920): 'What happens when a new work of art is created is something that happens simultaneously to all the works of art which preceded it. The existing monuments form an ideal order among themselves, which is modified by the introduction of the new (the really new) work of art among them. The existing order is complete before the new work arrives; for order to persist after the supervention of novelty, the *whole* existing order must be, if ever slightly, altered; and so the relations, proportions, values of each work of art toward the whole are readjusted; and this is conformity between the old and the new.' (Eliot, 1920: 50)

Bibliography

- Bauman, Z. (2000). *Liquid Modernity*, Cambridge: Polity.
- Benjamin, W. (1999). *Walter Benjamin: Selected Writings, Volume 2: 1927-1934*, ed. by H. Eiland, M. Jennings and G. Smith, transl. by R. Livingstone et al., Cambridge MA: The Belknap Press of Harvard University Press.
- Benjamin, W. (2002). *Walter Benjamin: Selected Writings, Volume 3, 1935-1938*, ed. by H. Eiland and M. Jennings, transl. by E. Jephcott et al., Cambridge MA: The Belknap Press of Harvard University Press.
- Benjamin, W. (2003). *Walter Benjamin: Selected Writings, Volume 4, 1938-1940*, ed. by H. Eiland and M. Jennings, transl. by E. Jephcott et al., Cambridge MA: The Belknap Press of Harvard University Press.
- De Certeau, M. (1984). *The Practice of Everyday Life*, transl. by S. Rendall, Berkeley, Los Angeles and London: University of California Press.
- Eliot, T.S. (1920/1976). *The Sacred Wood. Essays on Poetry and Criticism*, London: Methuen & Co Ltd.
- Fisher, M. (2013). 'Indirect Action. Some Misgivings About Horizontalism', in: P. Gielen (ed.), *Institutional Attitudes. Instituting Art in a Flat World*, Amsterdam: Valiz, pp. 101-114.
- Foucault, M. (1984). 'What is Enlightenment?' in: P. Rabinow (ed.). *The Foucault Reader*, New York: Pantheon Books.
- Gielen, P. (2009). *The Murmuring of the Artistic Multitude. Global Art, Memory and Post-Fordism*, Amsterdam: Valiz.
- Harvey, D. (1989). *The Conditions of Postmodernity. An Enquiry into the Origins of Cultural Change*, Cambridge MA and Oxford: Blackwell.
- Huyssen, A. (2001). 'Present Pasts: Media, Politics, Amnesia', in: A. Appadurai (ed.). *Globalization*, Durham & London: Duke University Press, pp. 57-77.
- Jameson, Fredric (1981). *The Political Unconscious. Narrative as a Socially Symbolic Act*, Ithaca NY: Cornell University Press.
- Koolhaas, R. and B. Mau (1995). *Small, Medium, Large, Extra-Large. Office for Metropolitan Architecture*, Rotterdam: 010.

- Lijster, T. (2013). 'Where is the Critic?' in: P. Gielen (ed.), *Institutional Attitudes. Instituting Art in a Flat World*, Amsterdam: Valiz, pp. 35–53.
- McLuhan, M. (1964). *Understanding Media,* New York & London: Routledge and Kegal Paul.
- Munder, H. en U. Wuggenig (eds.) (2012). *Das Kunstfeld. Eine Studie über Akteure und Institutionen der zeitgenössischen Kunst,* Zürich: JRP/Ringier.
- Rogoff, I. (2003). 'From Criticism to Critique to Criticality', on http://eipcp.net/transversal/0806/rogoff1/en
- Rule, A. and D. Levine (2013). 'International Art English', on http://canopycanopycanopy.com/contents/international_art_english

Elsewhere
Helicopters and Safe Places of Criticism

Max Jorge Hinderer Cruz

After moving from Berlin to São Paulo, not that long ago, I still earn a considerable part of my rather humble income by working as a so-called cultural critic or art critic. 'How exciting!' I hear some of my cultural and art critique friends back in Europe say, 'There is a lot going on in Brazil, isn't it?' – both are true, I guess, exciting and a lot going on, indeed. Others say: 'But isn't it a bit far away?' As much as I appreciate the loving care of my European friends, somehow I can't help thinking that most of the time Central Europeans overestimate their being central. And it seems to me that they're doing this in relation to a centre-periphery model that would seem highly outdated to most of the people all over the world, nowadays. Having grown up in South America myself, I wonder: far away from what? Far away from them? Far away from a particular given centre of the world? Isn't 'decentralization' a well-known concept to understand contemporary economy and life, at least since the end of the Cold War, if not since Copernicus, or Christopher Columbus? Well, my job offers still come from Vienna, Groningen, Madrid, New York, Mexico City, Rio de Janeiro, Seattle or Hong Kong. It all more or less takes place within the same system, a museum here, a magazine there, a university elsewhere. We're still talking about a globalized art world, aren't we? And isn't it true, and thankfully so, that perhaps especially in the fields of criticism, the so-called periphery has finally earned itself quite a few centre stage positions lately? I guess most of my friends nodding their heads as a sign of affirmation do know about globalization or the ideological global histories of corresponding centre-periphery models, yet eventually only one or two of them would be more precise about their concerns and come on out with the one question, the one question that is really bothering them: 'But isn't it dangerous?' – Now there you go! What does dangerous mean? Dangerous compared to what? Dangerous as opposed to what people making their money in the contemporary art context would consider being in a safe place?

Far Away from the Centre of the World?

Let me put it this way: When I leave my working place, I take the elevator 24 stories down, straight into the heart of São Paulo's city centre. While I watch the LCD display counting down to 0, it is as if I am passing through various layers of global history. And once I arrive on the ground floor, it seems that everything is real, and that it's all right here. Each layer has left its marks on each and every single one of us down here. You can taste it in the coffee that is being sold on the corner, you can see it on the dirty feet and faces of the homeless sleeping in the middle of the sidewalk, you can see it in the make-up of the trans-women working the street, hear it in their provocative laughter, you can smell it from the aftershave of the stock market brokers passing them by, you can count it by the missing teeth of the crack addicts asking for money, you can feel it in every pound of the overweight security personnel in front of every building, you can see it in the straightened-out hair of the new middle-class professionals with secretary jobs going for lunch, you can feel it hurting in the back of the rich old lady bending over to pick up the feces of her fancy hair styled white toy poodle, and you can hear it in the straightforward music beat escaping the headphones of a young tattooed graphic designer bumping into her while checking his smartphone. It's all true. The 500 years of colonization and its ongoing genocide on the indigenous population, the ongoing destruction of the Amazonian rain forest and the environment, the sugar cane plantations, the coffee empires and slave trade, the African diaspora, the gendered division of labour and its global chains of production, the violence of the Industrial Age hidden under the veil of progress, the Shoah, the Jewish, Italian, Japanese, and Korean migration of the twentieth century, the Bolivian, Haitian, and Nigerian migration of the twenty-first, the War on Drugs, the War on Terror, the hollow friendliness of the service industry, the capitalization of our desires, the velocity of the digital age, the icy winds of finance capital and gentrification that blow through the streets of the city centre, the ultimate bankruptcy of bourgeois values, the failure of the Worker's Party (PT) government, and the political disaster we call a parliamentary opposition. It's all real. If there was a centre of the world, wouldn't it be a place like this right here, where all these layers of global history are inseparably intertwined?

When I arrive back at my desk after taking the elevator back up again, the street noises are so far away that I feel rather disturbed by the sound of the cooling fan of my computer blowing like crazy. It sounds just the same as it did in Berlin. Here though, every now and then it is drowned by the sound of a helicopter passing by at eye-level.

Helicopters and Safe Places

Well, to be fair, statistically you are more likely to get killed in the streets here than in Berlin. São Paulo covers an estimated urban area with about 20 million people, most of them living in highly segregated environments and the contrast between super rich and super poor is horrifying, and visible everywhere. Being South America's largest city, it could very well be that São Paulo is not only the richest, but also the poorest one. Certainly this extreme contrast is more visible here than in most other cities on the continent. It doesn't take much to understand that the criminality in the streets is only a logical consequence of this disparity. Still, the city centre in particular is also one of the most diverse places to be found on this continent, and despite its bad reputation, all sorts of people of all social classes do move around here, at night too, walking.

However, it's no coincidence that São Paulo is said to be the city with the most dense urban helicopter traffic in the world. Now, I believe that if the more-than-99% of the population who cannot afford helicopters for everyday use (bringing kids to school, etc.), could actually afford it, they would most probably buy helicopters too. And they would probably do so not only to escape the horrifying ground traffic, virtually at all hours, every day, but also because it is part of the everyday life rhetoric of politicians, and of the middle and upper classes, to state that it's dangerous out there in the streets, at any time, any day. Accordingly, the idea of moving around in helicopters must seem pretty comforting.

That's when it struck me: having thought about what I assumed to be a general crisis of cultural criticism after WWII during most of my professional life, it took moving to São Paulo, and coincidently getting a working studio place with a view up in a high rise building in the city centre, looking at helicopters passing by, to make a striking observation about myself, my situation working as a cultural critic, and about the safe places of criticism in general. Like in a caricature, a strange mix of lived experience and theoretical knowledge I had acquired over the years seemed to come together in one grotesque figure. I thought:

Of course! Rather than suffering a jet set syndrome, most cultural and art critics, both in Europe and in South America – at least most of those I meet at international conferences, strolling around at art fairs and biennials – may probably be suffering from a helicopter complex instead. For most of the art and cultural critics this may apply in one of two following ways, if not in both at the same time: 1) the critic hallucinates him/herself into the social condition of talking helicopter talk about art and culture, that is to say, they hallucinate themselves into the sense of security and sovereignty that helicopter owners might have performing their social standing in relation to the world down there (whether talking about art and culture or not, that doesn't actually matter). And/or, 2) they hallucinate themselves into the condition of literally being able to see everything as from above, like on a map, and thus they think they are able to understand and explain everything from an objective point of view, from a so-called 'critical' distance.

Both ways, criticism suffers from a distorted imaginary representation of its relationship with its actual conditions of existence. Or to put it simply, most critics often appear to me as being far off from reality.

Far Away from Crisis

After passing through my own personal helicopter experiences, sitting on the 24th floor of a high-rise building in the centre of São Paulo, I cannot but realize that if I am far away from anything, it is that I couldn't be further away from *de facto* diagnosing a crisis of criticism, even if I wanted to. Regardless whether my observation is right, and the helicopter complex is the expression of an acute state of disorder of criticism, it is certainly far away from constituting a crisis. It's just the way neoliberalism works. How could I ever have thought that contemporary criticism was in a crisis, while me, myself, I was bursting with critical impulse, as were my friends with whom I shared and discussed ideas, and all of us were publishing ceaselessly – often unpaid – in international media? How could I have pulled myself out of my own observations? Isn't the *locus* of critique inseparable from its *modus operandi*? Doesn't the critical or even pessimistic talk about criticism that is being produced and reproduced by a vast catalogue of scholars and critics during the last decades contribute to making criticism a booming business? Probably there has never been as much criticism as nowadays. Aren't the flourishing international art market, the growing number of galleries, of independent art spaces, of museum shows, of fairs, of biennials, of visitors, the new emerging magazines, the emerging critical and curatorial study programmes at the universities, and most of all, the raving moralists criticizing criticism itself, and the many volunteers that read and write about them, aren't they all producing a constantly increasing demand, and thus a constantly increasing production of art criticism of all sorts and in all variations?

I would propose, if we really wanted to diagnose a crisis of criticism, that we might well start by assuming that said crisis is certainly not generated by a lack of criticism – at least not in a quantitative or symbolic sense. On the contrary, it rather seems as if the perpetually repeated complaint about a lacking *quality* of criticism would reaffirm the necessity of criticism to be constantly performed. To get back to our helicopter image and the safe places, we may think that a criticism turning around itself, eternally biting its own tail, has probably found itself the safest place of all.

But let's not forget that if the jet set syndrome was the buzz of the art world's much acclaimed globalization process, the helicopter complex is its clinical condition. And the very basic experience of taking an elevator, or throwing a stone, may already teach us that everything that goes up, must come down at some point. Criticism may ultimately produce its own crisis of overproduction, and taking into account the omnipresence of the economic imperative and management vocabularies dominant in the neoliberal art world and its spaces of negotiation these days, criticism may very well become nothing more than its own constant self-evaluation process, in order to secure the competitiveness of the market place. And when the helicopter comes down, it will necessarily have to pass through the different layers of global history, or at least will get tangled up with everyday trouble, and eventually crash into the ivory ruins of criticism that bourgeois culture left behind, and that, at last, will fulfil the function of marking the boundaries of new spaces of criticism to come.

Summing up, regarding my work there's one thing I have definitely learned by moving from one side of the world to the other: regardless which geographical spot, representational regime, identitarian politics, critical tradition or formalism the individual critic has made his/her centre of the world, the critics' ultimate challenge will remain the act of leaving their own safe places. Whether talking about art and culture or not, doesn't actually matter. The choice lies ultimately with criticism itself – with us critics. That doesn't mean we will have to sit and wait for the helicopter to come down unwillingly. But it is certainly an option to bet that it will.

Spaces of New Social and Art Criticism and Their Re-Conditioning

A Few Theses from the Post-Yugoslav Context

Vida Knežević
Ivana Marjanović
(Kontekst Collective)

The following text is not going to give a general overview of the state of art criticism in our region today. No matter whether today the traditional figure of the art critic (as a universal authority to analyse and valorize art events and art works) exists or not, that figure is not crucial for what we do in arts and what we want from arts. More precisely, it is not decisive for our conception of the practice of social and art criticism and for our understanding of the function and role of contemporary political art criticism and political art practice. Our starting assumption is that the creation of a critical discourse is always also a social practice, which Miško Šuvaković conceptualizes as 'criticism in the context of cultural critique', that starts by 'problematizing the contextualization of art work or practice, thus shifting the focus from the "art work itself" to conditions and circumstances in which the art practice as a cultural and social practice is being performed' (Šuvaković, 2010b: 298, our translation).[1] However, having said this, it does not mean that our intention is to put the art production aside. According to Šuvaković, criticism is a 'theoretical and practical discipline that initiates, recognizes, articulates, follows, mediates, and theoretically interprets the actual art production and the life of a world of art' (Šuvaković, 2010b: 296, our translation). Therefore, 'criticism is, in relation to *art practice*, a secondary discipline since it articulates, speaks and writes about art', while it is 'a primary practice in comparison to other theoretical disciplines in art', because by collaborating with other actors it is taking part in 'the constitution of the actual *world of art* and its place in a given culture and thus, in society' (Šuvaković, 2010b: 296, our translation).

Our point of departure is based on our own experience of working collectively since 2005 and on our research and observations of neighbouring practices. Initially our curatorial practice was related to founding and running the programme of the Kontekst Gallery in Belgrade, from 2006–2010. In the same period, it expanded and developed as Kontekst Collective with various related activities (curatorial, theoretical, artistic, activist) including more actors. From its inception, it was (as the name implies) context-oriented, interested in social-transformative processes and left-oriented politics.[2] Special interest was directed towards culture, art and political initiatives and collectives that were active in the post-Yugoslav condition.

We will expose below the elements of the grammar for 'new art criticism' and point out today's spaces for it. In doing so, we will conceptualize the notion of social criticism and art criticism as a political, contextual practice related to arts that at the same time exceeds the field of art. It is new in the sense of intervention and turning away from the dominant mainstream paradigm of art, but still relies on the historical heritage of critical practices. Furthermore, this kind of criticism can be, at the same time, a primary activity, independent from art practice but related to it. In that sense, art criticism may not necessarily depend on the existing art work; it can itself initiate its creation. This practice takes on different forms and materiality, depending on a concrete situation and it creates spaces of varying temporality: from art institutions to magazines, exhibitions and activist events and places. The spaces of criticism and art criticism, initiated in this way, sometimes overlap with spaces created by social movements (for instance, anti-racist protests against demolition of Roma settlements in 2010 or the current organizing of the Left in which various social actors take part, many unrelated to the field of art). Finally, this practice is contingent but has its effect here and now.

Kontekst, its Struggles and Spaces

Kontekst Collective is an autonomous organization whose work consists of the processes of interconnecting critical theory and practice and the field of arts and culture with wider social action. In our current practice, we are interested in the research that we conduct together with artists, and other actors; we conceptualize research projects, exhibitions, and works of art and realize them in collaborative processes beyond the dominant division of labour. Furthermore, in practice, it is important that our political position is clear enough to be understood by a broader audience and not only by those 'properly educated' and thus capable of reading it. Through our critical approach to the social reality, direct intervention and persistence to initiate discussion on topics that are rarely discussed we are trying to destabilize the most retrograde and conservative socio-economic and political processes.

We started our work at the beginning of 2006 within the framework of the long-term project Kontekst Gallery. This project was initiated within the programme line that was called Youth Forum within the municipal cultural centre Centar za Kulturu 'Stari grad' (Cultural Center Inner City), in an attempt to transform a part of this centre into a place of autonomous education and research in the area of contemporary visual arts and culture.

From August 2007, Kontekst Gallery developed within the framework of the non-governmental organization for contemporary art and culture – Kontekst, but still as a programme of the cultural centre. In 2008, Kontekst Gallery's work gained wide attention with the organization of the exhibition *Exception, Contemporary Art Scene from Prishtina*, which was disturbed during the opening evening by extreme right-wing and state actors and became a national scandal (we will come back to this later).

In March 2010, the establishment of the new cultural institution Ustanova kulture 'Parobrod' took over the cultural centre 'Stari grad'. Due to the pressures in the form of an official demand to vacate the working facilities, as well as the unwillingness to communicate of the new management, we decided to end our work in this space. However, our decision to close Kontekst Gallery was primarily the result of our disagreeing with the policy of the new (neoliberal) cultural institution.

After the closing of Kontekst Gallery, we started a long-term research project and action *Kontekst, Struggle For Autonomous Space*.[3] It was dealing with reviewing and re-evaluating dominant cultural policies and the possibilities of creating and preserving autonomous critical cultural and art practices in a world of contemporary capitalism. Also, this project problematized the function, structure and role of public cultural institutions and the possibilities of their redefinition in accordance with the requirements of the complex present moment. It also re-evaluated their relationship with independent initiatives in the field of contemporary art. The project was structured as a set of modules, which included research, a debating programme, art projects and a publication.

Project *Kontekst, Struggle For Autonomous Space*, among other activities, led us to different experiments and attempts at finding a new actual space for our intervention in concrete reality. Thus we entered into different negotiations and actions, from participation in initiating and problematizing the squat 'Inex Film' through signing and the contract with the Municipality of New Belgrade on the use of a community space to an attempt to restructure the relations with the city institutions at Magacin space. At the same time, the situation we found ourselves in also provoked us to engage in the concrete socio-political-economical context in which we work and live, to deliberate over the work and production conditions, as well as the place of a worker in the cultural sector within the economy. From October 2013, together with a group of political activists, we have initiated the community centre October. This space has become a hub for one part of the left-wing scene in Belgrade.

Principles of the New Social and Art Criticism

In order to discuss spaces of new social and art criticism it is necessary to formulate the principles under which such spaces are created. This is important because their conditioning represents the field of antagonism that is not given by 'interpellation' – by the way, the dominant ideology (of reproduction of relations of exploitation) forms us as subjects (Althusser, 1971). Here, it is about the new conditioning, or better yet re-conditioning, that happens through the struggle for circulation of knowledge coming from alternative worlds, which have existed 'ever since'.[4] New spaces are instituted or taken over, appropriated from the existing conservative or neoliberal institutional landscapes. Thus, temporarily or for a longer period of time, they start affecting the re-formation of subjectivity, the conditions of its production and organizing.

Although it may seem self-evident, it is important to stress (as it is often neglected) that spaces of new criticism are *also* settings for affirmation, creativity and action. Here we would agree on '*ruthless criticism* of all that exists' (Marx, 1843) but it is not seen as a final destination. Criticism is a tool for exploring, sustaining and expanding alternatives, and not a tool for the production of dead ends and paralysis of enunciation and organization. As Marx said 'ruthless both in the sense of not being afraid of the results it arrives at and in the sense of being just as little afraid of conflict with the powers that be.' And he stated that in the context of creating alternatives: 'we ... only want *to find the new world* through criticism of the old one' (Marx, 1843, emphasis ours). So, criticizing the old world should not make us forget finding and struggling for the new one.

In order for the new social and art criticism to be effective and to create or take over spaces, it is necessary for it to be contextual, in the sense that it addresses a concrete historical and contemporary geo-political context; it reflects material conditions of its own production and of existing social relations for the purpose of destabilizing and changing them; and its subjects constantly try to demystify the uniqueness of their own profession in the social division of labour.

New Art Criticism is Always Socially and Historically Contextual

New art criticism is always contextual as it takes into account the socio-political context from which it speaks. It is established as a negation of the existing order, i.e. as a 'criticism of conformist logic, that denies the reality of contradiction' and as 'criticism of an established system of living, that denies its own presumptions and possibilities'. (Marcuse, 1966: 7, our translation).[5] In our case, it is about the landscape of post-socialist Yugoslavia where the process of capitalist restoration is the common denominator of all the states that were created by the break-up of Yugoslavia. This landscape plays a semi-peripheral role within capitalist Europe nowadays.[6] This 'exterior' is constantly present and is being reflected directly or indirectly by the critical practice itself. It is in constant conflict with liberal, neoliberal and conservative ideological narratives that are presented as having no alternative and which are, in reality, two sides of the same coin.

Additionally, new art criticism is attempting to 'brush history against the grain' (Benjamin, 1940) and place it in relation to the concrete social and political reality of post-Yugoslav space. This is of special importance when having in mind the domination of retrograde and revisionist approaches to the reading of local history and art history. A telling example of the new criticism can be detected in the following statement by the Prelom Collective which was, during the 2000s, publishing the *Prelom* (Break), periodical for images and politics:

> Even though Prelom has its center in Belgrade, it is a Yugoslavian publication – with collaborators from Ljubljana, Zagreb, Novi Sad, Sarajevo, Prishtine, and Skopje – and represents a collective effort to problematize, theorize and fight against various, heterogeneous and paradoxical forms of contemporary peripheral neoliberal capitalism. Words and images like Yugoslavia, partisans, Socialism, Marxism, Communism etc. invoke something which is – for a specific reason – nowadays considered scandalous; actually it is a taboo, even though it could be seen as a mere prank. But the articulation of those words and images – that is, the *tendency* they represent – introduces an active practice of rethinking and reinventing

> revolutionary politics – something that is in fact foreclosed by today's neoliberal 'rationality' as a relic of those rebellious, naïve and digressive past times. (Grlja and Vesić, 2007)

A new critical practice takes into account the heritage of progressive and emancipatory art practices incurred during the twentieth century (or even earlier, in the nineteenth century), which are mostly connected to avant-garde and neo-avant-garde art.[7] As Marcuse stated, critical thinking is closely linked to avant-garde art; both have a tendency to 'break the power of facts over words and not to use the language of those who establish and impose facts and benefit by it' (Marcuse, 1966: 10, our translation). Critical practice also relates to emancipatory social and political practices of which the geopolitical space mentioned above is full. These are: left-wing social movements between the two World Wars, People's Liberation Front and the partisan movement, Anti-Fascist Front of Women, the practice of self-government, the policy of nonalignment and Third-Worldism, feminist activism, political practices of student cultural centres, et cetera.[8] For some time now, the referential frame of the 1960s and 1970s has been in focus in local art critical spaces. However, it is necessary to draw attention to the suppressed history of networks of solidarity actions of various left-wing groups between the two World Wars (student and youth groups, workers' initiatives, women movement, art collectives, et cetera). This period is very important for what happened after WW2, i.e. after 'the constitution of communist Yugoslavia not on the basis of liberal-democratic concept of people's sovereignty' but 'from a very different democratic principle – the revolutionary one' (Buden, 2003: 53, our translation).

One of the examples of Kontekst Collective's art practice was the production of a radio drama and audio installation *On Solidarity: Why It Is Important to Reflect on the Student Protests of the 1930s* (2012)[9] as well as the video *On Solidarity* (2013) in support of and solidarity with student protests and blockades. These were based on the principle of plenum as a direct democratic student body that occurred at the universities of Belgrade, Zagreb, Ljubljana, Rijeka, Novi Sad, and other cities in the region in the course of 2011.[10] Even though it may not be a universally known fact, student protests based on the principles of direct democracy were also a very popular form of organization in the revolutionary student movements at the universities of Belgrade and Zagreb between the two World Wars. Our work and research went in the direction of actualizing a part of the forgotten history of the revolutionary student movements in the Kingdom of Yugoslavia, and emphasizing the students' interconnectedness, struggle, communication, and solidarity, which often exceeded the limits of the student movements.

Working contextually in the post-Yugoslav space also implies discussing complexities and contradictions of socialism. It involves the difficult task of dealing with nationalisms that went hand in hand with the collapse of Yugoslav state, related to the restoration of capitalism in Eastern Europe. In Yugoslavia this happened in a very tragic way with the state of exception, apartheid regime, 'death worlds', rape and genocide.[11] Therefore, working in the post-Yugoslav space means re-establishing those never entirely broken ties of movements across what once was Yugoslavia, such as the leftist, artistic, feminist, gay and lesbian and later queer factions, that played a crucial role in 1990's anti-war movement.[12]

Reflection of the Process of Production

New art criticism takes into consideration the reflection of structural conditions of the institution of art and its production. This means that the place of its actors in the social division of labour and in the concrete socio-political reality, as well as the institutional frame of not only production but also of distribution, presentation, representation, and consumption matters a lot. The local condition of the present post-Yugoslav institution of art is worsened by austerity measures and economic pressures on the cultural sector. The most recent case in Belgrade is the decision by the city government to transfer *October Salon*, one of the most respectable and important annual manifestations of contemporary art in Serbia, to the biennial art show.

These measures imply the withdrawal of public funding, commercialization and commodification of spaces that were once more open to criticism.[13] Moreover, flexible working conditions and their precarization have become a daily routine in which the new art critics find themselves, side by side with the artists and other actors in the world of art. They have become increasingly aware of the uncertainty of work and earnings, and are increasingly worried about the lack of health insurance and pensions, the precariousness of their lives, and the next assignment.

Therefore, it is necessary to go back to the political-economic analysis in the sphere of art in order to demystify today's capitalist relations of production. In the performance that Kontekst Collective created in 2012, *A Sketch for the Possibility of Art against Neoliberal Capitalism*, we refer to and paraphrase a manifesto made by the artist Mirko Kujačić in 1932, in order to draw parallels in our analysis of the position of cultural workers today: 'Even though it constitutes a minority, the privileged class, which has a firm grip on material resources, harnesses art for the purpose of further reproduction of its capital, making artists, by means of their funds and demands, their employees, providing them with a piece of bread for which they are obligated to cough up their creativity. Otherwise, their art will not get paid for, they lose their place, ranking, and consequently the means of sustaining their bare lives. Any isolation without a compromise is prevented.' In the framework of an invitation to take part in a project[14] that dealt with historical struggles in former Yugoslavia, Kontekst Collective elaborated the above mentioned points that were the subject of the two-year project *Kontekst, struggle for autonomous space.*

Past practice shows that it is not enough to deal with these processes only by thematization and content determination, as Benjamin clearly stated in *The Author as Producer* (Benjamin, 1934 [1970]). It has been obvious (then and now) that a large part of political content ends up being recuperated and incorporated into yet another media spectacle. Moreover, these topics are desirable and go hand in hand with a liberal discourse of human rights and EU integration. This is especially the case with large exhibition projects, such as the representative biennial exhibition, the exhibition format that is becoming increasingly dominant and whose production frame is often not transparent (Vuković, 2014).[15] Although thematic frames (of criticism) of these biennials are full of political content, at the same time they hardly reflect on the concrete production relations that the curators are part of (the question of unpaid labour, budget distribution etc.)

Furthermore, new art criticism is trying to demystify the artistic and creative process, which by glorifying its uniqueness fogs the relations of production (fetishization of work) and puts artists and other 'creative professionals' (including the critics) in competitive relationships. Although more and more ('intellectual') workers are forced into precarious living and working conditions, such positions often remain mystified and not reflected upon. According to the members of the Radical Education Collective from Ljubljana, one of the consistent examples of new art criticism in the region 'the atomization of workers, which prevents collective action, is looked upon as autonomy, unpaid work is looked upon as a common practice in the world of art production, and false promises about getting a permanent job one day, provided that one endures the insufferable conditions, are looked upon as 'networking' and developing one's own reputation. The erasure of a boundary between free time and working hours is looked upon, at the theoretical level, as "development".' (Piškur and Pureber, 2011, our translation). Additionally, flexibilization of working relations encourages competitiveness among those that offer labour, whether they be institutional or non-institutional self-organized cultural workers. This consequently prevents solidarity among them and it is also the reason for hardly having any organized political actions and protests.

The new art criticism practice does re-actualize historical and local struggles in the art field against bourgeois conceptions of 'pure' art and the 'genius' status of the artist and translates them into a contemporary context. As with an individual artist's example, such as the case of Mirko Kujačić, several collective initiatives in the 1930s highlighted the struggles and resistance to bourgeois art conceptions in their statements: 'Through a misinterpretation of the work of the artist in our society, the erroneous belief that the artist is a being outside the social process of work, as well as social economic relations, has been formed. However, it is indisputable that the artist's work is conditioned by the economic relations in society. Even those who have claimed and assured us that "a genius is born" out of misery, must see clearly, if they would pay only a little attention to reality and are not professional illusionists, that artists have all of the essential human characteristics – namely, that they eat, work, and live.' (Motivi bojkota, 1936, 'Cvijete Zuzorić' – zahtevi umetnika [The Motives for Boycotting 'Cvjeta Zuzorić' – the Artists' Demands], our translation). A similar situation applies to other workers in art (critics, theorists, et cetera).[16]

The New Art Critic – An Intellectual Like Any Other Intellectual. The Place and Role of the New Critic in Contemporary Struggles

Taking into consideration the above-mentioned question on the reflection of relations of production, inevitably a new question is imposed – the place of a new art critic in them. On one hand, our starting point is Gramsci's assumption that all men are intellectuals although not all have this role in the given production process. On the other hand, we take into consideration Benjamin's thinking on the attitude, positioning, and subjectification of intellectuals in political struggles, certainly having in mind that today's socio-political context is very different and that, unlike the former one, it does not have a representative of political action it can identify with. Antonio Gramsci analysed the character and role of intellectuals in the reproduction of hegemony (both traditional intellectuals, such as priests, and organic intellectuals, i.e. those created by new classes, such as the bourgeoisie). Reflecting on the potential of intellectuals in the process of building a counter-hegemony, Gramsci exposed: 'All men are intellectuals, one could therefore say: but not all men have in society the function of intellectuals' (Gramsci 2010: 9). Or more precisely:

> Each man, finally, outside of his professional activity, carries on some form of intellectual activity, that is, he is a 'philosopher', an artist, a man of taste, he participates in a particular conception of the world, has a conscious line of moral conduct, and therefore contributes to sustain a conception of the world or to modify it, that is, to bring into being new modes of thought. (Gramsci, 2010: 9)

Benjamin's reflection on the problem of the positioning and subjectification of 'intellectuals' (Benjamin, 1934 [1970]) in political struggles, especially the deliberation of their relation toward the proletariat as well as the matter of organization, brings us to the question: is it possible, and if so how, to translate this to today's concrete critical practice. One possible direction would be that the production apparatus no longer be supplied with new content. Alternatively, new social and art criticism provides a consistent structural analysis of the production and the material conditions in which the art system works, one that includes the perspective of the political-economic analysis. Also, and not less important, is to always deliberate and discover new ways of changing that production apparatus. So, 'it is about more thoroughly changing the relation to the order of truth production in a way that transcends the figures of artists and intellectuals, even if they are specific'. (Raunig, 2006: 98).

The institution of art thus presents itself as a homogenous whole composed of 'professionals' with a common interest, masking the existence of class relations (inside and outside of the system). The existing division of labour in the art worlds is, in most cases, taken for granted to such a level that class awareness doesn't even exist: a cleaning lady should clean and should be paid less for that work, and so on. At this point, we would insist that the practice of new art criticism is working on abandoning class related exclusion, and on creating a work landscape where the existing hierarchy of labour has room to change, exactly because, as Gramsci said (and we make a small adaptation), *all people are intellectuals*. Discarding the class-based discriminatory set of values can be done not only by entering but indeed inhabiting new spaces of art criticism, as well as other spaces of criticism (social movements' spaces) where ideas such as those formulated by Gramsci do circulate and are *taken seriously*. Once there, an art critic, an intellectual like any other intellectual, 'embodies critique' (Garcés, 2009: 203-210) and takes part in modifying the existing conception of the world (including its existing class structure). When thinking about future art institutions in the light of the project of the invention and development of the institution of the commons and its components, Gerald Raunig too points out a differentiated and hierarchized connection between workers in art institutions (curators, security guards, directors, cleaners) and he stresses the necessity of seeing precarity from that complex and not isolated perspective of the art field, working thus on solidarity and change (Raunig, 2014: 82). Therefore, the discussion on the lives and jobs of those working in the field of art is not to focus only on that field but rather to connect it with precarious living and working conditions of all other workers.

Procedures and Work Organization of the New Art Criticism

In order to maintain existing spaces of criticism and create new ones, it is important, besides maintaining the above mentioned principles, to take into account the question of the methodology of work and its organization. The emphasis on a strategic change of work frames and perspectives plays a role here as well as contra-hegemony relations of collaboration in which the main concept is *working with*. New spaces of criticism are created that go beyond narrow guild and professional limits by establishing political and solidary networks of collaboration with other actors, collectives and initiatives. Collective work models, characterized by political discussions of work procedures, from critical self-reflection to politicization of friendship are inseparable from such critical practices.

Working With as a Political Choice and a Strategy

An art critic creates spaces for criticism together with artists, and/or other critics, activists and interested subjects, often changing, blurring and hybridizing professional boundaries for political and strategic reasons. The concept of collaboration practiced here is *working with*. *Working with* tries to abandon the top-down relationships in art worlds that are the outcome of professionalization, experts' authority and symbolic capital accumulation, often reproduced by all sides that take part. That means rejecting some of the existing codes of communication (also in critical spaces) such as exclusiveness, arrogance and careerism. More precisely, it means getting rid of a-sociality or, better yet, strategic sociality (selective socializing to boost one's own symbolic capital, i.e. socializing only as part of professional interest and benefit). Also at stake here is freeing oneself from a hidden but profound disgust with anything that has to do with lower classes and popular values.

When new art critics curate an exhibition, they invite certain artists for political and strategic reasons: they want to contribute to making certain knowledge visible, expose it in an ex/position. They want to make a position *together with it*, relating it to works of others and their own concept. In that sense the *name* of the curator is indeed not crucial here. They never perform this work alone. A telling example of taking a political position together through the medium of an exhibition was the formation of a temporary curatorial collective (in which we also took part) from 'Serbia' that collaborated with a group of artists and theorists from 'Kosovo' on realizing the project *Exception – Contemporary art scene of Prishtina*. The exhibition was meant to be the presentation of Kosovo Albanian artists who were almost unknown in Serbia due to the conflicts over the sovereignty of Kosovo, the post-war blockade of information and cultural racism. This exhibition opened in the beginning of 2008 in Novi Sad in the Museum of Contemporary Art Vojvodina, but it was prevented on the day of the opening in Kontekst Gallery in Belgrade by the violent action and protest by extreme right-wing actors and police. Nevertheless, it triggered a large-scale public discussion both in Serbia and Kosovo. Many people took a stand and formulated their own opinion, on that very moment, about the art works, the exhibition, the curatorial work in forums, films, blogs, online news, TV shows and printed media.[17]

The art critic, in the role of curator, *working with* artist(s), has 'the curatorial function' of 'organizing the ex/position' which means 'organization of public sphere', of 'debate that breaks out among those standing around' (Marchart, 2007: 164-165). This means 'to construct a counterposition to the dominant position from which an antagonism can then arise' (Marchart, 2007: 166). Organizing a debate means organizing or trying to organize conflict or antagonism.

Besides curating, the art critic occasionally creates art pieces together with artists working on a common project (we have been practicing that with much delight and joy). In those situations *working with* becomes a very intense practice of fluidity, hybridity, and blurring of borders. Intersecting knowledge from art history, art theory, art criticism and arts is a fruitful condition for the advancement of ideas on how to articulate critique. One example of that practice is the *Sex, Work, and Society* research exhibition (Ljubljana and Belgrade, 2007). Within this framework we produced a publication, curated the show, but also exhibited art works that we created together with artists involved in the exhibition: an audio installation and a questionnaire in the form of a poster project.[18] Another example is the exhibition *Without Borders – Some Critical Reflections on European and Global Border Conditions* (Belgrade, 2009) which came out of an open call for a workshop conceptualized and organized by the h.arta group from Timisoara, and Kontekst. In this situation we ceased to work as curators and worked as equals together with the artist collective h.arta and all the people who took part in the workshop, conceptualizing and producing an exhibition in the course of the workshop.[19]

The above examples of *working with* are a matter of choice. But, in some situations *working with* can be engendered as an urgency and reaction to the state of exception in nationalist/racist/patriarchal capitalist states. An example is the formation of the RUK group (Workers in culture group), that temporarily existed as a community of art critics, art theorists and artists gathered around the prevented exhibition *Exception – Contemporary art scene of Prishtina* (Knežević et al., 2008).[20]

When writing about art, critics do not write because they have a completely distant position from which they can valorize and categorize. Neither is their motivation to profit from it, to be the first to write about it, to be the one who discovered it, the one who performs 'the best', who provides the most controversial interpretation of it (which sometimes, in competitive contexts of art criticism, appears as a tendency). Rather, they want to zoom in on it, concentrate and focus their own thinking. They do so in order to learn something from it, to get involved with its aesthetic, political and textual undertakings, just like in an ex/position, ex/positioning it in the format of a text that has a different materiality and temporality. They write because a certain artistic and cultural production fascinates them, motivates their actions, affects their ideas and creativity, and in that sense, it is the practice of *working with* that specific production.

Collective Models

Referring to the title of Stevan Vuković's research project 'Kolektivni modeli' (Collective Models) on Fluxus and conceptual art in the former Yugoslavia, presented in a series of talks in Kontekst Gallery in Belgrade in 2006, we would like to emphasize that a new art critique creates spaces for criticism through the collective models of work (Knežević and Marjanović (eds.) 2008: 123-124). This cannot be done as an individualistic venture. The collective creation of ideas, work groups, concepts, art works, exhibitions, books, lectures and texts is a necessary procedure for creating spaces of criticism.

Decisions are never made by the individual self; they are negotiated among multiple individuals. Collective models of work imply a different mode of production than the individualistic one. They require more time, discussion, exchange of ideas, work on the self in terms of detecting and giving up domination mechanisms. That means developing patience, understanding, and respect for the others' opinion, even when one disagrees, working on your own openness and readiness to reconsider your own positions, instead of regarding the self as the ultimate carrier of truth. Working collectively brings conflicts as well. Ideally, clashes and contradictions are publicly communicated with the outside world and (though they often remain hidden) because they are relevant to advancing the debate in the same way the final 'products' are. An example can be found in *Prelom* magazine under the chapter: 'Prelom i prelomi Preloma' [The Break and Breakings of the Break] where harsh theoretical and ideological disagreements among editors and authors are exposed to the readership. (Buden et al., 2008/9: 5–57).

However, collective models of work and complex means of production of alternative knowledge and practices imply often affective encounters of love and friendship that collectives are largely based on. They take us 'venturing into unknown territories, taking risks that could lead to something new, understood as an experience of intensity, as a rupture with the commonplace' (Piškur, 2014: 5). Therefore, they are not only collectives of working people but also collectives of possible and impossible friendships. Although rarely thematized, it is the situation of affective relationships in collectives where very intense political processes are happening. In that sense, Bojana Piškur claims: 'Friendship is thus a form of emancipation, not in the sense of political correctness, consensus or search for some universal truth, but as a constant discovering of what we are and what we become in the processes of friendship' (Piškur, 2014: 5).

Collective models of inhabiting spaces of criticism, remind us time and again of Gramsci's observation that all men and women are intellectuals. For Gramsci it was clear that artists are intellectuals, but in contemporary art worlds this fact is often obfuscated by the creation of hierarchies with those who hold and perform theoretical knowledge at the top. This unwritten rule and material mistake is to be corrected as part of spaces of criticism. All knowledge is valuable. Collective models may seem as nothing new or special – we have collective models of work in all kinds of commercial and non-commercial companies and organizations. Even in art, as pointed out by Bojana Cvejić, the 'types of collectivity and collaboration practiced today' do 'represent a sustainable model for continuous collaboration that does not question its foundation and methodology or seek political social action' (Cvejić, 2005). She further states: 'Collectivity and collaboration, thus, no longer appear as viable models of experimentation and critique as they are already subsumed under the institutional order and a cultural policy trend.' (Cvejić, 2005).

However, we are not talking about random collective models in art worlds. Our collective models are strictly concerned with critique and social transformation. Even though, as Cvejić rightly argues, that depoliticization of collectivity takes place (and one has to keep in mind that her field is contemporary dance and theory where collective productions are more standard than in visual arts), still in the global worlds of art and theory, creativity and invention have been mostly related to individual merits. This kind of reasoning is either the outcome of a bourgeois perspective or the consequence of critical survival in precarious working conditions. Other authors point this out as well: 'Though collaborative or collective work has long been accepted as normal in the kind of artistic production that requires ensemble work, such as in music, in the context of visual art under which the individual artistic talent reigns, such loss of singularity of the artist is much less the norm, particularly under the operative conditions of capitalism.' (Enwezor, 2004). In that sense, when collective models are taken politically, and they often are, this logic of depoliticization is at the same time interrupted and this also happens in spaces of art criticism.

The case of our collaboration with the h.arta group may be used as an example here. The project was funded by the Austrian residency programme Kultur Kontakt and was related to its presentation. Initially, we were asked to curate a show for which we could select artists from the archive of the residency programme. We selected only the h.arta group (with whom we had previously collaborated) to work on a project that would make more sense to us. In the meantime, we realized that the whole framework was connected to the celebration of the fall of the Berlin wall and *openness* of European borders. We took this information, which we did not have from the beginning, to reflect on the question of borders of the 'fortress' Europe at that time. Hence, for us and the participants something that might have been a presentation of a residency institution turned into working on urgent political issues. In Serbia these topics are often obfuscated through the internalized neo-imperialism of the phrase 'we want to become Europe' – as if we are not already part of it and as if western Europe would be a democratic paradise. In this example, something that could have been a classical curatorial collective project (of two curators working together and with numerous artists) turned into a non-classical curating and artistic practice where the entire content of the exhibition was produced by all participating actors.

Furthermore, for these collective models we relate to the history of collectivity, which has been 'a crucial strategy of the avant-garde throughout the 20th century' as Enwezor points out (Enwezor, 2004). Enwezor looks at this practice from the *artistic* perspective, rightly defining 'collective or collaborative practices (that is the making of an artwork by multiple authors across porous disciplinary lines)' which 'generate a radical critique of artistic ontology' (Enwezor, 2004). Our perspective is from a different position: from that of 'curators' who cannot be seen anymore as performing what is usually understood as curatorial work.

Finally, collective models do not imply a collectivity dogma and in no way are they proclaiming collectivity as the essence. It doesn't mean that authors working individually are not contributing to the collective spaces of criticism, but there is a difference between working individually for collectivity and working individually for individuality. Isolation and single productions are necessary processes in creating spaces for art criticism.

Concluding Remarks

The practice of new art criticism does creates spaces and not just a few. There are many of them, they are multiplying and they are creating not only a cartography of survival but a road map for living, for us who create and inhabit them, but also for others who feel attracted by such spaces and relieved when inhabiting them. These spaces, working on re-articulating politics and restructuring societies, tell us time and again not only that another or different world is possible, but that we already partly live in one of such worlds. Or, in other words, to quote the title of Oliver Resler's art work: 'There must be an alternative' – we would say that alternatives are already there. These spaces, together with others, are providing the realm for cultivation of social relations different from dominating ones (framed by neo-liberal capitalism, neo-imperialism and the nationalist state), for different models of loving and living.

Notes

1 Šuvaković is referencing the numerous practices that rely on post-colonial, post-socialist, late capitalism, feminist and queer studies. See: (Šuvaković, 2010b: p. 298).

2 The changing character of our work is mirrored in various definitions others have given it: post-activist curatorial practice (Šuvaković, 2010a), contextual art (Group Terms, 2010), belonging to 'Independent artistic associations' (Dedić, 2012).

3 See: https://kontekstprostor.wordpress.com/

4 An interesting study on historical contestations of dominant social relations and beliefs, where for instance heretical movements are interpreted as social movements of middle ages, can be found in the book by Silvia Federici, *Caliban and the Witch: Women, the Body and Primitive Accumulation,* 2004.

5 Or as Marx claims: 'Just as one does not judge an individual by what he thinks about himself, so one cannot judge such a period of transformation by its consciousness, but, on the contrary, this consciousness must be explained from the contradictions of material life, from the conflict existing between the social forces of production and the relations of production.' (Marx, 1859).

6 See: Srećko Horvat and Igor Štiks, Welcome to the Desert of Transition!: Post-Socialism, the European Union, and a New Left in the Balkans. 2012. http://monthlyreview.org/2012/03/01/welcome-to-the-desert-of-transition/

7 See: Suzana Milevska, *Gender Difference in the Balkans: Archives of representations of gender difference and agency in visual culture and contemporary art in the Balkans*, 2010; Pavle Levi, *Cinema by Other Means*, 2012; New Media Center_kuda.org, *The Continuous Art Class. The Novi Sad Neo-Avant-garde of the 1960s and 1970s*; Zorana Dojić and Jelena Vesić (eds.), *Political Practices of (Post-) Yugoslav Art: retrospective 01,* 2009.

8 See: Gal Kirn, 'Conceptualisation of reproduction and politics in the work of Louis Althusser: case of socialist Yugoslavia, 2012'; Slavoljub Cvetković (ed.) *Omladinski pokret 1919-1969.* [Youth Movement 1919-1969], 1969.

9 See: http://urbanfestival.blok.hr/12/en/2012/08/12/kontekst-kolektiv/

10 The key goals of these protests were related to the possibility of achieving publicly financed education that would be accessible to all, as well as to defend the autonomy of the university and the possibility for student self-organization.

11 See: Sezgin Boynik and Minna Henriksson (eds.) *Contemporary Art and Nationalism: Critical Reader*, 2007.

12 In relation to the former one should be critically attentive as the liberal, civilizing discourses of the 'West' and 'Europe' often materialized here.

13 See: the eipcp's online edition *the post-yugoslavian condition of institutional critique*, 2008.

14 *Oktobar XXX: Exhibition–Symposium–Performance* was curated by Jelena Vesić, Pančevo, Serbia in 2012. It was conceptualized as a processual re-enactment – involving critical reading, interpretation and actualization – of questions initiated and contemplated within the experimental counter-exhibition *Oktobar 75* that took place in the Student Cultural Center (SKC) Belgrade. In October 1975, various cultural workers active in SKC – critics, gallery owners, curators and artists – decided to publish their critical statements on the concept of *self-managed art* in relation to the *workers self-management* as the official programme of Yugoslav socialist state politics. For *Oktobar XXX* various actors from the independent and left-wing intellectual, artistic and activist scene were invited to speak about art and society from their different, and sometimes opposed, positions. More: http://bijenaleumetnosti.rs/2012/index.php?pid=1&news=45

15 For sure this is not only a local phenomenon. On how the archives of the most influential European biennial exhibitions are gated, see the text by Vesna Madžoski, 'Exorcising the Ghost of Europe: Manifesta Biennial of Contemporary Art and the Failed Rhetorics of Democracy', 2013: p. 279. A counter example is the 11th edition of Istanbul Biennale curated by WHW curatorial collective in 2009, when the statistical information and finances related to the production frame were rendered, by curators, transparently. Example taken from: Vuković, 2014.

16 See the exhibition text 'A Few Remarks on 'Minor Matters' by Kontekst Collective (Vida Knežević and Marko Miletić), 2013.

17 The exhibition was curated by: Vida Knežević, Kristian Lukić, Ivana Marjanović and Gordana Nikolić; Artists: Artan Balaj, Jakup Ferri, Driton Hajredini, Flaka Haliti, Fitore Isufi Koja, Dren Maliqi, Alban Muja, Vigan Nimani, Nurhan Qehaja, Alketa Xhafa, Lulzim Zeqiri. See: *The State of Exception Proved to be the Rule*, a video documentary of the prevention of an exhibition, by Eduard Freudmann and Jelena Radić, Serbia 2008, 84 min., Serbian with English subtitles

18 Curators: Ivana Marjanović and Vida Knežević (Kontekst Gallery, Belgrade) Participants: (artists and activists from Belgrade and Vienna): Jelena Radić (Belgrade), Goca Belić (Belgrade), Milica Ružičić (Belgrade), Maja Savić (Belgrade), Julia Wieger (Vienna), Elke Auer (Vienna), Esther Straganz (Vienna) and Eva Egermann (Vienna). www.galerijalkatraz.org/?p=1531

19 See:http://workshopwithoutborders.wordpress.com/2009/10/10/without-borders/.

20 More about the exhibition and the RUK group, see: Vida Knežević, Kristian Lukić, Ivana Marjanović and Gordana Nikolić (eds.), *Free And Sovereign. Art, theory and politics. A collection of essays and interviews on Kosovo and Serbia*, 2013; Vida Knežević, Svebor Midžić, Darinka Pop-Mitić, Branimir Stojanović and Milica Tomić (eds.), *7. Februar. Glasilo Radnika u kulturi* [7th February. Magazine of the Workers in Culture], 2008.

Bibliography

– Althusser, L. (1970) 'Ideology and Ideological State Apparatuses', in: *Lenin and Philosophy and other Essays*. New York and London: Monthly Review Press.
– Benjamin, W. (1940) 'On the Concept of History' www.marxists.org/reference/archive/benjamin/1940/history.htm, (accessed August 27, 2014).
– Benjamin, W. (1970) 'The Author as Producer.' *New Left Review* I/62.
– Boynik, S. and M. Henriksson (eds.) (2007) *Contemporary Art and Nationalism: Critical Reader*. Pristina: Institute for Contemporary Art 'Exit' & MM – Centre for Humanistic Studies 'Gani Bobi'.
– Buden, B. (2003) 'Još o komunstičkim krvolovcima ili zašto smo se ono rastali' [More About Communist Slaughters or Why We Actually Parted?] *Prelom/Break*, in: *Journal for Contemporary Art and Theory*, no. 5. Belgrade: Centre for Contemporary Arts.
– Buden, B. et al. (2008) 'Prelom i prelomi Preloma' [The Break and Breakings of the Break], in: *Prelom*, no.8/9. Belgrade: Prelom Kolektiv.
– Buden, B. et al. (2008) *The post-Yugoslavian Condition of Institutional Critique*, http://eipcp.net transversal/0208, (accessed August 27, 2014).
– Cvejić, B. (2005) 'Collectivity? You mean Collaboration' http://republicart.net/disc/aap/cvejic01_en.htm, (accessed August 27, 2014).
– Cvetković, S. (ed.) (1969) *Omladinski pokret 1919-1969.* [Youth Movement 1919-1969]. Belgrade: Mladost, 1969.
– Dedić, N. (2012) 'Focus Issue on Serbian Art in the 2000s. Interviews.' www.artmargins.com/index.php/5-interviews/681-nikola-dedic, (accessed August 27, 2014).
– Dojić, Z. and J. Vesić (eds.) (2009) *Political Practices of (Post-)Yugoslav Art: Retrospective 01*. Exhibition catalogue. Belgrade: Prelom kolektiv.
– Enwezor, O. (2004) 'The Artist as Producer in Times of Crisis.' http://kit.kein.org/book/export/html/249, (accessed August 27, 2014).
– Federici, S. (2004) *Caliban and the Witch: Women, the Body and Primitive Accumulation*. New York: Autonomedia.
– Garcés, M. (2009) 'To Embody Critique. Some Theses. Some Examples,' in: *Art and Contemporary Critical Practice: Reinventing Institutional Critique*. Raunig, G. and G. Ray (eds.). London: MayFlyBooks.
– Gramsci, A. (2010) *Selection from Prison Notebooks*. New York: International Publishers.
– Grlja, D. and J. Vesić, Prelom kolektiv (2007) 'The Neoliberal Institution of Culture and the Critique of Culturalization', http://eipcp.net/transversal/0208/prelom/en, (accessed August 27, 2014).
– Group Terms, DSC. (2010)'Contextual art in the countries of Eastern Europe: Approaches, diagnoses and treatments of the problems.' www.antijargon.tkh-generator.net/wp-content/uploads/2011/05/contextual-art.pdf, (accessed August 27, 2014).
– Horvat, S. and I. Štiks (2012) 'Welcome to the Desert of Transition!: Post-Socialism, the European Union, and a New Left in the Balkans.' http://monthlyreview.org/2012/03/01/welcome-to-the-desert-of-transition/, (accessed August 27, 2014).
– Kirn, G. (2012) 'Conceptualisation of reproduction and politics in the work of Louis Althusser: case of socialist Yugoslavia.' Ph.D. diss., University of Nova Gorica, www.ung.si/~library/doktorati/interkulturni/21Kirn.pdf (accessed August 27, 2014).
– Knežević, V. et al. (eds.) (2013) 'Free And Sovereign. Art, theory and politics. A collection of essays and interviews on Kosovo and Serbia', in: *Free And Sovereign. Art, Theory and Politics. A Collection of Essays and Interviews on Kosovo and Serbia*. http://napon.org/slobodnisuvereni/en/text/01_en.pdf, (accessed August 27, 2014). Hard copy published in Serbian language: V. Knežević, et al. (eds.)(2013) *Slobodni i suvereni. Umetnost teorija i politika. Knjiga eseja i intervjua o Kosovu i Srbiji*. Cenzura, Novi Sad.
– Knežević, V. and I. Marjanović (eds.) (2008) *Kontekst Archive 06/07/08*. Belgrade: Kontekst.
– Knežević, V. et al. (eds.) (2008) *7. Februar. Glasilo Radnika u kulturi* [7th February. Magazine of the Workers in Culture]. Belgrade: Radnici u kulturi.
– Knežević, V. and M. Miletić, Kontekst Collective (2013) 'A Few Remarks on 'Minor Matters'. http://camera-austria.at/camera/uploads/2013/09Exhibitiontexts_Ausstellungstexte_Kontekst.pdf, (accessed August 27, 2014).

- Madžoski, V. (2013) 'Excorcising the Ghost of Europe: Manifesta Biennial of Contemporary Art and the Failed Rhetoric of Democracy,' in: *Kunst und Ideologiekritik nach '89/Art and the Critique of Ideology After '89.* E. Birkenstock et al. Bregenz: KUB-Arena, Kunsthaus Bregenz.
- Marchart, O. (2007) 'The Curatorial Function,' in: *Curating Critique*, ICE Reader 1. Marianne Eigenheer (ed.) Frankfurt: Revolver.
- Marcuse, H. (1966) *Um i revolucija. Hegel i razvoj teorije društva* [*Reason and Revolution. Hegel and the rise of social theory*]. Sarajevo: Veselin Maleša.
- Marx, K. (1843) 'Marx to Ruge, Letters from the Deutsch-Französische Jahrbücher' www.marxists.org/archive/marx/works/1843/letters/43_09.htm, (accessed August 27, 2014).
- Marx, K. (1859) *A Contribution to the Critique of Political Economy*. 1859, www.marxists.org/archive/marx/works/1859/critique-pol-economy/preface.htm, (accessed August 27, 2014).
- Milevska, S. (2010) *Gender Difference in the Balkans: Archives of representations of gender difference and agency in visual culture and contemporary art in the Balkans.* Saarbrücken: VDM Verlag.
- 'Motivi bojkota 'Cvijete Zuzorić' – zahtevi umetnika' [The Motives for Boycotting 'Cvjeta Zuzorić' – the Artists' Demands]. Istorijski arhiv Beograda [The History Archive of Belgrade], 1936; Fond 'Cvijeta Zuzorić', predmet 103 [The 'Cvjeta Zuzorić' collection, item 103], 1936.
- New Media Center_kuda.org. (2005) *The Continuous Art Class. The Novi Sad Neo-Avantgarde of the 1960s and 1970s.* Frankfurt am Main: Revolver.
- Piškur, B. (2014) 'Politicization of Friendship,' in: *Politicization of Friendship*, exhibition catalogue. Ljubljana: Moderna galerija.
- Piškur, B. and T. Pureber, Radical Education Collective Ljubljana (2011) Statement in the text: 'Beleške sa debate' [Notes from the Debate] created as participants' notes from the panel discussion 'In the Engine Room: Working Conditions in Cul-ture', held at the Cultural Centre Rex in Belgrade, 26th June 2011, http://rexpro.b92.net/mvm/engineroom.html, (accessed May 09, 2014).
- Raunig, G. (2006) *Umetnost i revolucija. Umetnički aktivizam tokom 20. veka* [Art and Revolution. Artistic Activism During the Course of the Twentieth Century]. Novi Sad: Futura publikacije.
- Raunig, G. (2014) 'Occupy the Theater, Molecularize the Museum!,' in: *Truth is Concrete. A Handbook for Artistic Strategies in Real Politics.* steirischer herbst and Florian Malzacher (eds.) Berlin: Sternberg Press.
- Vuković, V. (2014) 'O problemima politizacije umjetničkog polja' [On the Problems of Politicization of the Art Field]. *Bilten*, 25th April, 2014. www.bilten.org/?p=581 (accessed August 07, 2014).
- Šuvaković, M. (2010a) 'Art and Activism in YU and Ex-YU 1968-2008,' in: M. Park et al. (eds.) *Reality Check: Art & Activism Reader*, 7-13. Belgrade: Akademija. http://lisatorell.com/bilder/ny/_10_reality%20check%20cat.pdf, (accessed May 09, 2014).
- Šuvaković, , M. (2010b) *Diskurzivna analiza: prestupi i/ili pristupi 'diskurzivne anlize' filozofiji, poetici, estetici, teoriji i studijama umetnosti i kulture*. [Discourse Analysis: Transgressions and/or Approaches of 'Discourse Analysis' to Philosophy, Poetics, Aesthetics, Theory and Studies of Art and Culture]. Belgrade: Orion art.

The Apparatus of the Mind

John Ellingsworth

First, an introduction: I got into cultural journalism when I started working for a publication covering physical and visual theatre sometime around 2006 (when I was still reasonably fresh out of university), and from there wrote reviews for five or six years before grinding to a halt. For most of that time I was also running my own online magazine (focused on contemporary circus, just about the smallest niche in the performing arts) and doing my level best to turn that into something resembling a job.

I had a lot of ideas for this: I tried contextual and display advertising, affiliate marketing, referral schemes, syndication. I even built an online network that could serve personalized ads targeted by location and interest. Some of these things worked a little bit, but none at anywhere near the scale I needed to put myself on a salary. At the same time as I was floundering on the business side, my magazine was becoming successful by other measures – it was respected within the sector, it had a solid audience, and I found it easy to connect with the international sphere and to find support to travel to events around Europe. So for a while, at the start, it was possible to concentrate on the things that were working and to not worry too much about the parts that were failing. I had a sort of monastic faith that my editorial rigour would eventually be rewarded.

During those first years I made a living through freelancing – pulling editorial jobs mostly through the profile and contacts that I had built up by doing the critical stuff – but gradually I came to resent the amount of time and energy it took to scrape by in my professional life. This feeling peaked in my third year of being an editor, and after some intensive thinking my answer – which at the time seemed to me quite rational and logical – was to produce a print magazine. I told myself that that way I could establish a direct financial relationship with my readership and create the necessary conditions to pursue journalism as an act of service – the thing I most wanted to do. As it was, I wrote and printed my magazine, it wasn't successful on the level I needed it to be, and I lost money and put myself in an even worse position. From the depths of the ensuing funk I wrote an essay about journalism and media models which I felt achieved some fiery and exceptional rhetoric but which didn't really achieve much of anything outside of that.

So after losing money on the magazine and shouting at the sky, I dropped out for a number of months and worked on other things. Eventually I came back to the world of arts journalism and criticism, but with the feeling that I needed to try something different. I decided to stop writing reviews, take several steps back, and appraise my situation with the broadest possible view. How could I undertake work that was rigorous and meaningful within a sustainable career?

The point of telling you all this here at the start is to try to show you that questions concerning the place and structure and forms of critical practice are not only of distant interest to me. Instead they are highly practical questions that I ask myself constantly and that direct the course of my professional life.

Given the chance to write – or to speak to you – on this subject, I'd like to forget about rhetoric for once and to shoot instead for something flat, simple and, perhaps, useful: here's everything I've learned, here's everything I think.

A Piece of History

I think most of today's criticism is following a model that is out of date.

Reviewing and critical appraisal grew up around a media system that was designed as an information service: buying a newspaper was a way of staying informed on current affairs, and reviews were like tiny windows onto the activities of the cultural world. A review contained two key lines of information: first, it was telling the reader, often in very literal terms, whether or not they should visit the exhibition, watch the film, buy the record; second, for readers with a broad interest in a certain art field, it was a way to survey the landscape and keep an understanding of how things were evolving/developing on a national/international level.

Buying the newspaper was the only way that this information would reliably come to you. The alternative was that *you* had to go to *it*: you had to clear the diary and attend all the performances yourself, or drop in on some sort of highly specialized professional meeting each week and wander from person to person asking their opinions on things and gathering up all the information. You could get recommendations from friends of course, but probably these were harder to come by at a time when you weren't constantly in touch with your acquaintances and their recent experiences and opinions. In some sense the critics were your agents in the field – you could rely on them for intelligence and situational analysis, and you would develop a relationship with them which would include a sense of how their personality was reflected in their reports and general angle of approach.

But now that the genie is out of the bottle – now that information is not only free but has *been* freed – the critic is in a different position. It is not possible anymore to hold a monopoly on information; the critic is no longer a gatekeeper – or at least the gate is much, much smaller. Arguably there is a curatorial position for those who sift through and highlight information, but this is partly performed by social networks (where you are naturally building connections based on likeness), plus curatorial influence doesn't necessarily correlate with specialist knowledge: a theatre sells more tickets off a sunny tweet from Stephen Fry than a review in a leading newspaper.

In some arts this shift in critical power has been ameliorated by the way digital technology can tie media to purchase: if you read a review of an album and it sounds like your jam then you can buy it and listen to it on the exact same connected device that you used to look at the review in the first place. That original function of the critic as a provider of commercial recommendations is thereby partly preserved. But in the performing arts, my own sector, we have to contend with the fact that most of the things we write about have an extremely small window of relevance: shows usually play in one place at a time, often only for a few nights and with a limited capacity, and so the whole problem of what criticism is *for* is much sharper.

As a sector, we are talking about it all the time. Back when I was writing reviews I'd be asked a couple of times a year to speak on the role of the critic or the future of criticism. I accepted a few of these invitations, and a certain hopeless circularity emerged as, from one panel to another, over many months and seasons, I would wheel out the same tired points. I had a list that I had come up with – nothing especially insightful – that included: the critic mediates between artists and audiences in the case of complex work; the critic documents the artistic field, witnesses artistic movements, and traces lineage; the critic provides context, provides feedback; the critic enriches a reflective culture and plays a part in promoting humanistic values; et cetera, et cetera.

Taking any of those points individually I could see that they were worthwhile – I do think that it is important to document artistic work, that context is meaningful, that inviting audiences into reflection is valuable – but I came to feel that reviewing and criticism (which, again, was shaped long ago by a commercial function) wasn't ideally suited to any of these things.

So the approach that I began to take myself was to try to be as mechanical as possible in separating form from function. I wanted to take my original list of services that the critic performed and then build projects and activities around those points as specific goals. So if, for instance, my aim was to document artistic process I asked myself what was the *best* way to do that? I wanted to have exceptional clarity of purpose, and, with an eye to sustainability, I wanted if possible to tie each strand of my practice to a specific growth area in media or the arts to increase my chances of finding paid work.

Mediation: Content Services

A year ago I was at a conference with representatives from around 50 theatres and venues in the UK, and among the scheduled sessions was a talk delivered by the Head of Marketing at the Roundhouse, one of the largest performing arts venues in London. He was talking about selling tickets, and he said that what they were finding, at the Roundhouse, was that reviews were becoming less and less important. He said that the venue was itself taking over from reviews with its own content – that they were able to 'remove risk at the point of purchase' through the provision of their own media: audience reaction videos, trailers, a Twitter feed, Facebook comments, blog posts, etcetera. As he said this I looked around the room and every person I could see – so managers and programmers from venues all over the country – was studiously making notes.

Things have only accelerated since then, and today most venues and organizations understand that they need to internalize some of the functions that were previously performed by the media. For some this is intimidating; others are probably quite excited by the prospect of being able to keep their communications relentlessly on message. Regardless, you can look at their current efforts in this sphere and it's clear that (a) the venues themselves mostly aren't very good at the work they've inherited, and (b) the smaller ones are pushing the responsibility of content creation onto the programmed companies, who are also not very good at it and don't have a lot of time to invest in developing the requisite skills.

The problem is that, particularly in smaller organizations, responsibility for this new work tends to fall on the marketing department, who are used to writing traditional copy that hypes an event by creating a clear image of it – a miniature brand. For some forms of experimental art the rules and expectations are a little different, but the closer you get to the mainstream the more imperative it becomes to create a perception of high value around an artistic work. This, in turn, prohibits showing weakness. Suggesting, for instance, that a performance differs wildly from night to night, and that some nights it is powerful and other nights it falls completely flat, is not a strong marketing message because it increases, rather than reduces, a potential customer's sense of risk at the point of purchase.

To put it another way, traditional marketing is trying to do all the thinking for you – it wants to present an artistic work, or an experience, as a 'sure thing'. This style of communication works fine for announcements and press releases, but in contexts where you expect debate or discursive writing the information it presents is stretched very thin. Even when you take out the pressure of sales there can still be a communication vacuum. I follow a couple of art schools on Twitter, and when they promote the work of their students it always has the same cheerful, safe tone – things tend to be 'lovely' or 'great' or 'terrific'. You can almost watch the words hollowing out, because at some level the goal is to avoid the possibility of ever being misinterpreted. Twitter distils the problem by concentrating it within a limited medium, but it can happen in blogs and on other communication channels as well – organizations have this glass-eyed, surface-y engagement with even their own cultural products and activities.

Obviously it is not always appropriate, or at least not easy, for a school to publicly express opinions on the competence of student work, but assessment of quality is just one facet of a sensitive response – you can have opinions about character and influences; you can have an emotional response; you can think and interpret.

Some larger organizations are realizing this and creating editorial positions within their communications departments. What they are trying to do, fundamentally, is to initiate conversations around the work they present – to create a discourse around art and then to host that discourse on their own platform. (Or if the conversation spins out into other areas of the Internet then they want the threads to lead back to them.) From the pragmatist point of view of a marketing department this is just another way of drawing readers to a venue/festival website and getting them into the top of a sales funnel, but, regardless of the end goal, the skills of the critic – a person who can relate to art, interpret it, frame it in terms of a wider field (in other words, *talk* about it) – are highly relevant.

The first wave of collaborations between critics and presenters, at least here in the UK, mostly took place within live art – a genre of performance that often invites, or even requires, mediation through its own conceptual nature.[1] The practice of 'embedded criticism' briefly became popular, which would sometimes mean little more than a critic writing reviews to be hosted on the festival website, and other times would entail the critic following the process of a company (i.e. getting down and dirty in the rehearsal room). But as the embedded model was iterated on, and spread outside live art, the discordance or internal friction between art criticism and art presentation threatened to shake the whole thing apart. How could a critic form a legitimate response to a work when they were being paid by a body that had a financial interest in a *positive* response?

Today the number of collaborations between critics and presenters is increasing, but usually in relationships that ditch the reviewing format (which is built around judgement/assessment/analysis) in favour of more loosely interpretative writing or journalistic pieces that centre on the voice of the artist (e.g. a series of interviews). At the same time the core work is not so different: if the key skill of the critic is articulation then they are still performing this work, just in another form and to another end.

I can understand if you would rather not go near a marketing department. Questions of independence and integrity are deeply personal and, in my own view, wholly specific to the situation at hand. But if you've got the stomach for it, this area of work is growing rapidly. It's happening more and more: festivals commissioning critics to edit in-house magazines, run blogs, curate discussions – to mediate between cultural activity and audiences.

Context: (Online) Education

I often said, when asked, that part of the role of the critic was to 'provide context'. Now I wonder what I actually meant by that. I never stopped to really examine it, but I think my sense was that context was the ability to perceive an artwork in relation to the wider art field that gave rise to it. In theoretical terms, this meant approaching the work of criticism with almost a curatorial mindset – arranging each art experience in relation to every other and keeping an orderly mental record of connections and sympathies. In practical terms, within a review, it generally meant explaining to people that what they thought was bold or original was actually derivative and poorly executed.

In the performing arts, where contextual knowledge is relatively inaccessible (in the sense that you can't attend a performance from the 1960s in the same way that you are able to watch a classic film whenever you like), the knowledgeable critic is both needed and, in a sense, irrelevant. Needed because their frame of reference is unique and irreplaceable, and irrelevant because what is the point of providing context to a reader if it is just a matrix of historical facts within which they have no intellectual agency?

It could be useful to distinguish between the provision of context – i.e. giving the reader the tools to distinguish/compare/cross-examine – versus the exhibition of context – showing that you, the critic, know more than the reader by punctuating a text with references. The latter approach is really only a manifestation of seniority/authority, and is probably the reason why so many artists are aggressively against comparative analyses of their work, insisting that they want the audience to experience the art work alone, in a kind of aesthetic vacuum.

Still, the further you turn from an exhibitive attitude the clearer it is that context fulfils an educative purpose, and critics who are interested in this branch of their practice often drift toward teaching. In the realm of pedagogy, 'context' is the field of knowledge, which the teacher has undertaken to pass on to the student. It has a practical purpose in bringing another person into a more sophisticated and nuanced relationship with art. This has always been true, but the growth of online learning (and particularly highly iterative platforms such as Coursera, edX and Khan Academy)[2] is opening up a new space for the critic.

On some level education is only communication – communication of ideas, knowledge and enthusiasm, from teacher to student, from student to teacher, and between students as peers. And in the twenty-first century, broader communication trends have radically altered the ways in which information is recorded, stored and transferred from one person to another. To keep pace, the online education sector has been creating platforms that embrace the principles of open access, that recognize the participative role of the spectator/reader/user, that fully engage with the opportunities of mixed or transmedia storytelling, and that understand the role of social networks in connecting, parsing and even enhancing networked information.

Putting it another way: the skills needed to be an educator and those needed to work in media have never been closer. Online education is still an emerging field. It is a new/experimental space, with even very large institutions still working out what methods are the most effective. The humanities have been lagging behind the sciences (partly because scientific learning and assessment is more programmatic) but are starting to catch up, and the interpretive/analytical nature of arts education opens the way for creative approaches to the attainment of learning outcomes.

I think that those who enter this space early, and grapple with its fundamental possibilities and limitations, will attain a valuable position for the future.

Documentation / Reflective Thinking: Convergence

Another item on my list that I never gave enough thought to was the idea of 'documentation'.

In the performing arts many artists do not document their work at all or else they document it poorly. Asked to keep a record of their artistic process (usually to report to funders or provide a venue with some of that discussion-feeding content) artists will often simply place a camera in the corner of the room. This creates *a* document, but it is one-dimensional; it attests to the existence of the work, the process, but can be of little use to those who want to reflect on the context of a creation or engage with the implicit knowledge and decisions that inform its shape, structure and material.

This weakness in documentation creates a space for the critic, but I think there are two key questions to grapple with. First, how do you document something as complex, messy, diffuse and multifaceted as artistic creation? Second, how do you address that documentation to artists, researchers or audiences who want to increase their artistic knowledge?

My own sense is that documentation is in a stronger position to answer both these questions if it engages with the most recent and progressive developments in digital media, and if critics working in this area embrace the concept of convergence.

The idea of a 'convergent newsroom' has been around for some time. Put simply, this is the idea that, in the online age, the different forms or aspects of media production have started to converge within individual journalists. So where once you would have had separate people working on writing, audio, video, art design, etcetera, now it is one hack with a broad suite of skills. As upstream practices flow back into the mainstream, it seems inevitable to me that critics will eventually have to follow suit – just as they have become accustomed to self-publishing, promoting themselves through social media, and so on.

But it is also useful to think of convergence in respect of the media being produced. So instead of having a video in one part of a website, text in a blog, audio in a podcast, those elements are being combined within single pieces. In the last two or three years we have seen a real explosion of experimentation in this field. Media producers, from big newspapers to online television channels to independent creators, have started to tell stories by combining text, photography, audio-visual materials and interactive elements with highly iterated visual and user experience design. Not all of these experiments are successful, but the best merge art and journalism in creating a new form of engaging multimedia writing.[3]

This can actually take many different shapes, and just because an article includes different media doesn't mean it has to include them all equally. It is normal for a piece to have a dominant quality, led by the leading competency of the producer – so you have image-intensive articles produced from the perspective of a filmmaker or photographer, and others that interpret the visual elements as rhythmic interruptions to a textual narrative.

I don't know how to qualify 'good' documentation within the arts field, but when I ask myself what I want a document to be I tend to think of something thick, something rich, something that carries a sense of time and place. I also think of it as having a number of layers, and a modular quality, to fulfil different levels of interest and engagement.

This thinking has partly come from trying to anticipate what researchers or other interested parties might be looking for in the future. So imagine, for instance, a performance researcher who is looking back to an obscure show from the 1980s. This person hasn't been able to get in touch with the creative team, so all they've got to go on is whatever documentation they can dig up. Of course this person isn't going to find one review and then stop there, satisfied. Instead they will collect all the reviews they can find, as well as posters and programmes and flyers. They will look for production images and video, try to find interviews, visit the original venue. They will gather together lots of different pieces in order to flesh out their sense of what the performance event was and what it felt like.

The opportunity that exists is for critics to collect the different facets of a documentary record (what the performance event was) and to marry that with an intelligent sense of how those elements can interrelate to reflect an artistic experience (what it felt like). To some degree this entails expanding a sense of the critic's role out to an editorial or curatorial function – the emphasis shifts from judgement of the artistic work towards an assessment of how best to represent it. The critic is still interpreting the work in deciding what information it is relevant to include, but some of that responsibility is shifted onto the reader as they dig through documentary content.

Editors are already doing this work to a small extent: if a website publishes a feature and includes a gallery of photos they are going one step further in providing documentation. However, there is still space for development because the majority of critics/commentators are approaching work from the same angle and with the same level of engagement – you have different intellectual and critical responses, but usually from the same basic position (having seen a show once, from the audience). It is broad, but not deep.

My own ideal is for an artistic document to reflect an experience so intensely that I can feel some piece of it myself. To date, multimedia writing has mostly grown and evolved within features journalism, but it has mostly had the same goals: to create immersive works, saturated with a sense of a particular environment, that are explored as much as they are read.

Taking the practical view, another reason for critics to engage with multimedia writing is that it brings together a set of skills that are not widespread and that are therefore easier to sell as bespoke services. Anyone can write an article (though quality will vary), but not every organization has the competency to produce advanced digital media.

The door is wide open, I think, and the sooner you engage with this stuff the more valuable you make yourself.

Recognition / Iteration: Reviewing

Finally, returning to the start, I think there are a couple of functions for which the traditional reviewing form is well-suited.

Foremost, it is the ideal way for a writer to establish themselves within a particular field and to build authority. In the performing arts, at least, venues are generally very open to providing review tickets, and writers can always volunteer with established magazines/websites when they are starting out. There aren't many barriers to entry besides time and motivation, and then – even if traction is declining among general audiences – reviews will usually be read by the artists they cover (and then perhaps shared with friends and peers). After you've been reviewing for a year or two your name becomes known, and if you've been doing the work consistently then certain qualities have probably started to attach to your name (hopefully a sense of trust, rigour, fairness). This awareness starts with the artists but gradually spreads to venues and presenters and others working in your chosen sector.

The other major benefit of reviewing is that you see a lot of work and you iterate constantly on what is essentially the same mental process: the process of responding to / reflecting on / articulating artistic work. It is a kind of mind training, and through it you also naturally develop a foundation of knowledge to contextualize work. The problem, I think, is that reviewing only takes you so far. In practical terms, it becomes a career dead-end, and in intellectual terms it traps you in repeating the same task over and over. There is a point at which personal growth/benefit flattens out, or begins to climb only incrementally – and maybe for that reason it is better to see reviewing as a training ground and as the first step towards another kind of critical work.

It is a way to prepare a network and build trust that can support future projects, and it is a way, if you like, to prepare the apparatus of the mind. After that, you have a lot of options for what you want to do.

Notes

1 A couple of examples... In 2010, Hannah Nicklin was commissioned as a correspondent at the festival In Between Time (www.inbetweentime.co.uk) – she was a sort of roving reporter responding to the programme and everything surrounding it. In 2011, SPILL Festival (www.spillfestival.com) had a thinker in residence, joined the next year by a writer in residence (critic and curator Diana Damian). The writer Mary Paterson (www.marypaterson.tumblr.com) worked a lot with arts festivals and producers around the same time before moving on to work more directly with artists.

2 Coursera (www.coursera.org) partners with a lot of HE institutions to offer courses; edX (www.edx.org) is likewise working with a lot of universities and was founded by MIT and Harvard. Khan Academy (www.khanacademy.org) is independent and emerged in a rather extraordinary way from one educator's YouTube channel. All three are very large: Coursera has around 7 million registered users, edX more than 3 million, Khan Academy around 10 million active users per month.

3 A couple of the most successful for me would be *The Guardian*'s 'The NSA Files' (www.theguardian.com/world/interactive/2013/nov/01/snowden-nsa-files-surveillance-revelations-decoded#section/1) and Grantland's 'Out in the Great Alone' (www.sports.espn.go.com/espn/grantland/story/_/id/9175394/out-great-alone). The Journal Setinel's Pulitzer-nominated 'The Course of Their Lives' is a nice synthesis of some of the current design trends (www.jsonline.com/news/health/The-Course-of-Their-Lives-Medical-College-of-Wisconsin-students-gross-anatomy-class-225058322.html#!/the-first-cut/). With the emphasis on film the *Hollow Documentary* project (www.hollow-documentary.com) is best-in-show. Specifically from a documentation angle one of my favourite pieces is Polygon's 'Street Fighter 2: An Oral History' (www.polygon.com/a/street-fighter-2-oral-history).

Part 2

Institutional and Professional Shifts

'Un-Common Sense' Social Critique and the Struggle over Commonality

Christian Höller

Is common ground a word or just a sound? Lou Reed – 'Good Evening Mr. Waldheim', 1989

In what ways is critique related to the idea of commonality? Is the work of the cultural or social critic, in its sometimes quite heterogeneous flavours, indebted to a notion of the 'common' or 'collective'? Can commonality in any meaningful way be considered a guiding principle behind critique's manifold tasks and endeavours? In order to tackle this complex of questions we need to first take a closer look at the various meanings embedded in the term 'critique' and examine their specific articulation with regard to 'the common'.

To start out with an example from sociological discourse, it seems that for quite some time, starting as early as the 1960s but reaching back to the school of 'critical theory' in the 1930s, critique was crucially informed by an idea of social commonality. Thus, critique – in its more emphatic, objectivist sociological mode – was intricately linked to the notion of a higher, mostly hidden truth – a truth that, once uncovered by the potentially all-knowing critic, would shed some light on what might be good, or liberating, for *all*; or in other words: on what the unifying bond or kernel of a truly liberated society and its individual members might consist in. Along came the more self-reflexive approach of a 'critique of critique' that would cast some serious doubt on that very mission, which is trying to look for a higher commonality based on the empirical evidence available. Listening closely to what individuals, or social agents, had to say about their particular positioning in a given society was deemed more illuminating than putting those very agents under a general suspicion: the suspicion of being blinded, manipulated, or poised by whatever manipulative means the governing regime has at its disposal, therefore inevitably living in a state of 'false consciousness'. The critic, according to this second school of thought, might be better off listening in on the beliefs and feelings of his or her 'popular' informants – better, that is, than knowing right in advance that such beliefs and emotions cannot help but be elusive.

Both strands of critique – the one of 'critical sociology' and the 'pragmatic sociology of critique' (as this opposition is usually called)[1] – seem to be oriented towards a common horizon, though. A horizon, which despite the obvious methodological differences of the two approaches delimits the sort of 'common ground' that a given society is capable of providing. Is it possible – both critique *and* the critique of critique appear to be asking – to bring to the fore the truth behind society's overall functioning? To lay bare that seemingly ineffable and perhaps mysterious core that both the richest rich and the poorest poor (to put it in those extremes) are willing to share? Whatever the exact answer to this question might turn out to be, and also putting real-existing, seemingly unbridgeable social differences to the side for a moment, 'common ground' plays a central role here: either as the kind of shared basis to which individual agents might be blind, but by which they are nevertheless crucially governed (which is roughly the take of the sociology of critique); or (as the version of critical sociology has it) as the sort of societal bond that individuals have explicit beliefs and ideas about, which might themselves turn out to be elusive fantasies or ideological myths. Commonality in this sense, whatever its exact perimeter may be, appears to be the basis of societal cohesion, or the cohesion of any of its subsystems, be it politics or any other field. Critique, on the other hand, is exactly the kind of playfield or process, working within a more clearly circumscribed perimeter, in which the tenets (tacitly or explicitly 'believed') of such commonality are either deliberately established or wildly contested.

Enter the notion of 'common sense', which has to be considered as a central element of social commonality, in psychological as well as in ideological regards. However, instead of providing the kind of unifying core behind the (critical or uncritical) orientation towards a 'true-for-all' commonality, the realm of common sense is exactly where things start to radically diverge again. Sometimes viewed as a unitary, predominantly stubborn and largely conservative entity, it should perhaps more aptly be regarded as the site of a far-reaching discrepancy: on the one hand, the set of beliefs, attitudes and prejudices voiced or tacitly held by hitherto silent, sometimes radically dissenting subgroups of 'the people'; on the other hand, the allegedly all-encompassing, foundational and thus largely undoubted tenet of society as a whole – the kind of thing that everybody willing to be part of that society is actively or passively prepared to share. Today, the former finds growing expression in criticism 'from below', supported by proliferating digital media facilities giving rise to a 'vox pop' that exhibits sometimes radically individualist or 'particularist' tendencies. The latter, supposedly serving the task of providing 'common ground' for society no matter how big or small, is apparently caught up in ever more empty proclamations (made by official politics or institutional representatives), and appeals to hold on to the supposedly shared values of commonality. In order to arrive at a clearer notion of how critique (or the work of the critic) is related to such diverging ideas of commonality, this discrepancy is more fully explored in what follows.

Critique and Common Sense

How exactly should the relationship of critique and common sense be conceived – especially if one wants to arrive at a notion of criticism that is neither (in populist terms) too inclusive nor (in a more elitist regard) too exclusive? Is critique the necessary 'other' of a commonality mostly made up of popular beliefs that are themselves dominated by nasty stereotypes on the one extreme, or by a sort of profound folk wisdom on the other? Is its task mainly a 'negative' one, namely to correct and put things right with respect to widespread false beliefs, evil prejudice, or persistent popular 'doxa'? Or, to view things from the opposite perspective, can it only be the everyday opinions of everyday people that will set things straight for a sustainable criticism – no matter whether we are dealing with politics, economics, culture or other fields? Must, in other words, critique in its various manifestations first and foremost listen in and pay close attention to the beliefs of ordinary folks, their shared interests – their *common* sense, so to speak? This latter option seems to be particularly apt for critical approaches (such as cultural studies in their classical outline) that are not negligent or dismissive of realms such as everyday, popular, or vernacular culture.

Stuart Hall and Alan O'Shea, in a paper written shortly before Hall's death in February 2014,[2] have tried to tackle the vexed problem of common sense and the question how it might be meaningfully related to a substantial form of critique. The critique they have in mind is, needless to say, the one aimed at neoliberalism, which has come to dominate Western societies from the 1970s onwards. In fact, most analyses today assume that it has, or is about to become the one and only remaining (worldwide) ideology, with less and less spaces for alternatives.[3] Since people living under its regime were hardly simply seduced, or manipulated in other malevolent ways so that they would accept it, there must be other mechanisms at work that account for its stupefying success. Hall and O'Shea, in their approach, look at the realm of common sense in order to find out how this ideology could become so extensively adopted. But here, things are far from simple, since the appeal to common sense, frequently aired by, for example, politicians looking for consent, exhibits a kind of circular, self-fulfilling structure: it is as much invoked as a *cause* (the alleged reason why ordinary folks 'really' want this and that) as it is – in the very same instance – projected as the desired *effect* (what people are supposed to want in order to keep the existing power structure intact). Hall and O'Shea draw on the notorious (in this case British) example of welfare cuts, usually legitimated by an overall austerity agenda – to which, as we have rhetorically been accustomed to over the years, there is supposedly no alternative. They supplement this example from the realm of politicians' discourse with debates about fairness as they have been pursued in online forums of the British tabloid press.

The findings are quite telling: With respect to the latter (readers' comments), common sense does in fact expose a much more complex make-up than usually implied by politicians' speeches ('And let this be our message – common sense for the common good,' as David Cameron exclaimed in an address on April 24, 2011). In fact, it can be claimed that common sense does not possess a conclusive or somewhat cohesive structure at all. This is where Hall and O'Shea invoke Antonio Gramsci's famous outline of common sense as not utterly 'critical and coherent but disjointed and episodic'[4] – although it does seem to possess a certain logic, as well as an inherent bundle of historical layers ('stratified deposits', in Gramsci's terms). An elusive object hard to grasp by theoreticians (or observers of public opinion), it is all the more fleeting as it is continuously evolving and transforming itself, constantly adapting to novel situations, as it were. Far from being immobile and rigidly conservative (as social critics of a certain flavour would have it), it is 'strangely composite' by containing 'Stone Age elements and principles of a more advanced science, prejudices from all past phases of history ... and intuitions of a future philosophy.'[5] Fundamentally contradictory as it is, common sense finally 'contains critical and utopian elements' as well and Hall and O'Shea, in their way of mobilizing the potentially liberating and democratizing elements within it, go on to stress, at its core, 'a sense of unfairness and injustice about "how the world works"'.[6]

This sentiment, no matter whether it is thought of as mere intuition, a battery of tacit beliefs, or rather a set of explicit principles or cognitive fixtures, goes by the term of 'good sense' (*buon senso*, in Gramsci's original wording). It is exactly this element or kernel within common sense that might provide the steppingstone for a different strategy – different from politicians' usual invocation of it for largely conservative means. How exactly this strategy for change and alternative might be pursued, especially with regard to the shaky, contradictory and highly incoherent make-up of common sense, is left open by Hall and O'Shea. Still, in order to make it operative for a potentially emancipatory agenda, a necessary first step might be to open it up and snatch it from the claws of an altogether reactionary understanding (common sense as the primary site of prejudiced belief and stereotyped bias). The sort of potentiality at its core (namely a widely shared sense of injustice and unfairness) could thus be considered the primary seed for a more full-blown social critique – a critique taking as its departure not the higher truths that only theoreticians and experts are capable of seeing, but rather the manifold voices that common sense, in all its contradictory and incoherent structure, instantiates in the very first place.

The Rift within Common Sense

Before addressing the utopian kernel within the 'strangely composite' complex of common sense, it is worth taking a closer look at its internal rift. That split, or radical divergence as one might call it, does in fact manifest itself on two different levels. One can for instance differentiate between (on the one hand) common sense in the form in which it is instantiated by the multiple voices and components that actually constitute it; *and* (on the other hand) the overall, more unitary and generalized notion of common sense, the wholesale package so to speak, which is readily referenced by politicians and commentators in the media. And which, not to forget, is in a continuous process of being constructed, undone and reconstructed – instead of being a neatly packaged given.[7] A closer look might reveal the many gaps and divergences that occur on the first side of that bigger divide.

As Hall and O'Shea point out in their close reading of common sense, the latter – even in its 'vox pop guise' – is hardly ever exposing a unitary or monochromatic gear. For sure, the myriad of online comments on the welfare cuts/social fairness debate that they investigate exhibit all the stereotyped, even blatantly racist traits that one is tempted to expect right from the beginning. Talk of 'benefit scroungers', 'welfare fraudsters', or 'Romanians and Bulgarians ... panting at the bit to get here for either jobs or benefits'[8] is just as widespread among the comments as are more deliberate and reflected assessments. The latter include, again not utterly surprising, wholesale attacks on politicians and managers as the real 'scroungers', more modest proposals about a 'decent living wage for everybody', or the pinpointing of the ideology of competitive individualism, today penetrating *all* of society, as the real crux of the problem. Leaving aside the question whether online forums can legitimately be regarded as a form of democratic public debate (and not just the poor *ersatz* public sphere that some critics see in today's 'shit-storm' culture),[9] the plurality of comments nevertheless sheds some illuminating glow on the actual make-up of common sense.

For what it's worth, the gathering of voices and opinions in online forums can be counted as a kind of measurement of the width and expansiveness of common sense. Even if 'good sense' (in the Gramscian understanding mentioned above) may only account for a tiny section of that expanse, the various, often heterogeneous forms of criticism aired 'from below' are in fact the sort of bedrock on which common sense is built. And on which it might be unravelled and undone, one is tempted to add. For the sometimes radically diverging opinions, drawing on a wide and uneven multiplicity of sources, from the depths of expert knowledge to sheer amateurism or affect-laden expressiveness, constitute nothing less than the actual spectrum of common sense at a certain time. The 'voice of the people', sometimes glossed over in popular media as if it were a unitary, common call, thus exposes itself as fundamentally at strife: a cluttered ensemble of 'dissensus'[10] that can hardly ever be regarded 'as one'. In fact, the particularist and individualist tendencies within the broad spectrum of 'vox pop', no matter how progressive or reactionary the thrust behind them, generate a peculiar field of struggle – notwithstanding the mapping that official politics is trying to make of it; or, for that matter, the kind of instrumentalization politicians are keen to undertake.

That battlefield, however, is equally marked by the more consequential 'hegemonizations' propelled or aimed at by the larger forces in society. In fact, the struggle over common sense that lies at the base of all democratic hegemonic endeavours is as much using bits and pieces of what can be gathered from 'the voice of the people' as it is attempting to actively articulate them into a certain constellation (and thus bring it into existence). This points to the second, as it were, opposing side of the higher-level split within the notion of common sense referred to above. When politicians take recourse to talk of 'common sense for the common good' or, somewhat more pointedly, 'a system that matches effort with reward instead of a system that rewards those who make no effort',[11] the intended manoeuvre becomes quite obvious: to gloss over actual differences with respect to the question what a contemporary welfare system should look like; to pretend, by declaration, that a partial, 'proper' meaning can be retrieved out of diverging attitudes vis-à-vis the common good; finally, to put in place the ideology of competitive individualism backed up ('thanks' to the ongoing crisis) by seemingly unavoidable austerity programs.

In this respect, the appeal to common sense (or commonality generally) serves a clear task: to make sure that there are, at least theoretically, some shared assumptions that all (or most) members of a given society can potentially agree upon; to hit upon the kind of bedrock that is urgently needed in a 'society under siege', as Zygmunt Bauman has famously called the scenario in which the social is more and more endangered by the double pressure of intensifying globalization processes *from above* and the equally increasing fragmentation into more and more incommensurable lifestyles *from below*;[12] to rhetorically stipulate a sort of foundational ground, onto which the heterogeneous social multitude can be mapped – or, to put it in more positive terms, can inscribe itself. From a critical perspective, it seems easy to dismantle or deconstruct such ideological hegemonization (for example, the notion that there is allegedly no alternative to an all-encompassing competitive individualism that needs less and less backing through state support). What is trickier, though, is to figure out how (and why) such hegemonization successfully filters back into, and persistently settles itself in the 'vox pop', which makes up common sense in the very first place.

Here we touch upon a crucial feature that seems to lie at the heart of the debate over contemporary neoliberalism. As Jeremy Gilbert points out in his book *Common Ground: Democracy and Collectivity in an Age of Individualism*, neoliberalism promotes – not least through a tendentious hegemonization of common sense – a certain set of assumptions: assumptions which treat 'all creative agency and potential rationality as properties of individuals rather than of groups, which are in turn understood only as fetters on the freedom and mobility of individuals'.[13] According to that school of thought, all substantial forms of collectivity, sociality, or for that matter, democratic participation are considered as 'fetters' on any true liberation of human experience and accomplishment. Gilbert traces this line of reasoning back to Hobbes' 'meta-individualist' conception of the Leviathan, which initiated a powerful strand in modern political thinking running through modern group-psychological theorizing right up to, alas, the persistence of neoliberalism in the present. Contrary to that tradition, Gilbert outlines another, more 'critical' line of thought that favourably considers 'sociality as a condition of dynamic multiplicity and complex creativity, and [is] against any assumption that collectivity can only be understood in terms either of a simple aggregation of individuals, or of a homogenous and monolithic community'.[14]

Regardless of how the heavy terms invoked here ('multiplicity', 'creativity' and so on) might be spelled out in empirical detail, it should be acknowledged that this outline provides a particular reading of the fundamental split within common sense. While neoliberal reasoning, according to Gilbert, is deeply suspicious of any articulation of commonality (or accepts it only in the form of aggregated but in fact isolated individuality), the 'logic of collectivity' puts things radically different (this being the crucial aspect in which Gilbert is elaborating and in fact expanding Hall's and O'Shea's take on the common). Not only does it imagine instantiations of 'the common' as crucially characterized by heterogeneity and potentially 'infinite relationality', it also takes the multiplicity of voices as the building blocks of that very 'common'.[15] As the active constituents – not only to be unearthed but in fact to be constructed, worked on – of the common. In other words, the widely shared belief in atomized individuality should not simply be considered as the only remaining commonality there is today. Things should rather be viewed the other way round: having a certain feature or situation in common (and recognizing this as such) could, instead of being a dead end, crucially point toward a new social singularity. Who else but the singular and for the most part isolated individuals are bound to give rise to a new form of commonality (without any preconception of how that commonality will look like)? So where does this (admittedly rough-cut) scenario leave the practitioner of critique – especially when it comes to properly addressing the project of a newly emerging commonality?

The Rift within Critique

The overall picture that emerges with respect to a workable notion of critique on the basis of considerations so far, can be sketched as follows. We have, on the one hand, the critical address of, or general orientation towards a supposedly intractable common sense that seems in constant need of amelioration, correction or amplification. The professional critic, as it were, has to provide exactly these lacking resources, i.e. the tools and means for 'commoners' to better understand what he or she gets so readily outspoken about (for instance in online forums). If, on the other hand, the notion of common belief, prejudice, doxa et cetera is conceived differently (viz. in the vein of the old Gramscian understanding laid out by Hall and O'Shea) the overall critical task may change as well. It is then not so much a matter of putting things right (of correcting false beliefs so to speak) that the critic should primarily aim at, but – following a more fine-grained notion of commonness – a more immanent kind of labour. Acknowledging their position right in the midst of the battlefield of common sense, not above or underneath it, critics would have to abandon all transcendental entitlement or pretension, locating their claims on a par with other voices emanating from an increasingly fragmented public.

This is the sort of ground plot on which the deliberations of individualism and collectivity as pointed out above (and elaborated by Gilbert) come into play. For the obviously dated understanding of the transcendental critic (the 'traditional intellectual' in Gramsci's terms) is itself based on a highly individualist conception. Even if he or she is speaking in the name of a higher collectivity – which has become rare among contemporary intellectuals – his or her profile is one of enforced singularity: like a lone observer, floating above the uneducated masses, detached from dirty realities down there but through such detachment able to claim a more distanced, more objective view than anybody else.[16] Pursuing this admittedly rough-cut vision for the moment, the positioning of the second kind of critic (the immanent or embedded one, the 'organic intellectual' according to Gramsci) is of a much more collectivist (or in Gilbert's terms: relational) stance. Finding him- or herself amidst the crisscross streams and vortexes of popular opinion, the embedded – or should one say entangled? – critic cannot help but hold on to nearby anchors or currents, thus amplifying certain tendencies in the broad flow of common discourse while attenuating or consciously dismissing others.

With respect to dismantling or undercutting the deeply entrenched neoliberal assumptions touched upon earlier, the emerging scenario looks as follows: In an extreme regard, a detached and distanced view cannot help but accept the increasing atomization of the social, emanating (as it does) from a highly individualized position itself. Competitive individualism, even if it is identified and denounced as the general culprit responsible for most evils in today's societies, is hardly ever challenged by such a detached, 'high-profile' view. In fact, the distanced, transcendental critic seems to perfectly fit that very scheme even when he or she is justly castigating its nasty qualities of competitiveness and individualism. The more immanent, 'infinitely relational' perspective cannot do away with the ideology of individualist competitiveness either. Still, its embeddedness within a consciously acknowledged (and not straight-out negated) 'collective defined by its multiplicity, heterogeneity and complexity'[17] provides an altogether different starting point for recasting the relationship of sociality and individuality. Taking its departure from within a myriad of atomized particulars (one tiny bit of which it occupies itself), and moving through all sorts of potential or tentative gatherings/groupings, it might itself epitomize a possible way of overcoming those very starting conditions. By embodying a living model how to connect, share, and exchange bits and pieces of commonality, it might point towards a new, emerging collectivity (however shaky and instable it may be).

Of course, this is fairly utopian talk. However, returning to the central question of this essay, one might slightly reframe its general outline: Should critical expertise consciously take its place in the parade of particularist expression exemplified by the sphere of vox pop mentioned above, while at the same time orienting itself to a more general perspective? Or is the professional critic first and foremost obliged to hold on to a potentially universal perspective (even if such a view may have become less and less credible due to its increasingly empty proclamations)? Should, to pursue the latter track, the work of the critic be primarily premised on the articulation of a 'good-for-all', potentially 'all-inclusive' common sense? Or should it rather concentrate on gaining a foothold in partial and sometimes unpopular 'un-common sense', and attempt to move on to a 'more common' common from there? That second option – to jump ahead – might in fact turn out as the epitome of critical work, given that it takes its departure not from a perspective somehow abstracted and high above the social body, but rather from within its heterogeneous and fragmented assemblage. But before moving on to explore that seemingly paradoxical option, a few remarks should be made about the fallacy of the 'good-for-all' if it is aired from a detached, socially abstracted position.

The appeal to 'common sense for the common good' can be viewed, as pointed out above, as a kind of battle cry to hold on to neoliberal norms, especially if it is voiced from a privileged position within society. On the other hand, the wholesale critique of that very proclamation (unmasking it, as it were, as an ideological premise) will only have very limited effects, none of which is likely to filter through to the actual level where 'common ground' is being formed and constructed. For commonality first and foremost comes into being by the everyday articulation – dispersed, wildly fragmented, sometimes unpredictably converging, taking place on many different levels (from informal private conversation to public expression in online forums). It is that very disjoint and incongruous articulation that sutures together (and thus mistakenly 'unifies') the bits and pieces of common sense, which resist being readily available,[18] or easily retrievable as some higher social authorities are tempted to think. Taking a stand, either in all too positive or all too negative terms, vis-à-vis or above such wrongly unitized and thus normalized commonality only demonstrates the fallacy that such over-generalization is apt to produce.

Coming back to the two different models of critique, the upshot can be summarized as follows: Occupying the vantage point of a detached and distanced, wholesale condemnation (or reckless endorsement) of neoliberal assumptions seems to be in danger of losing touch with the 'acting out' of, or 'struggling' with those very assumptions on a daily basis. Furthermore, such a vantage point inadvertently fosters and endorses a higher-level individualism, which a thorough critique of neoliberalism wants to unravel in the first place.[19] By contrast, taking sides, or at least acknowledging the embeddedness of one's own position in the overall make-up of commonality may embody an altogether different approach. Taking into account, or consciously choosing as one's starting point the inextricable entanglement in the folds and niches of common sense attests to a much more collectivist stance. The subtle repercussions of competitive individualism are of course not banished by taking this route, but they might lose a good deal of the intractable hold which they exert even on their critical rejection. In fact, they may start to look like a gear that one could try to strip off and leave behind once the gates or assemblages of a newly forming collectivity start to open up. 'Common sense for the common good' can thus take on a radically different meaning, based on these two premises: that one is willing to pursue one's critical work from *within* common sense (and accept to be on a par with its multitudinous other instantiations), and that the common good is not something that exists beforehand but is rather a 'project' that has to be brought into being.

A Taste of Un-Common Sense

'[The] individualist conception of human life is promoted in a classically ideological fashion, informing a range of discourses and practices, from education policy to popular television programming, wherein it is presented, not as a particular way of looking at the world, but as simple common sense ... .'[20] This is how Jeremy Gilbert circumscribes the working of 'simple' common sense with respect to the penetrating effects that neoliberalism produces on various levels of everyday life. The task of the (embedded, as it were) critic would nevertheless consist in going beyond a mere unmasking of that very 'promotion'. While the *embedded* critic conceives common sense predominantly in terms of its existence on a representational level (its representations on television or in education being prone to criticism), the *entangled critic* (as one might call him or her) would first and foremost acknowledge the fact that critique has to emanate from within that 'strangely composite' complex (which reaches beyond mere representation). The difficult task would therefore consist in the joint realization that while on the one hand, common sense is itself constantly in the making, in the process of unpredictably morphing into a different kind of constellation, it can, on the other hand, only ever be transformed, i.e. undergo such morphing, if it is approached from amidst its very components. Which comes down to a realization that one's critical stance is always in some way partial, maybe partisan and biased, but by no means objective or sufficiently detached so that it could embody or declare the 'good-for-all'.

This is where the aspect of 'un-common-ness' crucially comes into play. Because the very acknowledgment of the critical position emanating from within the fractured and multiple 'stratified deposits' which add up to common sense ('simple' or otherwise) also has to take into account that commonality is always a construct, not a given. It may very well be that a whole 'range of discourses and practices, from education policy to popular television programming' reinforce a *particular* kind of commonality. Evidently, critique would have to tackle those very agents of reinforcement but still, there are two major limitations to be considered here: first, that what is being reinforced in the process is not some pre-existing entity but rather something strangely 'disjointed and episodic', something 'fundamentally contradictory'; and second, that the construction and/or reinforcement of commonness should itself be understood as one among various possibilities,[21] as a contingent 'particular', so to speak, that can be challenged, questioned, maybe radically undone or at least rudimentarily uprooted in the long run. In whose name or interest this process is conducted is of course highly contingent upon the dominant (or suppressed) ideology at a certain time. Suffice it to say that in the present moment, putting in place *different* ideological tenets than the ones supporting competitive individualism should rank high on the critical agenda.

Again, this may sound as a fairly utopian project (albeit in the emphatic sense of the term 'utopian' instantiated, among others, by the *Kilburn Manifesto*[22]). At the same time, it hits upon the interesting territory where the 'un-common' and 'good sense' meet. For the entangled critic, once his or her entanglement in the fractured layers of a composite common sense is reflexively acknowledged, cannot help but embody and thus articulate a position of un-commonness. The range of such a perspective can only ever be partial, no matter if it endorses the vision of 'fraudulent welfare abuse' or the need for a 'decent living wage for everybody'. By understanding this unavoidable partialness not as a limitation of critique but as its necessary precondition, its productive starting point, so to speak, this very un-commonness, can become an operative and possibly creative force. Especially by connecting to 'good sense' and enforcing the sometimes diffuse sentiment as to what unfairness and injustice are all about, it might contribute to the building (tedious and long-term as it may be) of a less and less 'un-common' but all the more encompassing commonality.

'Our ability to live with this incoherent structure may be due to the fact that the "stratified deposits" of common sense represent the outlook and interests of very different social groups ... .'[23] This diagnosis, expounded by Hall and O'Shea, points towards the multi-layered problematic any substantially critical work is facing today: that the outlook and interests of various fragments of society (however atomized or individualized they may be) are not something to be glossed over by critique but should rather be taken as a kind of empirical bedrock; that such outlooks and interests never fully homogenize into consistent or coherent structures but should instead be viewed as fractured and shifting 'deposits'; that, despite such fragmentation, there is a need to acknowledge these 'deposits' as integral to everyday life and practices of 'getting by'; and finally, that commonality is not a lost or hidden ground that only needs to be uncovered anew (e.g. from under persistent layers of individualist competitiveness) but rather a long-term project that involves quite some construction work alongside all unearthing efforts.

Common ground, to curtly summarize it, is an altogether shaky concept that is constantly in the process of losing its defining edges while at the same time regaining them anew; of potentially giving rise to the more un-common aspects embedded in its stratified make-up while simultaneously taking on novel, hitherto unknown contours. Which essentially leaves a twofold task for the critic: to acknowledge the un-common element in the common, and to start building a new common on the basis of such un-common insights.

Notes

1 See for instance Luc Boltanski, *On Critique: A Sociology of Emancipation*, Cambridge MA/Malden, 2011 (French original 2009), p. x; Nicolas Duvoux, 'The Empirical Sociology of Critique: An Interview with Luc Boltanski', in: *books & ideas*, February 2012, http://thesocietypages.org/monte/2012/09/01/an-interview-with-luc-boltanski-critique-and-self-subversion/ (last accessed January 2015); Ulf Wuggenig, 'Paradoxical Critique', *eipcp/transversal*, April 2008, http://eipcp.net/transversal/0808/wuggenig/en (January 2015); Robin Celikates, 'Systematic misrecognition and the practice of critique: Bourdieu, Boltanski and the role of critical theory', in: Miriam Bankowsky and Alice Le Geoff (eds.), *Recognition Theory and Contemporary French Moral and Political Philosophy*, Manchester 2012, pp. 160–172.

2 Stuart Hall and Alan O'Shea, 'Common-sense neoliberalism', in: *Soundings*, 55 (Winter 2013), www.lwbooks.co.uk/journals/soundings/pdfs/Manifesto_commonsense_neoliberalism.pdf (January 2015).

3 Cf. Stuart Hall, 'The neoliberal revolution', in: *Soundings*, 48 (Summer 2011), pp. 9–27; Stuart Hall, Doreen Massey and Michael Rustin, 'After neoliberalism: analysing the present', in: *Soundings*, 53 (Spring 2013), www.lwbooks.co.uk/journals/soundings/pdfs/s53hallmasseyrustin.pdf (this is the framing statement of the so-called *Kilburn Manifesto*, see www.lwbooks.co.uk/journals/soundings/manifesto.html, last accessed January 2015); Jeremy Gilbert, 'What kind of thing is "neoliberalism"?', in: *New Formations*, 80/81 (2013), www.lwbooks.co.uk/journals/newformations/pdfs/nf8081_intro.pdf (January 2015); see also David Harvey's meanwhile classic text *A Brief History of Neoliberalism*, Oxford/New York 2005.

4 Hall and O'Shea, 2013, p. 2.

5 Ibid.

6 Ibid., p. 3.

7 See Stuart Hall's earlier essay 'Gramsci and Us', in: *Marxism Today*, June 1987, pp. 16–21, www.hegemonics.co.uk/docs/Gramsci-and-us.pdf ((January 2015).

8 Hall and O'Shea, 2013, p. 15.

9 See for instance Byung-Chul Han, *Im Schwarm: Ansichten des Digitalen*, Berlin 2013, p. 9.

10 Cf. the elaboration of that notion by Jacques Rancière in 'The Janus-Face of Politicized Art: Interview with Gabriel Rockhill', in: *The Politics of Aesthetics*, London/New York 2004, pp. 52ff.

11 David Cameron in a speech on May 23, 2011, quoted in Hall and O'Shea 2013, p. 8.

12 Cf. Zygmunt Bauman, *Society under Siege*, Cambridge 2002.

13 Jeremy Gilbert, *Common Ground: Democracy and Collectivity in an Age of Individualism*, London 2014, p. viii.

14 Ibid., p. x.

15 Cf. ibid., p. 111ff. for an elaboration of 'infinite relationality' and p. 164ff. for a discussion of 'the commons'.

16 A similar argument is laid out by Jacques Rancière in *The Philosopher and His Poor*, Durham/London 2004 (French original 1983), especially in the chapter 'The Sociologist King', p. 165ff.

17 Gilbert, 2014, p. xii.

18 Cf. the deliberations on 'becoming' and 'possible worlds' in ibid., pp. 153ff. and 192ff.

19 See for instance Hall, Massey, Rustin 2013, Michael Rustin, 'A relational society', in: *Soundings*, 54 (Summer 2013), pp. 23–36, www.lwbooks.co.uk/journals/soundings/pdfs/s54%20rustin.pdf (January 2015), as well as Gilbert 2014, especially p. 31ff.

20 Ibid., p. 30.

21 Cf. ibid., pp. 192ff. As an aside, it should be mentioned that 'Uncommon Sense' is also the title of a 1945 science fiction short story by American author Hal Clement; almost needless to say, it is concerned with the struggle over (personal) hegemony in alien surroundings, cf. www.sff.net/people/hal-clement/uncommon%20sense%20by%20hal%20clement.htm (January 2015).

22 See www.lwbooks.co.uk/journals/soundings/manifesto.html (January 2015).

23 Hall and O'Shea, 2013, p. 4.

Criticism, Critique, and Capitalism

Luc Boltanski in Conversation with Robin Celikates and Thijs Lijster

What is the position from which critics speak, and on whose behalf? What is their function and responsibility with regard to the public? And how can they legitimate their authority? These questions, which are becoming increasingly urgent in debates on art criticism, are of course by no means unique to the figure of the critic. One might ask, and in fact one has asked, the same questions with regard to the specialist, expert or 'authority' in any other field. In fact, the position of the social critic has been on the agenda for some time in discussions within critical social theory and sociology. The French sociologist Luc Boltanski is one of the most prominent voices in these discussions.

In Boltanski's writings critique figures prominently, both as a question of method (what is the critical function of sociology?) and as a subject of sociological study (how do people 'do' critique?). A student and collaborator of Pierre Bourdieu, Boltanski was trained in the tradition of post-war French sociology, which saw it as its task not only to analyse systems of domination, but also to provide the dominated with an empirically-based understanding of their situation and ultimately with the tools for (at least cognitive) emancipation. As Boltanski came to realize in the course of his empirical studies, however, the tradition of critical sociology faces several theoretical and methodological problems. First, the dominated as described by critical sociology are themselves utterly oblivious to the forms of domination exposed by the sociologist. To account for this ignorance, the critical social theorist assumes that these actors suffer from 'false consciousness' or a distorted understanding of their own situation. This means, however, that sociologists necessarily underestimate, or even ignore, the critical capacities of the actors they are analysing, and at the same time overestimate the explanatory power of their own sociological approach. There is, in other words, an 'asymmetry between the sociologist enlightened by the light of his science and ordinary people sunk in illusion'.1 This asymmetry lies at the basis of a second problem. In Boltanski's view, critical sociology not only overestimates its own range of vision, pretending to know people better than they know themselves, but it also undermines its own emancipatory potential: the contempt for people's critical capabilities and practices ultimately robs critical sociology of an addressee.

In *On Justification* (2006 [1991]) Boltanski and his co-author Laurent Thévenot respond to these problems with what they call a 'pragmatic sociology of critique'. This pragmatic sociology of critique is not primarily interested in its own critical perspective, but rather in 'observing, describing, and interpreting situations where people engage in critique'.[2] This means observing situations in which actors find themselves confronted with indignation, stress, and social tests, and the ways in which they deal with these, especially in how they criticize each other and justify their actions. Critique, in this view, is not a meta-perspective, but a practice embedded in people's everyday lives.

As Boltanski came to realize in the debates that followed this 'pragmatist turn', however, this approach too has several drawbacks.[3] Placing the actors' own critique at the centre, the pragmatic sociology of critique made itself dependent on what Boltanski calls the actors' 'sense of reality'. Actors have a sense of what they consider 'normal', and this sense shapes the extent to which they experience feelings of indignation and anxiety, and hence the extent to which they are willing to criticize what they consider as the sources of these feelings. Although the sociology of critique might be right in arguing that critique is happening all the time, the scope of it is often quite local and limited. According to Boltanski, with the exception of revolutionary situations, 'ordinary people rarely call into question ... the general framework in which the situations that provoke their indignation and protests are inscribed'.[4] This also means that the sociologist might miss out on societal developments that occur over longer ranges of time, and that alter the very background against which people justify their actions. This is why, in his collaborative study with Ève Chiapello, *The New Spirit of Capitalism* (2005 [1999]) as well as in the methodological study On Critique (2011[2009]), Boltanski argues that sociology should also develop a 'sense of totality', that is a perspective from which the general framework within which acts of critique are situated can be questioned and criticized.[5]

Until now (and as opposed to Bourdieu), Boltanski has not written extensively on art and art criticism – although he was one of the contributing authors to Bourdieu's *Un Art moyen: Essai sur les usages sociaux de la photographie* from 1965 and in the 1990s started publishing his own literary work. His work, however, proved to be relevant to many discussions within and about the art world. In *The New Spirit of Capitalism*,

Boltanski and Chiapello distinguish between two kinds of critique: a 'social critique', focusing on capitalism as a source of poverty, inequality and injustice, and an 'artistic critique' that considers capitalism to be the source of disenchantment, inauthenticity, and oppression of personal autonomy. Traditionally, social movements had primarily depended on the first form of critique, while the second form belonged to the discourse of a minority group of bohemian artists and intellectuals, playing a rather marginal role. This radically changed in the 1960s, when artistic critique became the focal point of a large-scale social and cultural movement. Artistic critique now attracted a mass audience and became of substantial consequence, eventually even eclipsing social critique. In a kind of historical irony, however, capitalism – in the form of what the authors call its 'new spirit' – largely took on board and absorbed artistic critique, replacing traditional Protestant values such as austerity, ascetism, and a sense of hierarchy with 'artistic' values such as flexibility, autonomy, anti-authoritarianism and creativity. This process of integration left artistic critique empty-handed and called for a renewal of social critique – a project that, according to Boltanski, also calls for a renewal of critical sociology.

In his most recent project, Boltanski further develops the thesis that the form of capitalism emerging in the Western world during the last decades has in fact encapsulated the world of art. In an article written together with Arnaud Esquerre, Boltanski describes the 'form of the collection' as indicative of what comes after industrial capitalism with its standardized mass production.6 From this decidedly anti-idealist perspective, the art collection of the nineteenth century has become the model for the massively expanding contemporary market of haute couture fashion, gadgets, and luxury goods: circulating and collected commodities that have the aura of singular and individual works. It also serves as a template for the transformation of cultural and lived spaces into commodities, transforming entire cities into heritage sites fit for touristic consumption and patrimonial conservation. Again, this is a transformation of capitalism that, according to Boltanski not only shields it from critique but also neutralizes much of the critical potential art and aesthetics came to have in the course of the twentieth century.

For this volume, we asked Boltanski to reflect on the relationship between art criticism and social critique, on the different ‘regimes’ of art that emerge together with the new spirit of capitalism, and on the position of criticism within the contemporary art market.

Robin Celikates/Thijs Lijster – One of the main innovative aspects of your work, as you yourself have emphasized, is the transition from a ‘critical sociology’ to a ‘pragmatic sociology of critique’. This means that, as in your work with Laurent Thévenot, the sociologist is not the primary critical agent (in contrast to Pierre Bourdieu’s approach), but rather the one who charts or maps the critical activities of the actors. Where does critique stand today?

Luc Boltanski – I would like to begin with something like a preliminary. There is a tendency now in France, especially among philosophers, to try to rebuild the great divide between ‘us’ – the white, the occidental, the European – and ‘the others’. Of course, this divide can also be based on race or culture, but that has become difficult today if you want to remain a respectable intellectual. I think a very important but subterranean tendency nowadays is to build it on critique: ‘Of course, other populations, other countries, have a culture that is as interesting or as rich as ours, but our tradition has a specific trait which is the capacity to take this distance, from the immediate moment, and to develop critique.’ This leads to an opposition between ‘us’, who have critical possibilities, and ‘the others’ who are just subject to their belief. Against this tendency, I think it is very important to consider critique as a kind of anthropological competence inherent to social life.

RC/TL – So you see critique as an anthropological universal?

LB – Yes. Of course, it can take different forms in different societies. Of course, it can be praised and developed, or, on the contrary, refused. But I think that it is a kind of universal competency, and that you cannot imagine a complex social life without critique. Simon Susen, a German sociologist based in London, asked me: ‘But you have no anthropology, you are not able to base your assumption on an anthropology, so what is the basis of critique in your approach?’

I think the answer is very simple: it is the imagination. I reread, in this spirit, *L'Imaginaire* (1940) by Jean-Paul Sartre, and I think it is very interesting. With Sartre, the imaginary is very closely linked to critique. So I think this is the reason why it is very important to not just have critical intellectuals on the one side and the rest of the people who just believe things, on the other. The work of intellectuals is to totalize; they produce tools that make it possible to compare a local situation with an imaginable frame. This is something they can do because they have the tools of totalization.

The role of art criticism is different. Art, but also poetry – even the novel – and theatre are kinds of activities that can escape justification. I wrote several plays, and what is interesting is that you can make a character say the exact opposite of what you believe. Art, literature, poetry can explore alternative paths in language, bring things together like in a metaphor, without arguing. In the social sciences and philosophy you always have to give an argumentative justification for the things you put together. So you remain more easily in the frame of reality.

RC/TL – Would you say that art is more apt as a vehicle for critique than the sciences? Because it is the work of the imagination?

LB – I think it is not the same. Science and art have in common that they collect examples that don't fit with the definition. To produce definitions and qualifications is the work of institutions. They are always tautological. The classical example: 'A bachelor is an unmarried man.' And so you always need to confirm the definition with examples. But the list of examples is never finite. So you can always find an example that doesn't fit the definition. In *On Critique* I give the example of euthanasia. What about a woman who gives a lethal potion to her son who has aneuploidy: Is she a good example of a murderer? No. Is she a good example of a wonderful mother? Not exactly. So I think the first part of critique is to present examples that jeopardize the definition, the border of the definition. And you can do that with science or with art.

RC/TL – So is this something that is common to art, science, and intellectuals?

LB – In my book *Love and Justice as Competences* (1990 [2012]) there is a passage about moves that trigger the imagination: 'gestures'. A lot of political moves belong to the register of the gesture. And so it is not far from a provocation. It can be interpreted as a provocation or not. Ordinary people, or people who are doing politics, produce a lot of gestures, and part of the work of the social sciences is to register these gestures and to register all the interpretations developed around these gestures. Art, however, also produces gestures; gesture is the basis of art, of modern art, maybe of all art. And the role of criticism with regard to art is like that of the social sciences with regard to politics: to produce interpretations of the work of art as a gesture. The thing is that for the last twenty or thirty years, more and more frequently the artists themselves have been producing the interpretations of the gesture. The artist is more and more the one who makes the enigmatic gesture and the one who provides its interpretation at the same time.

RC/TL – In the recent art world, there indeed seems to occur a shift of social roles, as you notice, between artist and critic, but also between artist and curator. As for instance Boris Groys has argued, the curator becomes more like the artist, travelling around the globe and constructing exhibitions much like an artist constructs installations. Similarly, curators become like critics in so far as they define the framework in which a specific artwork should be looked at. At the same time, artists are often interviewed and questioned about their work, so that they are forced to deliver the theoretical fundament from which to consider the work – a role that used to be reserved for the art critic. How do you look at these kinds of shifts? What would be possible 'conflicts' and 'compromises', to put it in the language of the sociology of value regimes that you and Thévenot developed?

LB – I think that a good way to study this question would be to be attentive to 'trials' and 'affairs'. Is it completely true that what the curators are doing is more and more seen as a work of art? Someone who makes installation art is someone who creates meaning by putting things together and is the author of the totality produced by putting things together. Curators invent exhibitions, and put things together, producing meaning; they can then be seen as artists. But the basis of being an art object, is to be considered in what I call the 'collection form'. It is to be taken in the logic of the forbidding of reproduction: the distinction between original and copy or forgery. So you can prosecute artists who produce forgeries. But are there any trials about copies of exhibitions? Are there curators who start a trial against others because they have stolen elements of their exhibitions? The same goes for theatre directors: In France there are no more than one or two cases in which directors are suing colleagues because of how they have directed a play.

RC/TL – So one difference between the artist and the curator is that their work follows a different logic.

LB – I think that the day that it would be normal for a curator to sue a colleague for having made a copy of an exhibition or stolen some elements of it, would be the day that there is no longer any difference between artist and curator.

RC/TL – And with regard to the shifting roles between art and critic, or curator and critic, what would then be a 'trial', an 'affair', a test case, if you like? In your recent text on collections you say that the critic is 'shoved out' in favour of the collector, who is the important one who judges, instead of the critic.

LB – In my recent work on the form of the collection, I refer to Harrison and Cynthia White's *Canvases and Careers.* They describe a very particular regime of relations between art, money, and ordinary people. It shows the shift from the academic system – which was very close to the scientific system – to the new system, beginning with the impressionists, which they call the 'critic-dealer system'. What is striking in this system is the closeness of the different actors: artist, critic, dealer and collector. They know one another; they go to each other's homes. I call this the domestic regime of art. In this system, the artist is seen – and this is the legacy of the romantic artist – as a worker, who does not know what he is doing or what he is saying; who is just engendering things. The dealer goes to his studio, he sees wonderful things – for instance in Giacometti's studio, the wonderful tall design of Annette. He takes it. The critic is the one who makes the interpretation, the one who produces a narrative, about the artist, about the work, and most importantly about the relation between the artist and the work. He produces the engendering link between the work and the artist, which would become central in the evaluation of the work. Frequently, the critic is the friend of the artist, or the friend of the dealer and the collector; he has personal relationships with all of them. The collector puts the work in his home, if it is a painting or a drawing, or, if it is a sculpture, he puts it in the garden – so he lets it enter into his own intimacy. Usually, he will not sell it, at least for a pretty long time. So this is the regime that was successful in the twentieth century, after the end of the hope put in the academic regime.

RC/TL – So the academic system was followed by what you call the domestic regime of art. Would you now say that we are witnessing the end of the domestic regime of art? What would be its successor?

LB – I think that the successor looks like a mix of a state regime and a market regime.

RC/TL – Is the state, the museums, working together with the market, the private collections, to create this regime?

LB – Yes. Because the problem with the domestic regime is that the circulation of the work is very slow. For this reason I distinguish between the standardized way of evaluating things and the collection system of relations focusing on the singularity of the work. There is a third form, which I call the 'active form', when the object is seen as invested capital. In this form what is most important is the rapidity of circulation and liquidity. But liquidity demands that the tools and the instruments of the test are largely diffused and based on a relative consensus. I studied the stamp collection, which is very important to understand in order to grasp the new functioning of the art system. In the stamp collection the idea of the collection is pushed to its limits: the object is small, can be transported, and is described by catalogues. Its price changes, but within the range of value determined by the catalogue, made by experts, who are themselves connected to national institutions backed up by state guarantees. Suppose you have a problem with the police, you can ship your stamps to Brazil. Within the domestic system of art this would have taken considerable time – of course in 1942 you could ship your Renoir to Argentine, but if you have a more recent work, for instance a drawing by Michaux, I am not sure you could sell it very fast. In the new system the work must circulate more rapidly and more extensively, so the relationship between the name of the artist, and the mark on the work, and the interpretation must be much stronger than in the past.

RC/TL – But is the interpretation still necessary to make the work more valuable?

LB – I think the interpretation is still important, but the critic no longer has the monopoly on making the interpretation. The interpretation is still important, because it is part of the story, which gives the work its memorial value.

RC/TL – It seems, then, that the object's value is increasingly produced by a system in which the interpreter, the critic, the collector are engaged. You see this development critically from a sociological perspective, from which the art collection today appears as one of the main forms in which capital is stored; you point out that although it does not generate as much profit as, for instance, financial speculation, it is a very stable option for storing capital – and we guess this option is stabilized by this whole apparatus of collectors, curators, artists, producing meaning around it, and therefore it is highly effective for the new dominant class. But then one has to ask how, in the face of this system, a critical attitude can develop *within* the art system? What alternative standards are there for the critic to refer to, that go beyond this very closed system in which meaning is produced in order to store capital in a stable manner? You yourself say that this new form of the collection is very tricky, and also very ideological, because those involved say, for instance: 'I am just a collector, I love this object' – that is the official ideology of the collector, but at the same time when you look at the system as a whole in which circulation takes place, it has little to do with singularity and love. So there are these two levels: that of the experience of collectors, who say that they want to have the object in their collection because they love it, and that of the objective logic of the system, which is part of a larger transformation of capital. Since the traditional discourse of art has been integrated into the system it seems very difficult to criticize it.

LB – At the basis of the system of art is the necessary separation between those who are linked with the economic valuation of the work of art, and maybe profit directly from it, and those who are supposed to be linked only to the artistic valuation of the work. I do not know why this is the case, but this separation is very important. If both instances are the same, it is bad, after some time, even for the economic valuation of the work. In that case one could simply say: he says it is a good work of art because he has an interest in elevating its price. The price of the work is still supposed to be connected with its aesthetic valuation.

RC/TL – In *On Critique* you define institutions as 'bodiless beings', which are supposed to see objects from a transhistorical, outside view, instead of from a personal and subjective point of view. Should the critic also be a bodiless being in that sense?

LB – Yes, he or she has to be a kind of bodiless being. This is why I do not agree with what seems to be a common opinion today. This common opinion is that the traditional art institutions – the museum, the state, the critics, the referee system – no longer have any influence on the valuation of the work of art, that this value depends only on the actions of the collector. So, it is said, the same people are making the price and the value, and the price is now the only or the main symptom of the value. I do not think that is completely true. Although I think it makes sense to see this as an explanation of a certain change in the art world, it cannot be true. I think that you still need the actions of a bodiless being, or a state institution, in order to support the aesthetic value and the price of the work.

At the same time, it is surely the case that the actions of the collector are more and more important. Take the auction, for example, and the publicity of the price of certain works bought at the auction. The people who enter in competition at the auction take a risk of losing money. But in any case as a group they profit from it. Everyone who goes to an auction and who participates in an auction will lose some money. But that person also raises the value of all artistic goods in the world. So this is a kind of sacrifice for the collective. It assures and stabilizes the general value of the whole collective of works.

RC/TL – And in turn one does also profit from this. This is a long-term strategy.

LB – Yes, in the long term one does profit from this. Last week I spoke with a friend, Catherine Grenier, who is now the director of the Giacometti Foundation, and before that worked at the Centre Pompidou for a long time. My co-author Arnaud Esquerre was also there, just returning from the new Soulage museum in Rodez. Arnaud was astonished that a lot of 'ordinary' people were there. Catherine said that they came because they knew from the media about the price of the works. Their excitement was due to the distance between things that for them were nothing, and the price of the works. According to Catherine, today the shows of contemporary art are more popular than the shows of historical art, and I think there is something interesting in that. It is almost comparable to the diamond in Wilkie Collins' novel *The Moonstone*: it is the thing that is nothing, and that at the same time has the biggest value. This situation is produced not only by the market, but by the collaboration – and partly the opposition – between the market and all the work people engage in to produce a narrative around the work.

RC/TL – But the narrative isn't produced by the critic anymore.

LB – I think it depends on whom you call 'critic'. It is produced by scholars, journalists, curators, but all these persons are connected to the state.

RC/TL – That connects to the theme of what we call the 'displacement' of the critic; it is no longer the critic as in what we discussed as the artist-critic-dealer system, but criticism has somehow dissolved and been taken up by these different actors, who produce a narrative that gives the object its value.

LB – Criticism is a network of the actors, who collaborate with institutions, and actors connected with institutions, more or less connected to the state, in order to engender a narrative around the work and the artist, and connect the work and the artist – the career of the artist, the development of the artist, and so on. So criticism is still important, but it no longer simply revolves around the artist and critic of the domestic system: a lonely person who meets an intelligent friend in the salon. It is no longer about Proust listening to the sonata of Vinteuil. What we are confronted with is a *system* of critique.

RC/TL – If the art critic is so integrated into the system of the form of the collection, what happens to the idea of critique? Can art still have a critical role, or how do you criticize this system? It seems that the system includes a lot of the critical discourses that have been built up around art. You once said that the shift to the form of the collection – which includes the patrimonialization of society, turning everything into protected, cultural heritage – makes it very difficult to criticize since the collection is put together in the name of love of the art work, as patrimonialization happens in the name of our great cultural heritage. What could be wrong with that? And yet these developments are so entangled in new economic inequalities and the transformation of capitalism that one might want to criticize them.

LB – The main characteristic of the new critique is not being critical! It is the critique à *l'ancienne*, it is the reactionary critic, think of Jean Clair, who is still critical. But in general critics are no longer critical.

RC/TL – But what then happens to critique in the critical sense?

LB – The artist also stopped being a critical instance. I think the possibilities of critical art today are very poor.

RC/TL – Also because the criticality of art, so to say, is itself being commodified, thus even collected in some sense. Is there an answer to that? For the art world, for the critic, the artist, academia, the university? It seems like a deadlock.

LB – In the case of the domestic system, the collector used to put the work in his home; it was like letting somebody enter into his home. But now we have a different situation. What is very interesting are the attempts by artists over the last fifty years to produce works that would escape the market: land art, conceptual art, performance art. But everything has returned to the market. So certainly art that today would have the pretention to be critical, that has the pretention to be critique, can no more hope that it will succeed in exploring ways to escape the market. You know the typical attitude of a successful artist today: 'I am fed up with all these big shows; I will do a performance with a friend nobody knows in a room for just five friends. No money involved, we are our own producers.' But if what they have done is not acclaimed by *Le Monde* and *Libération* within two weeks they are very disappointed. The situation is completely deceptive. So it cannot be the attempt to escape the market that would help to renew critique. But then what could?

RC/TL – Wouldn't one possibility of the renewal of critique, now more in the social sense, consist in what you are doing in the new project: to show how the logic of the collection and thereby in a way the art system as a whole is implicated in this recent transformation of capitalism and the incredible concentration of riches?

LB – It would be important to rebuild what Marx did for the industrial economy, to rebuild all the cross-participation in the making of the price of things, and so to try to evaluate, to transform the work, papers, analyses, including that of the historians and philosophers of art, into work-time/working hours, and then into money. Stop ignoring that they are working for the 'machine'. To do that would be shocking. To say: you wrote a catalogue, what was your salary, and do you count in it all the years you spend previously studying other artists, and should we not raise the price?

RC/TL – Such an approach would then, for example, make visible how many actors that are not officially included are involved in producing the price.

LB – I think that if the system relies on the separation of aesthetic evaluation and monetary appreciation, one way of renewing critique would be to economize everything, to put everything 'on the bill'.

RC/TL – What would be the result of such a project, to show that the art system depends on a lot of free labour provided by people who do internships, students, et cetera?

LB – It would be very destructive.

RC/TL – Would that be good?

LB – It would be nothing if it is taken as a piece of art. If it would be taken as a piece of art and exposed, it would be like the blue paintings of Yves Klein, which were all exactly the same and yet sold at different prices. After the show, each buyer was very anxious about whether the one that was given to him by the artist really was the one he had chosen. The problem is that if a piece of art is critical and if it is a big success in the market, the price of the piece destroys the critical force of the work. If you make a work very strongly critical, the collectors appreciate it, and the price rises. The critical strength of a work is connected with sacrifice, it is a general law: you accept the risk you took by producing this gestural thing. So if the work is critical, it is connected with sacrifice, if it produces a lot of money, it is no longer critical.

RC/TL – What would be possible strategies to give contemporary art criticism a critical impulse? Would it make sense to use the same strategy you have used with regard to social critique? You have made the step from critical sociology to the pragmatic sociology of critique, and now you try to use a combination of both models: the actor's perspective, from the other perspective the 'sense of totality'. Could you think of a similar strategy for art criticism, i.e. that this sense of totality should also once again be part of art criticism? Perhaps indeed that art criticism should not just be directed at specific art works, but a kind of system critique? Would that be a way out?

LB – But then art criticism would become a kind of sociology of art. Its objective would be to reinforce the critical strength of critique.

RC/TL – So would you then agree with the discourse on the end, crisis or death of criticism? Or would you say that there should be a different kind of criticism?

LB – I think that what we call criticism in art is very fuzzy. You can have aesthetic criticism of art and the artist, you can have a criticism of the present system of selection of artists, or you can have a critique of what happens in society in general. But these are not at all the same thing. During the time of the historical avant-garde the three were constantly connected. I think that this is behind the sense in which you are using 'art criticism'. Why not have a kind of aesthetic discourse about aesthetic differences of the work, without the other two aspects? Maybe the connection of the three discourses is no longer possible, or it has become very difficult. Maybe the critics are naked, like the Emperor: they can no longer transform their aesthetic appreciation of the work directly into an attack of the system of selection and into a critique of society.

Notes

1 Luc Boltanski, *On Critique. A Sociology of Emancipation* (London: Polity: 2011), p. 23.
2 Ibid., p. 24.
3 See 'Sociology of Critique or Critical Theory? Luc Boltanski and Axel Honneth in Conversation with Robin Celikates', in: Simon Susen and Bryan S. Turner (eds.), *The Spirit of Luc Boltanski. Essays on the 'Pragmatic Sociology of Critique'* (London, Anthem: 2014), pp. 561–589.
4 Boltanski 2011 (see note 1), p. 32.
5 Ibid., p. 33.
6 Luc Boltanski and Arnaud Esquerre, 'La «collection», une forme neuve du capitalisme. La mise en valeur économique du passé et ses effets', in: *Les Temps Modernes,* n° 679 (2014), pp. 5–72.

Rethinking Institution and Critique

Hans D. Christ &
Iris Dressler

Two Question Marks

Two essays dealing with the potential of and the work on critique and freedom by the French philosopher Michel Foucault – *What is Critique?* (1978) and *What is Enlightenment?* (1984) – influenced us during the conception and naming of two exhibitions that explored the relationships between art, institution, critique and politics: first, with regard to a specific local conflict; and second to a more general reflection. These two shows were 'The Art of Not Being Governed Like That' (2010), quoted from *What is Critique?* and 'Giving Form to the Impatience of Liberty' (2013), quoted from *What is Enlightenment?*. The former was connected to the Württembergischer Kunstverein's explicit public position opposing the controversial, large-scale, traffic, urban planning and real estate project known as Stuttgart 21. The latter was an exhibition that took place as part of a collaboration involving the Württembergischer Kunstverein, the Wiener Festwochen[1] theatre festival and the Bergen Triennial.[2] Working independently, but with a certain exchange, both institutions investigated the intersections, exclusions and conflict situations between art, knowledge and politics. The focus here was not so much on the political or critical contents of art but rather on certain aesthetic methods, attitudes and practices in respect of their political and critical potentialities.

Against this backdrop, the following will reflect upon potential forms of critique, critical attitude and political action, with regard to both institutional and artistic practices. How can institutions, or, as Foucault would put it, 'institutions of government', question not only their own structures of governing but also demand of themselves 'not [to be] governed like that'?[3] What kinds of artistic methods resist this 'being governed', meaning – according to Foucault – a form of knowledge, action and being that is valid at a certain time, in a certain place? To what extent can institutions learn from art in this context, without co-opting it – the latter being one of the major concerns regarding institutional critique? Foucault demanded that the philosophical discourse should make an effort to 'practice ... a knowledge that is foreign to it.' He understands this 'as a kind of essay or test, by which ... one undergoes changes and not as a simplistic appropriation of others ...'[4]

Let it be noted in advance that our exploration of theory and our experiments with it, do not originate in an academic context, but in a curatorial and artistic one. When we quote Foucault in our exhibition titles it is not because these shows are about Foucault; rather, they are about the questions he bequeathed. It is a fragmented way of dealing with theory, schooled in artistic practices, which carries us away and contaminates these fragments with other things, sometimes to the point of unrecognizability. For us, theory is not an instruction for action, or something that has to be illustrated or something to cope with. Instead, just as art does in its own specific way, it creates an environment for thinking, which, in the best-case scenario, allows things to manifest themselves in different, unexpected constellations, under inverse postulates. It redirects our thoughts, allowing them to branch off and take detours. This annotation is not intended to make it impossible to challenge the following ideas, but to explain somewhat from which position and how we are talking. This text is not intended to submit an exhaustive or coherent treatise on art, knowledge, institution and critique, but to follow, in a more excursive way, certain theoretical ideas and thoughts about critique and (critical) knowledge with regard to certain artistic and institutional methods, practices and attitudes – and vice versa.

Talking Nearby

The 16mm film *Reassemblage* (1982) is the first film by the Vietnamese author and filmmaker Trinh T. Minh-ha. It is based on documentary footage that the artist filmed in Senegal. Trinh introduces it with the words, 'I do not intend to speak about. Just speak nearby.' In this film she questions the ethnological viewpoint and its supposed neutrality. Her introductory statement draws attention to a certain problem with power, which has to do with how knowledge is constituted and constitutes (e.g. race, class or gender). To the Vietnamese artist, Senegal is foreign. In order to be able to talk about the foreign or the others it is necessary to learn something about it / them and as we know only too well, this can be a catastrophe for these others. One could say that Trinh, instead of talking about the others, prefers to talk 'nearby' them, in their proximity, in order to protect them. She formulates a critical attitude directed at her own thoughts and deeds. She engages, as Foucault would say, with a knowledge that is foreign to her, without wanting to co-opt it.

In an essay on the poetics and politics of flamenco, the Spanish artist Pedro G. Romero reports how the informants of the so-called flamenco researchers made life hard for them by continuously lying to the anthropologists.[5] They turned the tables, as it were, meaning that, as the observed – and not, like Trinh, as the observer – they talked nearby, rather than about themselves.

The attitudes of both, of Trinh and the Roma, respectively the flamenco-people – attitudes that have to do with distance and digressing, with digressing from the truth so to speak – manifest themselves at the opposite poles of that power structure that is inherent in knowledge: that is, at the opposing positions of the subject and the object of knowledge. In both cases the power relation between these positions breaks up due to the refusal – on the one hand of the subject (Trinh) and on the other hand of the object of knowledge (Roma) – to correspond to it. In both cases it is about thwarting, if not sabotaging, positive knowledge, so that it does not direct itself against the object of knowledge.

Knowledge and Power

As Foucault points out in *What is Critique?*, however, the problem with the relationship between knowledge and power is not that a good knowledge (for instance, about the Roma, that is, the flamenco-people) might be misused by an evil power for bad purposes (such as their forced displacement) and thus be turned against its object. Knowledge and power are, according to Foucault, principally connected, because knowledge has to be equipped with power, that is, with acceptance and positivity, in order to function as knowledge and truth; power, in turn, must be able to invoke truth.

Thus, the question rather is why a certain element of knowledge – regardless of whether it is true or false – evokes the effects of power at a given time, in a given place; and, inversely, what makes knowledge acceptable in a certain epoch and a certain region.[6] Along these lines, critique would be 'the movement by which the subject gives himself the right to question truth on its effects of power and question power on its discourses of truth ... Critique would essentially insure the desubjugation of the subject in the context of what we could call, in a word, the politics of truth.'[7] Roma, who lie to flamenco researchers.

Foucault moreover does not regard critique as something that eradicates errors[8] in order to optimize knowledge. He believes that

> ... critique will no longer be practiced in the search for formal structures with universal value, but rather as a historical investigation into the events that have led us to constitute ourselves and to recognize ourselves as subjects of what we are doing, thinking, saying... . And this critique will be genealogical in the sense that it will not deduce from the form of what we are what it is impossible for us to do and to know, but it will separate out from the contingency that has made us what we are the possibility of no longer being, doing, or thinking what we are, do, or think.[9]

It is about the conditions and limitations of thinking, doing and being, about the contingent systems of order that affect our thinking, doing and being and about the breaks and gaps in this systems that first make change and, in this sense, critique, possible. The 'critique of what we are', as Foucault writes, 'is at one and the same time the historical analysis of the limits that are imposed on us and an experiment with the possibility of going beyond them'.[10]

Institutions of Government

What could this mean in reference to 'institutions of government', or, specifically, to an art institution such as the Württembergischer Kunstverein? In approaching this question, we would first like to join in with Simon Sheikh concerning the historical definition of that artistic practice referred to as *institutional critique* and 'respectfully leave that endeavour for the *Texte zur Kunst* and *October* magazines of this world'.[11] In the following we rather aim to outline what we understand and examine as and demand of a critical attitude of an art institution: an attitude that reflects both the critique of the institution – as it is articulated for example by artistic practices – and artistic methods as methods of critique. This attitude is not understood as a universal or fixed one, but as one corresponding to a process of permanent negotiation. Above all, learning from art means here, on the side of the institution, to try out other ways of thinking and doing, or – to speak with Foucault – the effort to practice a knowledge that is foreign to the institution and by which it undergoes changes, rather than co-opting the critique of the institution as formulated by art.

On the one hand, we will focus on the possibilities and limitations of a self-critical position toward the major fields of power and force of a Kunstverein:[12] the production of space, the gesture of showing or putting things on display, as well as the production of knowledge, discourses and social relationships. Here, the object of reflection is the institution itself and the ways that it governs. On the other hand, it is about inquiring the political spaces of agency of an institution: its own de-subjectification, its own objection 'to be governed *like that*, by that, in the name of those principles, with such and such an objective in mind and by means of such procedures...'[13]

Dilemma

Before we address these questions, we would like to take up yet another dilemma: that insoluble conflict and contradiction that appears as soon as a discussion around the possibilities and limits of critique against whatever kind of system, regime, or government comes up, i.e. the problem of complicity with – of being 'embedded in' – that very system one actually wants to criticize and change; and that problem of critique being absorbed by the criticized system itself, as for example Luc Boltanski and Ève Chiapello have shown in their often-quoted book, *The New Spirit of Capitalism* (1999). Boltanski and Chiapello here refer to the demands of the 1968 protest movements and the usurpation of these demands by capitalism. Those dilemmas can hardly be denied and it is important to be aware of them, without, however, falling into complete lethargy. For the capitalist or neoliberal system (or for the colonial or phallocratic or any other system) is neither almighty nor homogeneous, nor is it final or lacking in contradictions. If all of us are indeed fully embedded in these systems, then this all-encompassing cohabitation itself already explodes any thinkable homogeneity and implements within them the foundation of any critique.

In the worst case, the conviction that 'the critical interpretation of the system has become an element of the system itself', leads, as Jacques Rancière writes in *The Emancipated Spectator*, to an irony *against* critique in contrast to irony *as* critique. The former attitude reserves 'for itself the position of the lucid mind casting a disenchanted eye over the world'.[14] '... The machine can work in this way until the end of time, capitalizing on the impotence of the critique that unveils the impotence of the imbeciles.'[15] In this way, one is always on the safe side: one risks nothing, is not responsible for anything and is untouchable.

Instead of reinforcing lethargy[16] and *irony-against-critique*, we should keep in mind the fact that not only the system to be criticized can 'abuse' critique to achieve its own ends, but that it is also possible – and always has been – to reverse this kind of misappropriation and distortion. There is no usage (neither of goods and riches, nor of truth, knowledge or critique) that would be naturally owned by someone. Critique and political agency have to do with the incessant process of re-appropriation, of re-evaluating re-evaluation; with the constant battle over the order and partitioning of things, which are, as is preached from Foucault to Rancière, not natural, but contingent.

The constant repartitioning and redistribution of things through their 'inappropriate use', i.e., their *profanation,* to quote Giorgio Agamben,[17] is probably related to one of the strongest and most far reaching methods of art. Agamben himself refers, among other things, to the game and to art as practices of profanation, that is of undoing the untouchability of the sacred/ sacrosanct things[18] in order to return them to another economy (other than, for example, the economy of debt or consumption). We might understand art in this sense as a practice of inventing 'other', 'inappropriate' and 'false' ways of dealing with the 'sacred', untouchable order of things – with knowledge, meaning, values, symbols, politics, truth, goods, riches et cetera – and of shifting these things to other economies of knowledge, meaning, values, symbols, politics, truth, goods, riches ... than the reigning ones.

Let's get back to the question of what all this might mean with regard to an art institution's understanding of itself, its structures and shape: an art institution such as the Württembergischer Kunstverein, which is founded on a bourgeois tradition that is more than 185 years old. Although it is not one of the large museum machines, it nevertheless has annual revenues of around 1.3 million euros, 15 employees, 3000 members, an exhibition and event space of more than 1700 square meters in the heart of the city and a studio apartment and therefore can be counted among the established institutions.

Injustice

In our opinion the aim of critique here cannot, at any rate, be a universally valid model of an ideal institution, structure and infrastructure that caters to the needs of everyone and everything – and that finally would make any critique unnecessary. Rather and conversely, it is about understanding and accepting an institution as a place and a structure of permanent critique, that is of permanent negotiation and conflict among, for example, artists, institution and audiences. This conflict is based on a fundamental injustice, since one can never do justice to everyone. There is always something or someone that is left out, something or someone that has not and *could* never have been reckoned with. This injustice cannot be prevented, since it has to do with something unexpected, with a gap, a fault, a limit principally inherent to the institution. Anything else would be rather totalitarian. To put it another way, not aiming to do justice to everyone and everything means to remain – in this case as an art institution – assailable and touchable; which is not necessarily a weakness. It rather has to do with the accessibility for a common, an uncontrollable and unexpected use; a (re)appropriation by, as well as a constant negotiation with those that have not been thought of, by those, that criticize the institution's ways of governing.

In this sense, the goal of any critique of art institutions likewise cannot be to abrogate them, unless we assume that the goal of criticism is to eliminate sources of friction and conflict zones. To understand an institution as a source of friction and a conflict zone means to acknowledge that it always has one leg on the 'wrong' side, on the side of 'injustice', but to also realize that the space of political and critical action precisely emerges from there: from something that is contested and negotiated between the institution and its (unexpected) critics in the sense of dissent, not consensus. Thus, dissent, conflict, or de-subjugation are not things that an art institution could teach or provide either, but things in which the institution is constantly involved: and this not only as the one being criticized, but also as the one criticizing.

Contingency

In both cases – the institution being criticized and the criticizing institution – it is about what Rancière would call the 'fluctuating performers ... who ... give place to the nonplace';[19] about unexpected figures that are the first to note a certain lack. They show – as uninvited and unwelcome guests – what no one knew and *could* know about. It has to do with the limitations of thought. To devote oneself to this kind of uninvited guests does not mean devouring them, but to 'undergo changes' (Foucault), to be turned upside down, as the Indian author and curator Ranjit Hoskoté said, referring to the 'voice of the other'. This voice

> ... arrives suddenly and without warning; it disrupts rather than smoothing the textures of the listener's experience; it demands that the listener engage with its meaning in a full-bodied manner, placing his or her entire being on the hazard. The act of attending to such a voice, the voice of the Other, the sometimes sublime and terrifying Other, breaks and re-makes the attending self.[20]

Any art institution can and should itself become this kind of voice, this kind of uninvited guest, by doing and demanding something it is not supposed to do. In today's art world, this could be complexity, procrastination, confusion, or dissipation, meaning a certain form of the uneconomic, the inefficient and the lavish. Yet also, very specifically, it could mean taking a position in a local political conflict – something that is not required, since a publicly financed institution is supposed to maintain 'neutrality', whatever that is. And it could mean to 'prefer not to', that is to offensively resist those things that are explicitly expected of an art institution, such as to increase attendance, be compatible with the art market and the mass media, to maintain standards of professionalization, have a corporate identity, or to adapt to bureaucratic hoops. Nothing is more unbearable than an institution that always invokes the fact that its hands are tied ... It is about *dis*-obedience, instead of *anticipatory* obedience, for instance, when faced with censorship or the excesses of the copyright industry. All of this requires a certain willingness to take risks.

Dispositives

Another basic field of an institutional practice of critique and resistance in our view concerns the self-critical questioning of the major dispositives of power that an art institution provides and has access to: above all those dispositives sustaining the power of space, gaze, knowledge, discourse and social relationships. We are interested in a certain disturbance of the order of these power structures and dispositives: by relativizing and undoing the dominion over space, knowledge and discourse; by testing collective and multi-voiced forms of curating, or by bringing into play the limitations of our own thinking and actions. In the context of curating exhibitions this means, for instance, to refuse producing any sort of homogenous, uninterrupted, consistent narrative. We are interested in orbiting at ever greater distances around the subject of an exhibition – that is, in talking 'nearby', or circuitously, instead of addressing something directly. How could we create a sense of uncertainty and ambiguity toward what we are presenting: art or not art, high or low, artefact or documentation, real or fake? The exhibition *Giving Form to the Impatience of Liberty* was, for example, an attempt to negotiate the political spaces of action of art by presenting positions that contradict and exclude each other, without trying to reconcile the disputes. The artist Anna Oppermann has virtually elevated this position of 'both for and against', of not-deciding, into the main principle behind her ensemble art. She is one of the artists whose methods and ways of working have strongly influenced our attitude toward curating. We will get back to the methods as well as the critical and political relevance of her work in our final chapter.

Profanation

In our understanding, an art institution should be contestable and tangible, in the sense of Giorgio Agamben's already mentioned notion of profanation, that is of the 'inappropriate' use of things, which can undo their sacredness, their untouchability and especially their separation from common use.[21] This essentially presumes the awareness that in art perception, experience, meaning, knowledge, et cetera occur in the negotiation between artists, institution and recipients. Thus, an 'appropriate' use – in terms of an appropriate understanding and experience – of art cannot be controlled, neither by the artists nor by the institutions; the participation of for example the recipients is always at work and is not something to be – or not to be – provided by the institution. 'Warning. Perception Requires Involvement' is a slogan that the artist Antoni Muntadas writes on the façades of art institutions. He does not demand unconditional participation, but proximity and distance at the same time. Moreover, in our case, participation very specifically means sharing space, resources and infrastructure.

The Württembergischer Kunstverein

Common Space

We see the Kunstverein as a place for an open and also controversial discussion on the manifold methods and practices of contemporary art, as well as on the wide-ranging socio-political areas it refers to. Exhibition and debate, art and theory, research and production are likewise important. It is about a space of action that extends beyond the simple viewing of art, a space where art and the relations between art, artists, the institution and the audiences are subject to continual renegotiation: through conversations, debates, workshops, or workgroups, but also facilitated by access to books, journals and other materials and infrastructures. Among these infrastructures are, not least, the spatial premises of the Kunstverein itself, which are made available to local protagonists and groups for their own meetings, events and communication.

The main common space is the so-called Glass Tract, a transparent wing of the building that serves as entrance, foyer, archive, meeting and working place and as a space for manifold events. It is used not only by us, but also by political and activist initiatives, individual artists and artist groups, various local institutions, et cetera, whose activities are sometimes carried out in cooperation with us and sometimes under their own direction, sometimes in the form of private meetings and sometimes in the form of public events. These activities are completely uncurated. This common use allows any agenda, even though we do not allow just anyone into the building. Rather, it is related to a growing process, which at the latest began when we opened up the Kunstverein in the context of the conflict surrounding Stuttgart 21 and which since then has continued to expand, sometimes overlapping with our programme and sometimes not, in accordance with the interests and needs of various local protagonists and communities. A decisive factor in this development is the fact that there are hardly meeting places downtown anymore that do not require people to either consume or pay rent. By opening up the Kunstverein in this way, we not only started sharing space, but also allowed others a certain amount of influence on what kinds of content occupy this space.

Politicization

The Kunstverein is situated at one of the most central locations in the city, at the Schlossplatz, not far from the central train station and directly adjacent to shopping (a retail strip), leisure activities (a park), highbrow culture (the state theatre, the opera house, the Staatsgalerie, the art museum) and politics (tax authority, state legislature). Not least, this special location was one of the reasons why the Kunstverein took position in the conflict around the traffic and infrastructure project Stuttgart 21, since the controversy was mainly staged within the urban area described above. Furthermore, our involvement had to do with various interactions between the socio-political direction of our programme and the growing politicization that occurred among much of the population of Stuttgart by 2010 at the latest. The scale of this politicization was foreshadowed in the previous year, during another conflict that directly affected the Kunstverein.

In 2009, without any warning, the Kunstverein received a form letter from the city's cultural office, announcing that subsidies would be cut by ten percent. First of all, we were surprised by the total lack of any public debate and secondly, it was unclear who else had received this announcement. We published said letter on our web site and sent it to the press and all of our colleagues. The next step was a public meeting with other cultural institutions, where it was decided that there would be no division between the institutions affected by the announced cuts and those that were not. At the same time, the meetings with cultural policy factions were always attended by representatives of several institutions, in order to signal our solidarity instead of self-interest. Further ways of organizing arose so that the conflict would not simply be carried on with the city administration, but would also be made public. The patchwork of very different types of institutions – from the Fire Department Museum to the Opera, from the off-space to the State School of the Arts – and many private citizens who got involved, created a critical mass that ultimately led to a demonstration with three thousand participants. In the end, the cuts were halved and in some cases even completely rescinded.

During this phase, the Kunstverein postponed an exhibition, in order to concentrate its efforts on the political confrontation. This meant that, to some extent, it acted contrary to its mandate. The exhibition of the artist-members of the Kunstverein opened a few months later than planned, under the title *Art and Society,* at a point in time when that new conflict – which would soon instigate an uproar among a large portion of the regional population – was looming.

Since 2005, the annual members' exhibition of the Württembergischer Kunstverein has been conceived as an open format, each time related to a certain theme, but accepting all submissions. One group's idea in 2010 was to develop the exhibition architecture, using the remains of the displays from a large show about the history of the Ice Age, organized by the regional government.[22] Among other things, the group's concept included an agora for discussions, performances and more. One of the established components of the members' exhibition is that participants are also invited to suggest ideas for events. Nearly all of the proposals dealt with the protest against Stuttgart 21. Hence, it was the members who very consciously drew upon the main concerns of our programme that refers to socio-political contexts of art – and thus demanded to share in the Kunstverein's policy.

Stuttgart 21

I The Problem

Like other mega-projects of this kind, the traffic and infrastructure project known as Stuttgart 21 is founded on a combination of economic and prestige-based promises, lobbying and corruption. It is one of the so-called '21 Projects' that were called into being in the mid-1990s in several German cities, when the Deutsche Bahn (the German railways) was privatized, in order to artificially boost the company's capital base by auctioning off large tracts of inner-city terrains. Only the city of Stuttgart and the state of Baden-Württemberg resolved to realize the 21 project. Part of the Stuttgart 21 plan involves turning the existing train station ninety degrees and moving it underground, in order to improve the flow of traffic and to join up with the so-called European Main Street. As a matter of fact, however, Stuttgart 21 is mainly about the downtown property that will be gained by moving the train station underground. A new 'city district' is supposed to be built where the railway yard is now located. To realize this mega-project, parts of the historical station, which is a protected heritage site, was torn down and a section of a park where up to 250 old trees stood was cleared. Large sections of the city centre are going to be gentrified. It is still completely unclear whether certain aspects of the planned project, from fire safety to tunnel construction, are even possible, foreshadowing yet another fiasco on the scale of the Elbphilharmonie in Hamburg or the Berlin airport. The costs, which up to now have been estimated to be between 6.5 to 10 billion euros, will ultimately be borne by the public. Thus, we will be financing a project that will mainly benefit private real estate investors and the social classes that can afford downtown luxury living.

Solidarization

Ever since it was first announced in 1994, Stuttgart 21 has been publically criticized. After various attempts to stop it – such as the submission of a petition with 70,000 signatures – were simply ignored by politicians and administrators, resistance moved to the streets, reaching a critical point in 2010, when there were weekly demonstrations with up to 50,000 participants from all sectors of society. Areas of the park were occupied and the construction fence around the demolition sites at the train station were transformed day by day into a collective *Gesamtkunstwerk* made up of commentary, messages, collages, polemics, objects, slogans and much more. At first, the municipal and regional governments reacted with ignorance, then by defaming the protestors and using repressive tactics such as censorship – and when none of this helped, finally, on September 30, 2010, with excessive police violence (pepper spray, billy clubs and water cannons) against peaceful demonstrators.

During this phase, the Kunstverein publically took position against Stuttgart 21 and stood in solidarity with the resistance movement. One of the reasons for this, as mentioned before, was the Kunstverein's proximity to the sites where the public protest – reaching from weekly demonstrations to the occupation of the park – took place. In addition, the atmosphere at the time was characterized by intimidation, censorship and finally violence by the government of Baden-Württemberg under the state governor

Stefan Mappus and this made it absolutely necessary for the Kunstverein to take a political position – not just in reference to Stuttgart 21, but also in order to claim democracy, freedom of speech and freedom of the arts. It was necessary to play off the fact that a Kunstverein is a privately organized association, meaning that even though it is dependent upon financing from the city and the state, it is not directly subordinate to the city or state government. Whereas our colleagues at the state cultural institutions received a letter forcing them to take a 'neutral' position toward Stuttgart 21, no one was at least officially able to force us to adopt this kind of supposed neutrality – which, after all, means nothing but the suppression of criticism. After discussing the matter with the board and the staff, we decided to take the risk that, nevertheless, we could have been punished by budget cuts officially announced of being based on other grounds.

The Section

While the public protests against Stuttgart 21 continued to spread almost daily, we planned the exhibition *Re-Designing the East: Political Design in Asia and Europe,* initiated by the Japanese curator Keiko Sei. In six sections, the exhibition examined political resistance, activism and design in South Korea, Thailand, India, Hungary, Poland and the Czech Republic. Different curators from each of the local contexts developed the individual sections.[23] During the preparations for this globally oriented project, it seemed unbearable to us to keep the local conflict out of the exhibition. We decided to set up a seventh section devoted to the resistance against Stuttgart 21, which we opened at a slightly later time, as an exhibition within the exhibition. This section, or exhibition, entitled 'The Art of Not Being Governed Like That',[24] was developed in a collaboration involving the architect and urban scientist Yvonne P. Doderer, the artists Stephan Köperl and Sylvia Winkler and us. Besides these local participants, international artists such as Daniel G. Andújar, Noh Suntag and Dan Perjovschi contributed existing or new works. Perjovschi allowed the protest movement to make free use of the drawings he produced for the exhibition (also see pp. 8–9). Thus, for example, they reappeared in different variations and translations in the occupied section of the park.

The exhibition was conceived as an archive, documentation and installation that referred to major aspects of the protests against Stuttgart 21. The specific local events and developments were reflected in the context of general socio-political questions such as governmentalization, commodification, urban development, civil society and information policy. These key terms were dealt with in image/text montages that linked quotes from theory, media, marketing and administration, as well as in photographs, drawings, diagrams and videos produced within the framework of the protest or for the exhibition. Furthermore, a timetable was created that traced the development of Stuttgart 21 and the resistance against it back to the 1990s, historicizing the conflict in defiance of all those who insisted that this history had never happened.

The aim behind inserting this seventh section into the *Re-Designing the East* show was mainly to show solidarity with the protest movement and to defend ourselves against Mappus' increasingly anti-democratic policies. It was a refusal to remain neutral and a way of expressing our thoughts about this conflict, as one of many voices in the resistance to the conflict.

The extensive research done for the show was accessible to visitors in the form of an archive of files. All of the materials could be copied on site or taken home as a digital collection of data on CD. This archive encompassed a selection of theoretical texts, as well as information, documents and materials directly connected to Stuttgart 21, some of it coming from the protest movement itself: It was not about distributing knowledge, but about sharing it; it was an exhibition in which the curators, artists and a majority of the visitors had an equal share, where the roles of viewer and participant overlapped.

Opening Doors

Within the resistance movement itself, a broad network was formed in which a critical, yet decentralized and collective appropriation of knowledge of very diverse themes took place: the knowledge of environment, economy, transportation logistics, urban development, architecture, law, civil disobedience and much more. Increasingly, this necessitated regular exchanges among the various work groups. To do this, a room where people could meet and work was required. After receiving a request for such a room, we opened up the Kunstverein to the so-called 'action conferences', without imposing any conditions or interfering in any way. During the peak phase of resistance up to 700 people regularly attended these meetings, which not only took place in the Glass Tract, but occasionally spread to our exhibition space.

As soon as the Kunstverein opened its doors for the S21-action conferences, other requests for space from different groups and configurations of the protest movement followed. Parallel to our own programme, a great number of meetings, book presentations, press conferences and similar things organized by various groups also took place in the Kunstverein. This essentially formless, non-curated and not-programmed accessibility to the Glass Tract has lasted to this day and has extended to various social and cultural communities. Currently, events take place there almost every day.

Methodological Remarks or: What Art Institutions Could Learn From an Artist Such as Anna Oppermann

I Complexity

One of the artists whose methods, ideas and works were quite important for the development of our own understanding of a critical curatorial and institutional practice was Anna Oppermann, who died already in 1993.

'Somewhere in this world', she said, explaining her art ensembles, 'complexity must still be valued.'[25] The complexity of her works arose through and in an open-ended process of reflection, in which new configurations, twists and turns and intricacies were continually devoted to a problem instigated by a resistant object that was 'disconcerting or uncanny; ... confusing or even slightly mean',[26] an object that was not what it was expected to be: an unexpected guest. This object – a make-up mirror, for example, or the photograph of an old woman sitting at a kitchen table, or even garden cress – and the problems associated with it were reflected upon, expanded, shifted and rearranged in drawings, photographs, other found pieces, handwritten notes and newspaper clippings. These first arrangements, or, more precisely, ensembles, were documented from different angles and in a variety of media. These documents in turn were placed in the ensemble, along with other objects; then, everything was once again documented, arranged, expanded, documented ... all in an inexhaustible process. Oppermann was not concerned with getting to the heart of a problem, but rather in talking 'nearby', to quote Trinh T. Minh-ha once more.

She regarded her ensemble art as a spatial, material expansion of rhizomatic thought that is continually reorganizing, rearranging and relocating things and their meaning. As the Oppermann expert Ute Vorkoeper writes, she does not simply 'arrange ... objects ... in a new context, but ... in changing, growing contexts'.[27] This practice correlates with what Jacques Rancière calls – in opposition to the dialectical montage that generates shock and aims to reveal 'one world behind another' – a symbolic montage: that is, a montage that 'works to establish a familiarity' between 'elements that are foreign to one another'.[28] It is this staged familiarity among the unfamiliar elements that first creates a mutual irritation whose effects are unpredictable, allowing things to actually 'play around', become different and enter new relationships: to be redistributed in another, a new economy.

Oppermann's ensembles are constantly oscillating between the radical subjectification and fictionalization of a problem, comprising theoretical props, references to politics, psychoanalysis, sociology, economy, or the art world, polemics, public bashing, or self-incrimination. A subjective gaze and a subjectifying practice are at work here. Far from being haphazard, this subjectification has to do with not acknowledging things as they seem to be naturally given, with rejecting their – in Foucault's words – 'acceptability'. This artistic practice is critique in this philosopher's sense: as a 'movement by which the subject gives himself the right to question truth on its effects of power and question power on its discourses of truth'.[29]

The institution is understood by Oppermann as a space of negotiation, which she overtaxes in extreme ways: with the visual excess of the ensembles, which one can never quite fully grasp; with the complex, intricate references; with the density of materials and the manifold contexts that go beyond the work itself.

Oppermann writes about the background of her ensemble art: 'As far as the statement goes, I did not want to decide what to call more important or more successful: the actual object, the sketch, the conceptual examination or the finished image. Each part had something the others were lacking.'[30] The philosopher and literary theorist Joseph Vogl wrote about this inability to decide, this *zaudern* (hesitation, dithering), that it does not mark the opposite of action, but creates an in-between space of pure 'creative potency and contingency' at the threshold between action and non-action. *Zaudern* contains an inherent sense of resistance, because it turns 'against the irrevocability of judgments, against the finality of solutions, against the certainty of consequences ... and the weightedness of results ... *Zaudern* harbours the suspicion of complexity; it is aligned to an arithmetic that ranges from the hundreds to the thousands.'[31] This is precisely wherein the explosive force – a force that is deeply political – of Anna Oppermann's works lies.

Oppermann's works articulate critique also in a direct sense. Her ensembles are questions about otherness, or economy; again and again, they show up the art world of the 1980s dominated by *Malerfürsten* (painter princes) and an overheated market – its hierarchies, machismo, attention economy and protocols. All of this is negotiated in, for example, her ensembles *Pathosgeste – MGSMO 'Mach Grosze, Schlagkräftige, Machtdemonstrierende Objekte'* (Gesture of Pathos – Make Large, Compelling Objects that Demonstrate Power, 1984-1992) or *MKÜVO 'Mach Kleine,* Über*schaubare, Verkäufliche Objekte'* (Make Small, Straightforward, Saleable Objects, 1979-1992). With her proliferating ensembles made up of thousands of individual pieces, Oppermann does anything but make easily saleable objects. At the same time her large, space-consuming ensembles challenge that masculine-connoted 'top-dog-mentality' [Platzhirsch-Mentalität] (that continues to meet with success on the art market to this day), only to break it up ironically in works such as *Gesture of Pathos.*

Furthermore, Oppermann radically questions the ideological pillars of the museum: originality, immutability, authenticity, coherence, completeness and lucidity of the work, et cetera. Her work is 'institutional critique' to the core. Her critique starts already with the declaration of the public exhibition space as her studio, because a considerable portion of each ensemble is created in a long process carried out on the site where the work will be displayed.

One of the reasons that a Kunstverein – and not a museum – organized the first comprehensive, posthumous solo exhibition of Anna Oppermann's work in 2007 is that Oppermann bequeathed many problems to the museum as such. From classification to maintenance to the problem of installation, which evades any intention of an original, authentic and final reconstruction. It always requires a new, interpretative approach and in this sense, also a high degree of responsibility concerning interpretation, its inventiveness and relative validity. Presenting, that is re-creating her work means taking a position, instead of insisting upon neutrality. And it requires a certain uneconomical attitude toward time. We gave ourselves permission to close the Kunstverein for weeks, so that the curator, Ute Vorkoeper, could devote herself to the process of what she called 'interpretative reconstruction'.

Learning From Art, an Unexpected Guest

Both the critical questioning and the critical practices of an art institution do not develop out of the institution itself, because critique is always connected to the appearance of something that is not expected, to an unexpected guest demanding the seemingly impossible.

Hosting this unexpected guest, talking to and nearby it, is part of the conflict, part of the incessant negotiation of space, knowledge, thought, or action, which is at the core of any form of critique. Learning from art – here understood as the effort of practicing a knowledge that is foreign to the institution and by which the institution undergoes changes, instead of co-opting the critique articulated by art – can play a major role in this culture of dissent and critique.

Notes

1 The exhibition *Unrest of Form. Imagining the Political Subject* (2013), curated by Karl Baratta, Stefanie Carp, Matthias Pees, Hedwig Saxenhuber and Georg Schöllhammer.

2 The exhibition *Monday Begins on Saturday* (2013), curated by David Riff and Ekaterina Degot.

3 Michel Foucault, 'What is Critique?', in: Michel Foucault, *The Politics of Truth,* Cambridge MA: Semiotext(e) 1997, p. 29.

4 Michel Foucault, *The Use of Pleasure. Volume 2 of The History of Sexuality,* transl. by Robert Hurley, New York: Pantheon 1990, p. 9.

5 Pedro G. Romero, 'The Sun at Night. Preparatory Notes for Poetics and Politics among Flamenco and Modern Artists. A Paradoxical Place', in: *The Spanish Night. Flamenco, Avant-Garde and Popular Culture 1865-1936*, ed. by Patricia Molins and Pedro G. Romero, Museo Nacional Centro de Arte Reina Sofia, exh. cat., Madrid 2008, p. 77.

6 Foucault, 'Critique' 1997 (see note 3), pp. 52ff.

7 Foucault, 'Critique' 1997 (see note 3), p. 32.

8 Foucault, 'Critique' 1997 (see note 3), p. 25.

9 Michel Foucault, 'What is Enlightenment?', in: Michel Foucault, *The Politics of Truth,* Cambridge MA: Semiotext(e) 1997, p. 125.

10 Foucault, 'Enlightenment' 1997 (see note 9), p. 132.

11 Simon Sheikh, 'Notes on Institutional Critique', in: *European Institute for Progressive Cultural Policies*, 2006, see: http://eipcp.net/transversal/0106/sheikh/en

12 An art institution with no mandate to collect art.

13 Foucault, 'Critique' 1997 (see note 3), p. 28.

14 Jacques Rancière, *The Emancipated Spectator,* London/New York: Verso Books 2009, p. 37. Rancière here refers (among other things) explicitly to Boltanski and Chiapello's *The New Spirit of Capitalism*, London/New York: Verso Books 2006.

15 Ibid., p. 48.

16 Or 'melancholy' in Rancière's words.

17 Giorgio Agamben, *Profanations,* transl. by Jeff Fort, Cambridge MA: Zone Books 2007, p. 75.

18 In the ancient rituals, as Agamben points out, the sacrified meat had to be touched in order to be profanized, that is to be returned to the use of the community.

19 Jacques Rancière, *Disagreement: Politics and Philosophy,* The University of Minnesota, 1999, p. 89.

20 Ranjit Hoskoté, 'Notes Towards the Possibility of Transformative Listening', lecture transcript. See: www.initiative-humboldt-forum.eu/index.php?id=12.

21 Agamben 2007 (see note 17), p. 75.

22 Between 2005 and 2011 the state of Baden-Württemberg produced large, popular exhibitions in the building that also houses the Kunstverein.

23 See: *Re-Designing The East. Political Design in Asia and Europe,* ed. by Hans D. Christ and Iris Dressler, exh. cat., Württembergischer Kunstverein, Ostfildern 2011.

24 'The Art of Not Being Governed Like That', in: *Re-Designing The East. Political Design in Asia and Europe*, ed. by Hans D. Christ and Iris Dressler, exh. cat., Württembergischer Kunstverein, Ostfildern 2011.

25 Anna Oppermann 1998, quoted in: Hans D. Christ, Iris Dressler, 'A Commentary, Not a Foreword', in: *Anna Oppermann, Ensembles 1968-1992,* ed. by Ute Vorkoeper, exh. cat. Württembergischer Kunstverein Stuttgart and Generali Foundation Vienna, Cantz, Ostfildern 2007, p. 14.

26 Ute Vorkoeper, 'Therapy and Revolt of the Present', in: *Anna Oppermann, Ensembles 1968 -1992,* ed. by Ute Vorkoeper, exh.-cat. Württembergischer Kunstverein Stuttgart and Generali Foundation Vienna, Cantz, Ostfildern 2007, p. 30.

27 Ibid.

28 Jacques Rancière, *The Future of the Image*, London/New York: Verso Books 2007, pp. 56-57. Originally published in French as *Le destin des images*, Paris, 2003.

29 Foucault, 'Critique' 1997 (see note 3), p. 32.

30 Anna Oppermann, 'Lebensprozess und künstlerisches Vorgehen – wodurch wird mein Leben strukturiert?', in: *Pathosgeste – MGSMO Installation im Altonaer Rathaus,* Brussels/Hamburg 1991, unpag., quoted in: Ute Vorkoeper, 'Therapy and Revolt of the Present', in: *Anna Oppermann, Ensembles 1968-1992 ...*, p. 29.

31 Joseph Vogl, Über das Zaudern, 2008, p. 108. English translation from: *On Dithering: Motives of Suspension, Suture and Digression*, exhibition booklet, Württembergischer Kunstverein Stuttgart 2013, unpag.

Involvements in Art Criticism

As We Experience It and as We Claim It

Sabeth Buchmann
Sonja Eismann
Ines Kleesattel
Ruth Sonderegger

Ruth Sonderegger – I asked you to join this conversation because you are all engaged in art-criticism–both as theorists and critics. Moreover, I cherish your interest in practices of institutional critique as well as in the question as to whether institutional critique, especially in light of current attempts to historicize and criticize this artistic practice, has come to an end. Despite the fact that we have never before talked to each other in today's configuration, it seems to me that we share the assumption that the imperative to be critical, however problematic and ubiquitous, has corrupted neither all forms of artistic institutional critique nor all variants of critical writing and talking about contemporary art. This is all the more remarkable, as our backgrounds are rather heterogeneous. However, I may be wrong in assuming such agreement. But I did not ask you to participate in this conversation in order to re-affirm an already established consensus. In fact, it is rather your engagement with controversy, the fact that you embrace self-criticism and openness that motivated me to invite you to join this conversational experiment, of which the course and outcome are as yet unknown.

As we come from different disciplines, institutional backgrounds and generations, it might be instructive to start our discussion by talking about why we became interested in art criticism and how and/or why we started practicing it.

Sabeth Buchmann – In my case, the starting point lies in the late 1980s: Inspired more by pop writers such as Julie Burchill, Diedrich Diederichsen, Clara Drechsler and Jutta Koether than by certain journalistic or academic forms of art criticism, it was their radical subjective style that encouraged me to write. As for many others of my generation and milieu, the field of interest was not so much related to the art market as to all kinds of pop and subcultural activities, which overlapped with artistic practices. Furthermore, writing for me was an opportunity to absorb those contents and methods that came along with the import of French theory and Anglo-American cultural studies, especially regarding their manifold interfaces with art and politics. Another important background was the theatre and film group Minimal Club, which I cofounded with Elfe Brandenburger, Stephan Geene und Mano Wittmann in 1984 and which over the years expanded its activities by publishing books and *A.N.Y.P. – Zeitung für 10 Jahre*: This was a mixture of essays on art, culture and politics which appeared once a year – in accordance with its concept from 1989 until 1999. In a way one can say we were interested in diagnosing and/or evoking the spirit of that time beyond commercialized *Zeitgeist*-claims. For us, the 'newspaper' was a possibility to get into communication with those artists, filmmakers, theorists and activists in whose work we were interested. From today's perspective one could call this an interdisciplinary way of networking within the so-called self-organized field.

RS – I think that my entry point into art criticism was my frustration with philosophical aesthetics and its tendency to speak of art in the singular, i.e. a-historically and without sensitivity to geo-political contexts but nevertheless in a strongly normative tone. This frustration resulted in a turn to the history of art criticism. Following some hints in Th. W. Adorno's *Aesthetic Theory* and W. Benjamin's dissertation on *The Concept of Art Criticism in German Romanticism*, I turned to Friedrich Schlegel. There I found an approach that insisted on art criticism as the solely convincing basis of art theory. This was exactly what I was looking for in my search for a possibility to defend a critical and thus normative account of art works without ending up with a-historical norms of good taste. Moreover, I was intrigued by Schlegel's account of critique as something positive, an affirmative critique so to speak, i.e. his idea (much later taken up by Adorno) that only convincing art works deserve criticism and that this criticism should be directed at figuring out, indeed define, what convincing artistic practices were aiming at even if they had not achieved their aim.

Sonja Eismann – Although coming of age a bit later, I think for me the situation was similar to Sabeth's because I was, as a suburban teen in the late 1980s and early 1990s, influenced by the reverberations of 1980s radical subjectivities in writing that I was consuming in German pop culture and theory magazine *Spex*, but also self-published pop culture and underground fanzines that favoured a dissident, authority-defying and idiosyncratic mode of expression – which could sometimes border on the misogynist. Thus I was glad to become aware, a bit later, of nineties culture in the sense of political grass roots activism, Do-It-Yourself culture, and of course Riot Grrrl, although this movement, having never really crossed over to the European continent from the US and the UK, was not so much present as a distinct phenomenon at first, but rather as a diffuse discontent with and resistance against male dominance in so-called alternative cultural spaces. So, I think, for me the most important thing that had me trying to articulate myself in regard to cultural production was something as simple as having a voice – a distinctly female voice that could not believe that, after the efforts of Second Wave Feminists, not only female contributions to the arts were routinely neglected or trivialized, but that the same was happening in supposedly emancipatory subcultures. Another driving force for me was to have some form of critical engagement that was in opposition to what I was – or rather, wasn't – finding in academia in the 1990s. So I turned to subculture to engage in oppositional practices, being also interested in the debates that were instigated by the so-called German 'Poplinke' in the 1990s who were trying to merge aesthetic and political discourses.

Ines Kleesattel – My starting point was sort of twofold as I studied fine arts and philosophy at the same time and I was interested in social criticism from both directions, art and philosophy: On the one hand I grappled with the problem of how to deal with an explicitly socio-critical perspective *within* art works, without breaking them down to simplistic content or message. On the other hand I was concerned, similar to Ruth, with approaching art with philosophical aesthetics or theory in a more general sense. I wondered how to talk and write about art works and maybe specify certain aspects that are immanent to them, without explaining them in a reductive way, but rather starting a discussion about and also with them.

So the question of which connections between art and critique can enable emancipating forms of perceiving, thinking and encountering reality – which neither art nor theory could achieve on its own – became more and more important to me. And now I am working with Adorno and Rancière trying to combine their to some extent opposed approaches: while Adorno's materialistically oriented aesthetic of the work emphasizes the art work's socio-historically situated objectivity as a fundamentally critical formation of fragments of the existing world, Rancière's aesthetic of experience is rather idealistically oriented. It insists on the 'Emancipated Spectator', who has her very own individual understandings of the art work and thus experiences anti-authoritarian empowerment. In my opinion both sides are absolutely essential, since work and experience call for each other reciprocally. And an ambitious art criticism might be able to cope productively with the complementarity of the art work's specifically situated production and its potentially undetermined reception.

SB – I think it is important to consider the different starting points of art criticism in order to figure out the often diverging relations between the notions of art and critique: The ones who started off from a more practice-related field and the ones who – like me – felt the necessity to work with subjects and methods of the 'New Art History', of cultural studies and media theory; this approach might differ from problems and concepts related to philosophy, aesthetic theory, political theory and sociology. Of course, we witness manifold mixtures of both. One important difference between the two approaches lies in the ways of contextualizing and historiography, which of course show divergent receptions of art and its objects.

RS – My turn to art criticism testifies to what Sabeth just said. For my fascination with art has everything to do with my background in philosophy and in particular with my interest in Benjamin and Adorno. For both of them the possibility of critique is closely tied to art works. In their eyes, it is mainly artistic practices that perform and trigger modes of critique that are not totally complicit with the status quo.

However, the moment I turned to art criticism (along the lines of Schlegel, Adorno and Benjamin), the borders between art and culture seemed extremely blurred so that engagement with cultural studies became imperative. I felt the need to replace the question as to which critique artworks practice and/or trigger with the question as to what kind of critique different objects and practices ignite, irrespective of the question of their identity as art work, cultural product, political engagement. However, apparently the idea that there is more criticism in art than anywhere else did not totally disappear. This might be due to the fact that I was and am strongly influenced by early critical theory.

SE – I would totally agree with the claim that there is a somehow more open space for critical engagement to be found in art and art criticism, which is why I gradually turned to art as some kind of intervention over the years. Because the massive economic changes that we have witnessed. which are of course of paramount importance to the field of art as well, as we all know, have made the spaces for action or criticality much smaller or even less interesting when it comes to the entertainment complex. Just think of the demise of the music industry, the rise of the Internet and subsequent control mechanisms in cinema, et cetera. But I do think that, paradoxically, in art these spaces have even opened up more, accompanied by all the complications brought about by massive monetization.

IK – I'd like to cherish the idea that there is a specific, privileged space for criticism in art. Of course this is not so much due to a peculiar essentiality of art as such, but rather to institutional possibilities. For certain formats, as for example alternative documentary or experimental education, it is much easier (or even the only prospect) to get aid money and access to distribution channels within the art field than elsewhere. Naturally, this is a big problem as well, because to be labelled as art also means a belittlement for critical production. However, it allows certain productions that otherwise were very unlikely to be realized at all. I think those spaces of freedom and possibility, which exist despite and within the monetized art field, must be defended. This is where I spot an important task for art criticism: Art criticism can and must *distinguish* between different claims of criticality and advocate critical and emancipatory potentials *context-specifically* against an overhasty and generalist dismissal of the critical as it tends to recently be announced by Tom Holert, Helmut Draxler or Luc Boltanski. Furthermore, art criticism should help broaden the sphere of influence and potential audience of the productions consigned to art spaces. Unfortunately, mundane art criticism in common journalism barely lives up to such assignments.

SB – I see two central problems within the contemporary field of art criticism: On the one hand the often idealizing philosophical projections on art, which sometimes go along with neo-normative and/or over-determining claims regarding the highly charged interfaces between art and politics. Lyotard and Badiou, to my mind, are obvious examples of said projections. On the other hand, we face the problem of a much too affirmative and/or unengaged art criticism lacking specific concepts regarding aesthetic and social notions of critique as well as of its changing positions and functions within art history.

RS – I totally agree with Sabeth. When I wrote my PhD (in the field of philosophical aesthetics), I came to the conclusion that philosophers are either not interested in art at all or that they essentialize and glorify it. Philosophers have a strong tendency to expect art to solve all the problems that philosophy cannot resolve. For me, this was just the other side of discovering the necessity of making criticism the basis of art theory and cultural theory. In my view, criticism is rather the direction of an engagement or of an endeavour with its own failures and impurities than a clear-cut case like heaven or hell. As long as one follows the philosophical path of the question as to what is essential about (for instance) art works, institutional, social and geo-political questions seem of less or no importance. However, the moment one turns to a close analysis of concrete artistic or cultural production one cannot but become aware of institutional frameworks and geo-political contexts; not least because artistic and cultural practices themselves refer to them – often by way of critique.

SE – At this point it would be interesting to consider how Tom Holert, in the introduction to his new book *Übergriffe* [Trespassing], writes about the 'deskilling process' in the art world, which, according to him, leaves critics today greatly confused about their role. Before, he argues, they had some kind of normative power in regard to defining categories such as 'good' or 'bad', but now they are often forced to retreat into a kind of subservient position, providing merely descriptive accounts of the art works for their readership. And Helmut Draxler reckons that the art critic is an institution in him- or herself which, of course, makes it hard to criticize the institution from within (critique, he says, 'is never directed purely against power, but is always already a power itself' (Draxler, *Gefährliche Substanzen*, 2007, p. 120 [translated by copy editor]). So I would like to discuss the potentialities of writing about art from these points of view. Where do we position ourselves, what other diagnoses can we think about?

SB – There are various and contradictious genealogies of what happens in the field of art criticism today. Sonja just mentioned Tom Holert's and Helmut Draxler's position, which can be seen as exemplary for different directions and their changes. In Tom Holert's case, I would state an expansion of art and pop criticism onto the field of visual studies, science and political theory; in Helmut Draxler's case an expansion of social history onto the field of aesthetic theory and political philosophy. The question is how those shifts relate to institutional and economic dynamics within the sometimes overlapping, sometimes separated fields of art and discourse. Together with Andrea Fraser, Helmut Draxler was one of the first within the German speaking context to reflect on service culture as a dominant signifier for the art practice of the nineties. Their panel on 'Service Culture', which they organized in the Kunstraum Lüneburg in 1994, is already part of the history of institutional critique. Tom Holert, like some others associated with *Spex* and/or *Texte zur Kunst*, in the latter case first of all Isabelle Graw, together with Stephan Germer one of its founders, already count as 'institutions'. I don't want to exclude myself from the group of those who are either accepted or criticized for representing a certain power of definition (*'Definitionsmacht'*). However, the question is whether this has ever touched the art market and/or whether it still touches on it. And as much as art criticism seems to serve the desire for symbolic marketing, the shift from gallery deals to those of auction houses proves the opposite. Probably this also has to do with the shift from categories of aesthetics to those of ethics around 1968. By 'ethics' I mean identity policies and the critique of representation that I still would defend, but which came along with advanced forms of critique that are divorced from any material references onto the objects of art. It is very seldom that both aspects become linked in a way that responds to the difficulties and complexities of making art.

SE – From my experiences as a journalist who writes about culture in general, there is a growing pressure to be 'supportive' of the things one writes about – which on the one hand is due to the power of advertisers with their ever decreasing budgets, rewarding those critics who are more 'friendly' towards their products, but on the other hand there is also a call for solidarity or even complicity from the community of cultural producers, the imperative to 'stand together in times of austerity'. I find it really interesting that you said that the spheres of activity of critics like ourselves never really touch those of the highly financed art world of the collectors, because we all know that, on the other hand, there really is no outside to the art world that would be represented by critique – criticality being an integral part of the whole field. So although we as critics of specialized media outlets are of course far removed from the world of art as financial investment, we must also be aware that the performing of criticality is exacted by art institutions themselves for their constant renewal.

IK – This raises the question as to what kind of art criticism we are talking about here. Is it just the writing of the four of us (and our 'peers') or are we also talking about the pitfalls and potentials of art criticism in its most general sense?

I agree that the art market is barely touched by our writing, but it does make a difference if an artist is reviewed or not. Anyway, I really see a severe constraint in the 'preaching to the already converted' as we do by writing in magazines such as *Texte zur Kunst*, which are explicitly leftist and intellectually demanding and thus have a very limited, already specialized readership. Sonja's situation may be a bit different, as the *Missy Magazine* is not aiming for an already well-informed art audience; it might start a discussion with people who are not sympathetic with the presuppositions of the voiced critique from the very beginning.

Distribution via not so much specialized channels, maybe daily newspapers or school art education programmes, might have greater or at least different effects than remaining within the elitist field of 'art & discourse'.

SB – I am not so sure about the polarization of elitist and less specialized channels. Being often frustrated about the decreasing quantity and quality of art criticism in daily newspapers – which is, on the one hand, due to cost-cutting measures and, on the other hand, due to a seemingly increasing populism – I would insist on a specific knowledge, which of course should permanently reflect its premises, interests, and validity. Regarding the ongoing critical reception of *Texte zur Kunst* – but no less of *October, Afterall* or *Grey Room* – which in some regards I agree with, the magazine obviously continues to be a productive site of dispute and conflict. Furthermore, *Texte zur Kunst* is a symptomatic example of the dependency of art criticism on the dynamics of the art market as well as on institutional, academic and media booms – and it is always exciting and sometimes frustrating to see how critics and editors deal with them. There is no doubt that specialized art criticism can perform itself as a high-end, sexy discourse that comes to an arrangement with the ruling conditions. Therefore, in my eyes art criticism should keep in mind its own social history and its institutional position that provide both a position of power and a position of minority.

IK – But the issue of being elitist and talking to a very restricted community remains. Although I agree on appreciating the work of *Texte zur Kunst* for its self-/institutional-reflective debating practice, there's still the problem that no one reads this magazine who is not sympathetic to a theoretically sophisticated approach towards art *from the beginning*. Its texts are jargonized and they are based on a lot of implicit presuppositions. And if I write in a magazine like this, I have a very clear idea as to who I'm writing for – namely people 'like us', well-informed about contemporary art and its current discourses, interested in aesthetic and political theory and thinking of themselves as critical, open-minded and leftist. Wouldn't it be crucial to provide differentiated and ambitious alternatives to populist or mere descriptive journalism that are still somehow 'reader-friendly', i.e. accessible and comprehensible without expertise, maybe even appealing? Why is playing a providing role per se a bad thing, as Holert implies? After all, the important question is: who is providing *what* to *whom* in *which situation*.

SE – As I have already mentioned, *Missy* as a medium does see itself as part of a specific (political) community, which marks a starting point that is quite distinct from 'mainstream journalism', but also different from outlets such as *Texte zur Kunst* – as our readers are not perfectly informed, but *benevolently and critically interested*. So ours is a constant movement between the necessity of distance as a mode of criticality and the distancing from distance, which is an integral part of fan attitudes, a sort of suspension of disbelief. Dietmar Dath, in his book about Buffy the Vampire Slayer (*Sie ist wach. Über ein Mädchen, das hilft, schützt, rettet*, 2003)[She's awake. About a girl who helps, protects, saves], has as insightfully as drastically delineated the antagonistic, but equally blind spots of informed cultural studies versus nerdy fandom, which he sees to exist simultaneously in a kind of 'pop criticism with the will to explain', as the 'perennial stupidity of knowing too much and understanding too little'. He declares himself guilty of also having taken part in paving the way for a kind of analysis that is too often caught between the positions of the 'fanboys' with their affirmative 'But I like it!' and the 'learned ones' with an over-theorizing approach that does not even care to engage with their subject matter on a level of close reading ('Have these people ever watched a whole episode of *Buffy*?', he asks despairingly). A loophole out of this conflict might be not to hypostatize the evidences of fandom, but to problematize the complexities and the involvements of one's position in the cultural and creative industries.

IK – I'd like to think of art criticism as part of an emancipatory pedagogy that facilitates access to alternative perceptions of reality and to the utopian potential of aesthetic autonomy. Of course, neoliberalism doubtlessly does incorporate critical skills and perverts autonomy into precarity, but it could be precisely the task of art criticism to take a closer look on specific claims of criticality and autonomy and articulate differentiations here. Despite all justified wariness à la Boltanski, not *every* form and content of criticism is compatible with neoliberal profit motivations, and a lot of versions of autonomy and radical equality prove to be still very critical about existing hegemonies. I am convinced that art criticism – focusing on ever specific constellations – can help to discern and address such nevertheless resistant moments and thus open up a broader discussion, that goes beyond just subverting the art field. Admittedly, as art critics we are part of the game and therefore indeed entangled in ambivalences, like Draxler states, but this does not mean that there are no emancipatory prospects at all. Judith Butler argues that any critical-emancipatory agency must be based on acknowledging our entanglements and dependencies instead of longing for sovereignty. As art critics we could probably learn something from Butler here. As to a 'pedagogical' commitment, this certainly involves transforming art criticism into a more polyphonic and ever changing conflict (where something is at stake) rather than lecturing 'skilled' but in a monologue about good or bad art.

RS – I am very sympathetic to Ines' suggestion to experiment with knowledge and practices that emancipatory pedagogies have provided us with. Over the years I realized that (for me, having the privilege of being a teacher) discussing art works during seminars and workshops most of the times is much more fun than writing about them in isolation or in conversation with texts (at best) that others have written; and it is rewarding, too. For, on the one hand, doing art criticism together makes clear from the outset how contested, if not one-sided, experiences with art works are and that such contestation is an integral part of speaking and writing about art. On the other hand, it is fascinating to see how much substantial knowledge about the respective art works (art works currently on show in a context the group shares or that somebody brought to class) is in place already in groups of people that have come together more or less incidentally for a seminar or a workshop and to see how much more experiences and knowledge you can produce together if you take the time to listen to each other. Moreover, and probably most importantly, doing art criticism together time and again shows that one can learn to perform the kind of talking or writing that is called art criticism (in western aesthetics). This does not mean to disdain or deny the necessity of scholarly knowledge and expertise, on the contrary. However, much of such knowledge is made available to us today (and more should be made available) in ways that are not altogether different from the situation in the seminar-room I just evoked. I am primarily thinking here indeed of all the art-critical knowledge we can find on the Internet these days: knowledge provided by professional (mostly unpaid) critics, so-called lay(wo)men, aficionados, et cetera, plus, in some cases at least, fervent debates about the knowledge provided in this way. I certainly do not want to whitewash or belittle the fact that most of the scholarly or not so scholarly discussions and expert-knowledge we find on the Web are the product of unpaid labour. However, I think that some variant of unconditional basic income would be a better remedy for the precarity of most of today's art critics than re-installing the hierarchies between more or less professional journals and magazines.

SB – Since the exchange with others being involved in common discussions are basic to my writings, I usually prefer to work with editors; I can also see the advantages of blogs, because there are more and more issues that don't get considered by professional editors and dependent writers. But I doubt whether the multiplicity of voices is enough to change given power relations. Don't they just get distributed and dispersed in the way Foucault has described it? I am not sure whether this tendency brings with it an enlargement of the 'heterogeneous empirical totality of art works' of which Peter Osborne speaks and which tends to harmonize those social conflicts we observe under the condition of today's network economy. I am probably less optimistic than Ines about the broad effect of art criticism and, on the other hand, I am not so negative about addressing specific contexts with which I can enter into a dialogue on an equal footing. I would even stress this moment much stronger than *Texte zur Kunst* does in order to have a constant change of issues and discourses. However, this also means a loss of binding and continuous debates, which, as I assume, would be forced even more to reflect on mechanisms of in- and exclusion. Furthermore, I think that deliberate strategies of inclusion can produce the opposite and on the contrary diminish spaces of criticism: In my eyes, it is productive that *Texte zur Kunst* is such a controversial magazine. It lives, to a certain extent, from its negative reputation, which obviously evokes an ongoing process of objections.

RS – I do not want to play down the pleasure of having extended discussions with the editors of a magazine (or book) after completing the first draft of a piece of art criticism, even if such debates might be painful at times too. However, as long as these discussions are not made accessible to the readership they remain the pleasure (or burden) of a few experts who share a specific (professional) field. I had remarkable discussions with various editors of, for example, *Texte zur Kunst* but they remained 'behind the curtains'; for instance, on the question as to whether one should totally avoid the term 'spectacle' (in the late 1990s), whether excessive praise should be tolerated or even encouraged, whether contradictory or paradoxical statements in one and the same text are to be avoided, et cetera. In my view, the question is as to whether and how it might be possible to ignite the discussions Sabeth has with her fellow critics-editors among those who do not belong to the editorial board. What comes to mind here, is the idea of a polylogue, i.e. having several articles on one and the same exhibition, artist, diagnosis, institution, instead of just one; or to search for texts that consist of contradictory elements, such as Plato's *Symposium*. For on the one hand, any solitary piece of criticism involuntarily (or not so involuntarily) takes on the position of an objective judgment; on the other hand, it is no longer necessary to provide readers with more or less neutral information as to what is on show on which sites as art institutions provide abundant information in all kinds of media about their programmes. However, what is missing indeed, is self-critical debates. I would even venture to say that in the field of criticism, professionalism very much equals the openness to self-critique.

My plea for experiments with polylogues neither advocates spectacular debates for the sake of debates (usually between two big shots) nor should it be misinterpreted as relativism. However contradictory they may be, the arguments and claims of a polylogue do refer to each other critically instead of being indifferent and relativistic in relation to one another. Moreover, my idea of a critical polylogue envisions a space in which not only different approaches but first of all the powerful hierarchies between them become visible and are commented upon. To put it differently, to create spaces for criticism means to create spaces in which power structures become visible no less than, occasionally at least, alternatives.

SE – As an editor and publisher of an independent magazine that we chose to position on the 'free market' to reach more people than with, say, a feminist fanzine or blog, fully aware of all the ambiguities and constraints this decision entails, my colleagues and I are constantly struggling to put forward a potential third position that aims at reconciling the stances that you all so very well articulated.

We are thus oscillating between the sometimes – deliberately – awkward poles of conveying 'positive knowledge' about marginalized positions that might or might not be commodified, and criticizing criticality. We once ran an article about Michaela Melián's video work, featuring Silvia Bovenschen and Sarah Schulman, for Shedhalle, a long-standing, alternative art space in Zurich that is rarely mentioned in art criticism, in which Melián talked to these two co-organizers of a ground-breaking, now largely forgotten exhibition of women's art in Berlin in 1977 (*Künstlerinnen international 1877-1977*) – which already then represented largely forgotten art works by women. (Interestingly, Melián's work was taken up in an extensive article in *Frieze* magazine later on). This piece might be a good example of our belief that the binary dichotomy of artistic and social critique – which are of course ideal types of heuristic categories in Boltanski/Chiapello – should be regarded more dialectically, accommodating specific conditions and contradictions. Projects such as the e-flux reading group accompanying the showing of Rossella Biscotti's *The Trial* in New York in May 2013, where old (and new) texts by, amongst others, radical feminist and Marxist autonomist Silvia Federici were read and discussed, establishing links between the pressures of reproductive labour in the times of *potere operaia* in the 1970s and neoliberal globalization, are, in my opinion, further instances of an immensely productive way of examining marginalized historical positions for the production of contemporary criticism.

Part 3

Media and Identity Shifts

Feminist Critique
Open and Critical Enquiry

A Conversation between Katy Deepwell and Suzana Milevska

The invitation to join the editorial team of the book *Spaces for Criticism* and to suggest writers for submissions and conversations was a great opportunity and at the same time a challenge to my own understanding of the role of contemporary criticism today. It immediately became clear that while selecting whom to invite one also contemplates their understanding of the ways in which art criticism navigates and balances between the interpretation of art production and the critical analysis of the different cultural contexts and socio-political conditions that influence and shape the art production that criticism addresses. To me as a curator and theorist coming from a cultural context with a very limited space for any critical discussion about the need for gendering the art field and where feminist interventions are often dismissed as theoretical imports from the so-called 'West' it seemed a very relevant political intervention to address the relevance and possible influence of sparse spaces for feminist critical writing in various cultural contexts. To question the impact of the limited quantity of published feminist writing on the development of feminist art and women artists' practices in general was one of the main aims of this discussion.

Ever since Katy Deepwell, an art critic based in London, initiated and started editing the journal *n.paradoxa: international feminist journal,* this has been one of the rare periodical publications that has continued to provide space to women writers who in their texts focus on the art production and representation of art by women artists who are active on the international art scene but also in their local art scenes, wherever they are. The journal caters to an array of both established and young art writers who write about women artists' exhibitions and artistic practices, frequently presenting internationally unknown women artists from various corners of the world next to the works of the better-known feminist artists who even might have influenced their work and offering a trans-generational as well as a trans-national model.

I therefore asked Katy Deepwell to engage in a series of conversations about feminist critique and criticism and to publish the outcomes of our discussions here. The discussions, which took place via skype, e-mail and during our meetings, revolved around the lack of spaces available for representation and critical reflection about feminist art and artists, particularly in the international art contexts. We started our conversation with the assumption that if the international art scene is favouring male artists from various parts of the world, this multiplies when it comes to women artists and women writers on art who work in more conservative contexts: their voices and perspectives may be underrepresented in their local cultural context and this is reproduced again, in the international art scene.

Suzana Milevska – I'd like to start with an introduction and contextualization of our conversation. In this conversation we propose to focus on the specificity of feminist art critique over the last couple of decades and how it has affected criticism in general. When we first met (in 1996) the promise of the internet was so prominent that you initiated the first editions of *n.paradoxa: international feminist journal* in the virtual online space. Were there any additional reasons for this decision, apart from overcoming the institutional limitations of existing professional and academic journals dealing with feminist art and women artists, e.g. cross-cultural outreach? And how did this situation change later, when you moved the journal's content to the much more demanding printed version?

Katy Deepwell – In 1996, people were more optimistic about the possibility of the internet as a communication tool that might profoundly encourage exchange and dialogue between people (and not just elites) as universities, government departments and services became linked up for the first time all around the world. In accounting for the internet as a space for art criticism, we have to consider not only the internet as it is today, but its historical development of use in the last 20 years and this is not a technological story but a cultural one. The 'public' vision of the internet as a vast resource and a library of information was only starting to be realized by some major IT projects on library and museum collections: very few journals at that time had electronic forms or PDFs (which are now commonplace). People were willing to embrace this 'promise' and 'potential', even though we knew that the internet was a product of the military industrial complex of the US (and subject to surveillance as a result) and that matters related to computing and pornography were the largest subjects online at that time. What I saw in my initial searches in 1996 was the absence of not just art criticism, but feminist art criticism, from the online world – with the notable exception of discussion of new media projects which used the very tool with which they worked as a tool for communication in lists, journals and online forums. Museums had only just begun to use 'databases' to document and create digital archives and mainly used the internet as they do today as a marketing and corporate promotional tool. The shift since 1996 has been so profound in the explosion of 'data' and 'services' available to people via the internet from governments and business, particularly in libraries, but the public dimension of this has been reduced to incredibly rigid and highly formalized channels of 'delivery' and this has not changed, in spite of the hype surrounding 'social media'. There are formulaic methods and expectations about how we encounter things online and there is remarkably little experimentation. These developments have brought a profound change in how we interact with this online environment, falsely believing it to be a complete repository of all information and images (including our acceptance of a specific quality of image, screen-readable jpgs), but rarely ideas. Reading habits have shifted online, but only in so far as 'an article' or 'document' uses this form of delivery: its content remains unaltered, except by the minor addition of hyperlinks. At the same time, there has been a collapse of the 'review' into marketing and promotion: namely, the endless repetition of 'the same press release' on Facebook-type noticeboards, on websites, on blogs, on twitter feeds; or the circulation of meta-data, which accompanies new productions of a book, an exhibition or an event. There is a dreadful 'conformity' in publishing now, even on blogs (supposedly the new and democratic medium for anyone to express their opinion without censorship, even for those with almost no computing skills).

n.paradoxa's online history began optimistically at the beginning of these developments and at a critical moment in the development of cyberfeminism as a discourse. It was an experiment to create a site for international exchanges between women about feminist art criticism –

but it was an academic specialism that came at the tail end of many other kinds of critical, research and academic initiatives about this subject in the preceding two decades. I had no economic capital to become a publisher, so I decided on the net as a vehicle for ideas (using my cultural capital) and taught myself HTML in two weeks. Bloggers today have preformatted tools readily available to them to do exactly the same and do not seem troubled by questions of 'ownership' to their material or 'intellectual property rights'. I had ideas, information and a network of people in my field to whom I thought it would be interesting and who could contribute: *n.paradoxa* is a standard publishing model, just online. The art world, however, is not interested in reading outside print media (and this is still the case today), so I took the initiative to develop a print journal: as the 'proper' and 'professional' form for ideas – personally, I don't find this more demanding, just different and both forms present specific possibilities as to what can be done. Behaving paradoxically (like the philosophy of the journal), I continued the two separate forms for over 15 years and this genuinely confused people who read one but not the other or felt I should conform to the standard model of journal publishing, where the online version is only a copy or minor extension of the print into the digital realm. In 2011, I finally capitulated and today the online PDF is identical to the print, but in the preceding years (1996–2010 on the HTML site) this was never the case. I keep a very important part of the old online site up-to-date, including the resource lists of books, websites, exhibitions and other feminist art journals, even though these are now run from a database [www.ktpress.co.uk]. The policy of the journal was to create an intersection between feminist theory and writing about contemporary women artists, which would embrace international dialogue between different locations in the world, i.e. transcend the national dimension of criticism as it is constructed in national newspapers and art magazines, which are language-specific and generally distributed only nationally. Each issue (online) and volume (in print) was constructed to maximize the international dimension of these contributions. I chose the dominant *lingua franca* of the internet, English (also my mother tongue), being aware of the problems that this generates, but committed myself to publishing translations, where possible. So today, over 500 articles have been published from writers and artists living in more than 80 countries. The other driving idea was the expansion of this discourse by publishing only once about any artist or work, and because the journal was a platform that was not driven by the need to review the 'latest' show (i.e. journalism's topical agenda) or by a media/advertising financial model, it could do this as a way to reconsider feminism's legacy post-1970 in contemporary debates in the expanding field of contemporary art.

I would also like to ask you about whether an exhibition is a suitable space to open a dialogue for feminist art criticism. Conventionally, it is only the exhibition's review that is seen as critical reflection. But there are alternatives to this, in the exhibition itself, in the catalogue, in the talks that surround it. It seems that here too there is a shift in opinion in the last 20 years in curatorial praxis. You have also worked as a critic and art historian, separate from your curatorial practice. Do you mentally separate these activities, or see them as different only because they are produced in different critical spaces: a journal, a newspaper, an online website, a book or an exhibition?

SM – I have often thought about the potential of exhibitions and alternative spaces for exhibitions as platforms for voicing critical positions towards mainstream institutions. Over the last two decades, we have continuously faced the disappearance of differences and distinctions between the fine arts and media, a process that is also occurring in the relation between criticism and art. I have often re-examined the relation between these two, in my opinion, totally different professions. Curatorship, as a hybrid profession that establishes a more direct relationship between the critic or theorist and the artist, underlined this interactive intertwining of different professions and media. I see this tendency as a positive one, and from the beginning of my professional engagement in this field I have supported a more creative, more artistic form of criticism, which has brought me to the curatorial profession as being the most creative relationship between the artist and the art work.

In my critical texts I have mainly targeted the local institutional agendas for being elitist and not reflective in relation to contemporary art phenomena. However, ever since I started curating (in the early 1990s) my motivation was instead to simply criticize through my own practice by promoting a different and critical view to art, which otherwise was very limited and closed in the circle of institutional policies in Macedonia. I therefore curated exhibitions mostly in spaces that were not intended for exhibiting art and belonged neither to the official art institutions nor to the state and that, one could argue, functioned also as a certain art criticism. I did give up writing art criticism very early (only after four years of continuous writing critical reviews in daily newspapers) because in such small cultural contexts as Skopje and Macedonia it soon became obvious that I would encounter many instances of different conflicts of interests. Writing critically about the institutions and exhibitions curated by other colleagues that would often include art works by the same artists with whom I collaborated became very problematic. I still hold relevant the discussion about the limits of the use of curating art for the purposes of generating a critical art or art criticism, because it creates a kind of self-referential closed circuit. I'd like to go back to the warning that we owe to Theodor W. Adorno. Actually, it was Robert Lane Kauffmann who tried to re-contextualize Adorno's critique of Benjamin's striving for a philosophy, theory and criticism that would be closer to art, while pointing out that in Adorno's view this would mean that art would be expunging itself.[1] His critique was grounded on the discrete contradictions of the cognitive and social functions of art and criticism, and on the belief in their institutional differentiation. The absence of critical reflection on the part of theorists, when combined with a lack of critical attitude towards history and reality could only turn their work into a self-referential and self-indulgent game. For Kauffmann, this discussion had a particular relevance because of the inevitable difficulty to draw 'absolute ontological distinctions' between the language of literature and that of criticism,[2] but one could expand this by thinking further about the relation between, for example, conceptual art and 'institutional critique' art works and the art criticism about them.

Critical reflection is a responsibility of both critics and curators and the need for it is still one of the necessary layers that add to the complexity of the art world and I don't see it only in terms of writing critical reviews. For example, aside from the development of theoretical art discourse, I find organizing discursive events and publications that invite debates to take place about the most urgent critical issues far more productive than pronouncing the death of criticism.

I am aware that the curatorial practice cannot provide all the necessary answers to the recent contradictions in contemporary art, because of the promotional dimension that to a varying extent is present at the core of the curatorial profession. Curating, however, complicates this black-and-white picture of criticism, since it interferes and criss-crosses between art, theory and social context, thereby offering a better understanding of the issues of 'self-reference', social art activism and other aspects that in many critical texts have too limited potentials for direct impact. Therefore I find criticism necessary, both in terms of social critique of the art world and in terms of aesthetic reflections about various general developments of art and certain concrete art productions and media.

KD – How has your actual curatorial work contributed to developing your approach to criticism as a feminist? Is it possible to have a consistent 'line' in curatorial practice as a form of art critical production? Certainly, there are some notable feminists who have addressed this issue (Lucy Lippard, Marcia Tucker, Catherine de Zegher, Maria Lind, Silvia Eiblmayr, Bojana Pejic, Ruth Noack, to name a few). How do you see this situation in your own work?

SM – Ever since I moved on from writing art criticism and started curating, I have directed my critical curatorial practice towards working with women artists (although not exclusively) and towards curating from a feminist position. In that sense I want to believe that my curatorial initiatives inevitably have had a critical impact on the local art situation. For example, the texts that I have written as introductions to catalogues not only provide a contextual space for exhibiting to women artists but also to the artists who declare a feminist agenda and seek to make way for critical art practices that anticipated many socio-political issues in post-transitional and post-socialist societies, issues that at that time were not so present in art criticism and art theory. I still feel the pressure because of the obvious feminist agenda in my work. For example, I am aware of a difference in the pace of development of my own career and the careers of the curators who did not strive to change anything about the art system but only fully embraced it. I refer to my projects *Liquor Amnii* (1996) and *Capital and Gender* (2001). Particularly with the public cross-disciplinary project *Capital and Gender* I anticipated many urgent discussions, which have re-ignited lately, about the neoliberal economic turn in Eastern and South Eastern Europe. The project encompassed 17 art installations and participatory performances, as well as new media workshops, lectures and a theoretical conference that took place in the City Shopping Mall (GTC) in Skopje and the Museum of the City of Skopje.

The City Shopping Mall is one of the first covered shopping centres in Eastern Europe (built in the early 1970s after the devastating earthquake that hit Skopje in 1963). For almost a decade after the split of Yugoslavia and Macedonia's independence (in 1991), it was a dark and abandoned place, until it was revived in the late nineties. According to one of its architects, Živko Popovski (1934–2007), who spoke at the project's conference, it was designed with many different purposes. On the one hand, it had a social and public function (with a lot of social, non-commercial and community-oriented spaces such as a cinema, gallery, chess club, et cetera). But on the other hand, one of its main functions was to survey and control the successful local small and middle-sized businesses (wedding-gown makers, shoe and watch-repairers, sweets shops, etc.). What sparked my attention was that with the mall's economic revival in the nineties, the fully blown-up sexist imageries of the advertising billboards proliferated and overnight started dominating the public space of the centre, which had once been a gloomy and emptied-out space with only few advertisement posters.

This phenomenon soon revealed how fragile and susceptible the gender equality agenda from socialist times was, however heavily fought for through WWII and during the fifty years of communism. My questions then were (and still are now) how it was possible to have time reversed in such a short time and to go back to basic conservative rules of the patriarchal society without questioning them, as if meanwhile nothing had happened. Women lost the right to paid maternity leave of nine months, equal pay for equal work, and representation in political and social structures even when the quota system was still in power. Through the discussions, the newly produced art works and the publication for the exhibition it became clearer how the continuity of patriarchy was maintained long-term through very strong family structures, regardless of the changes in the political and social policy decisions.

At that time I was very influenced by the postcolonial debate about the 'unequal exchange' (e.g. in my introductory text for the reader *Capital and Gender* I referred to Gayatri Chakravorty Spivak's *The Critique of the Postcolonial Reason*).[3] Only later I came across Silvia Federici and the feminist debate about the reproduction of capital as unevaluated and unaccounted labour, Nira Yuval-Davis' concept of *transversal politics* and Chandra Talpade Mohanty's take on solidarity.[4]

However, already with *Capital and Gender* I was interested in the effect that the proliferation of overtly sexualized and sexist imageries would have on societal relations, with the neoliberal transformation of the public space. I focused on the transformative power of visual culture and media, both in positive and regressive terms. In this context I tried to use the most uncritical space, the space of the shopping centre, for opening up a critical discussion. In parallel, I also curated a conference in the Museum of the City of Skopje that revealed great tensions between art critics and curators with regard to gender issues and feminist debates. It was in this context that feminism (and your name as a feminist art critic was also mentioned!) was once again attacked for being a typical product of Western theory, as if feminism was not necessary in our region because of the equality gains of the socialist period.

In fact my project anticipated the opposite, and revealed exactly the falsity and simplicity of this argument which had been addressed already in the context of the debates about the transversal, intersectional and cross-national aspects of feminism.

Did the positioning of the critical framework of the journal as feminist also bring with it certain methodological demands on you as the editor and on the writers throughout the process of conceptualization of the journal? How was this negotiated with the need to also cover and present the work of a vast number of relevant women artists who do not consider themselves feminist? Here I particularly have in mind the older generation of ground breaking female artists whose artistic practice cannot be defined as feminist in theoretical and activist terms, even though it made a certain impact on gender awareness in various peripheral art scenes. Did this mean that the programmatic borders of the space of criticism had to be expanded depending on the general feminist political editorial agenda to present women artists and to offer ever more space for feminist criticism to women writers, even when they do not necessarily apply feminist methodology?

KD – The method of the journal is embodied in the title: *n.* – the abbreviation for noun/ thing; 'para' – beyond, 'doxa', what is mainly taught and known in the canon, as standard fare of curricula. What is this noun, this 'thing' called feminism? The problem we have is its constant diminution and marginalization and its reduction to one thing, one object, one method. For me, feminism has always been a heterodox, open, complex and contested field about women and, in relation to art, art criticism and art history – as well as women's studies, feminist theory and activism in the women's movement (we have more than 40 years of activities in this field in contemporary art). As an editor, I see it as a personal responsibility to maintain this diversity culturally, politically and geographically, because this is central to how debates within and about feminism should proceed. I don't have a singular line or a tack about what is or is not feminist art, and the journal does not advocate some pre-defined politically correct ideology. What I do insist upon is that all writers who contribute define what they mean by these terms and consider how they put them to use in their writings for this journal.

This approach is about opening up a space for women writers to explore the very definition of feminism in relation to the practices of women artists. It is not a closing down of this debate into definitive readings. If it was, then all we would be doing is repeating the demonstration of 'mastery' in the final definitive reading of a 'great' artist to which other critics and art historians can only pay homage: which is typically the reverent object of art criticism as it is celebrated in art history and how art historians 'use' critics' opinions. The question of what is the subject of feminism needs to be kept open, even when we are in the midst of disputes about what subjects count, who is dominant or worthy of exploration in the field, who seems to offer the most authoritative readings at any present conjuncture and even who 'owns' the field at any particular moment or in any location. *n.paradoxa* is a contribution to the much broader field of enquiries about feminisms, it sits amongst all the other occasional articles in other journals and special issues which address feminisms, amongst all the exhibitions and research projects on feminism, feminist art and contemporary art histories about women's art production, amongst all the books and websites. *n.paradoxa* is a node in a network, a concentration of activity and an intervention in pre-established meanings and understandings that are already in circulation. It is possible to construct a feminist reading of any art work (produced by either a male or female artist) and this goes beyond simply pointing to gendered distinctions in how art is produced, but this form of feminist critique is not the dominant mode in how art works are reviewed or discussed in our media today. The journal does prioritize women authors writing about women artists because this space is the one that mainstream culture continues to neglect and foreclose in its pursuit of the selective tradition and the next great 'thing' in cultural phenomena. This is the journal's tactic and how it makes its intervention about making visible women's labour in critical thinking on contemporary art: both in what is discussed and in how it is discussed. The journal also varies the forms of art criticism in relation to the standard 2,000-6,000 word academic essay, incorporating some writing experiments and interviews, but definitively different styles of writing. Again, this is a point about the dreadful conformity in publishing: why is 6,000 words the norm, 'the optimal form', for chapters/essays/serious articles or 800 words the norm for exhibition reviews?

SM – Another topic that I'd like to discuss is the potential of critical work in the framework of educational academic institutions. For example, I see teaching at art academies and university departments as a very important critical practice, because art history can be re-written in a critical way each time one mentions a certain artist or movement. Also, I have found precisely the possibility to introduce feminist reading of pre-established art history matrices to be an important intervention.

KD – Like you, I also teach and have done so in a variety of different roles since 1986 and am currently a Professor of Contemporary Art, Theory and Criticism at Middlesex University. *n.paradoxa* was my solution to the invisibility of contemporary women artists in the curriculum: it was to make it impossible to say – as many people did say when I was a student in the first part of 1980s – 'there are no women artists'. The implication was really no women artists 'worthy of study', particularly if, like me, you replied to such stupidities with 'but what about... ?' and reeled off a large number of women artists' names. So, we have the problem of which subjects are studied – by students and by academics – and we have the problem of 'how': which methods to use. I agree that the tools offered by critical feminist art histories often present the necessary shift in understanding needed for all students to engage with feminist questions or questions of gender (these two are different!). However, I worry that this may also leave the canon unchallenged, especially when these methods are presented as 'alternative readings' but the dominant selection of artists, subjects and movements remains the same. There is another dimension to feminist scholarship, which has been research on women artists themselves, and this involves making new archives, extensive documentation, building different collections: often outside museum collections in alternative institutions or library archives. There is now a new focus on the history of feminist exhibitions and initiatives, because there have been many and this trajectory is now desperately in need of critical and art historical attention and it is also revealing for the range of different experiments in exhibition-making that were undertaken in the last forty years. This work on what is often considered the marginal, the minor, or the peripheral has the capacity to challenge what is culturally dominant and revise it. Feminism is not 'over there', 'outside' or 'Other' as a form of knowledge: it is how we grasp, understand or conceptualize the world.

SM – This brings us to one if not the most relevant questions about the actual position of feminist critique at this very moment. In your work as a theorist and editor you have often referred to the impact of the feminist critique on art theory and criticism in general. One would have to agree with the assumption that art criticism inevitably could not continue as before, after the raised awareness of its previous limitations in terms of addressing the intersectionality of gender, race/ethnicity and class issues. However, there are still some bastions of art system's structures that haven't really changed much (for example, regardless the prominence of feminist critique, the lists of the major museum-run retrospectives of women artists are still very short, the lists of the best-selling artists hardly include women and the recent change of the curatorial team of the MoMA in New York turned it into a male dominated team). My concrete question here would be where would you see the most efficient influence of the feminist critique in terms of historic and methodological change of art criticism and whether things change only in an upward and positive direction? I have some doubts in this regard because of the recent return of conservatism and nationalism in most European countries (particularly in Eastern, Central and South Eastern Europe) which directly influenced and often reversed the already accomplished feminist agendas.

KD – I want to mention two of my essays. In the first,[5] I was preoccupied with the flattening of all discussion of feminism into the question of equal opportunities and the idea that feminist politics in the West is no longer needed, because some women have gained equality. Here, statistics about the shifting face of women's representation in the mainstream art world – if discussed at all – are seen either as a sign of progressive change or, if mentioned, immediately identified with an 'outmoded' politics. On a world stage, this false position implies that it is only women outside the West (or of non-Western origin, as migrants or refugees) who have problems with gender equality and the moral high ground is in helping these 'disadvantaged' women. This completely false position leads to some corrosive inequalities and hypocritical positions in the art world vis-à-vis which often well-funded and middle or upper-class women artists are foregrounded on the international art world stage as well as a certain prioritizing of works and artists whose subjects are 'abjection', 'suffering' and tortured/abused/objectified women's bodies. Feminism, in order to start to articulate its own position, has to tear down these misconceptions about subjects and artworks. The essay then addressed how two distinct conceptions of rights – one about equality attached only to notions of citizenship and the other about human rights as 'international' – were in conflict in the construction of these false positions.

In the second essay,[6] I was concerned with how, following a comment by Slavoj Žižek, we now have two dominant positions in art criticism about women artists. The first suggests that 'Otherness' is the only mechanism in and through which all women artists who are recognized as neglected or marginal to 'culture' can become a special subject worthy of attention (i.e. their placement as 'Other' reinforces a feminine stereotype). The second position, which exists simultaneously, holds that the question of feminism in relation to the position of women artists is no longer worthy of any discussion (so feminism and any question about gender in relation to women artists exists as a not-All, without Symbolism). So, the first position may give the illusion that feminist art history has been integrated into the dominant discourse about any/all women artists, but the second is the stark reality of feminism's liquidation from all discourse because gender equality is now an assumed and implicit norm and feminist politics is no longer needed in relation to questions of citizenship, globalization or critiques of neoliberalism (so writers are 'free' to carry on ignoring feminist insights about power, perpetuating male dominance and reproducing a typically androcentric bias in their debates). Discourse is not reality. The stark reality of persistent institutional discrimination against women artists from around the world, as well as in 'global contemporary art worlds' continues. Feminism remains an important perspective on contemporary political life. Neither of these two discursive positions I outlined is tolerable for contemporary feminists, but this is also why a feminist critique of the status quo and the position of women artists is still required.

SM – My final suggestion of a topic to be discussed has to do with the relation between spaces for criticism and the critical language in situations where systemic power overrides any critical voice of intellectuals, artists, curators, et cetera. Here I particularly refer to the powerful state and public art institutions that still monopolize the art scenes in some of the countries of Eastern, Central and South Eastern Europe and this became even more urgent during the fast transition towards the neoliberal institutional mechanisms and capitalism. Often the unique combination of nationalist and right-wing policies with their 'inherited' inert bureaucracy results in a complete de-professionalization of institutions and an inability on their part to initiate or lead any relevant activities. In your own view, what kind of spaces could one hope for, when the future of the critical language in the dominant society of control offers only a space for critical voices speaking political gibberish, or a kind of professional bubble where they speak only to the ones who understand the highly professionalized hermetic language of art criticism and all other voices are marginalized or silenced?

Most of us who live and work, and try to function outside the Western centres do not have direct access to the existing international art system to begin with. Neither do we have access to the language addressing art and to its development. We either work in concordance with our local rules and ambitions, or we strive towards presentation in global frameworks where different rules of the game apply – the rules of globalism. Therefore the globalism we have been experiencing over the past decade is less global for some entities. It is not easy to keep a balance between the local predispositions and authentic interests on the one side, and the demands of the global cultural network on the other.

KD – Everywhere there are reactionary and highly conservative forces and people who have deeply vested interests in maintaining the status quo or certain factions in political regimes. The art world and the academic world for that matter are no different. However, it is far from an absolutist regime, there are many markets, many spheres of operation, many different communities and many audiences. There are different kinds of cultural politics at work and many different constituencies competing for the relative 'institutional power' to name or authorize their account of the world, their advocacy of certain artists or ideas about art practice.

There are different positions in existence and different ways of negotiating this territory and of finding opportunities in which to act. I am not speaking here about a postmodern pluralism or some kind of neoliberal relativism in a free market, but about the art world as an agora:[7] a contested space in the past and in the present as its very condition of existence. There are many cynical and self-seeking publicists who are very good at 'making a splash' with their latest obsession or promoting their clique or professional concerns. They do not have a monopoly, even when they become the subject of popular discussion. There are always alternative undercurrents and networks as well as oppositional voices. If we see only what is going on at the centre as the only agenda and our only means of taking part is to adopt their agenda and interests, we will be silenced automatically because we already are positioned that way as 'marginal', 'ex-centric'; we need to think instead about changing the agenda altogether. When does any centre feel secure enough in its ideas not to feel marginal in other circles of influence or when does the marginal become powerful enough to see its ideas transform rather than exist as co-opted or tokenized by the centre? There is a struggle over the production of meaning as well as over the circulation of ideas in relation to circles of influence. Women artists are still trying to work out how to promote themselves in a culture in which their practice continues to be automatically 'minoritized'; spoken of in veiled or opaque language codes in relation to trends, for instance about 'the body' or their ethnicity; or even where their 'feminism', aka their politics, might be promoted as a specialized marketing tool for a unique selling point.

When we speak about art criticism, most people's first reaction is newspaper journalism : art criticism is thought to be the reflection on what's happening today and 'now' in terms of the latest exhibitions and immediate critical reactions to how good or bad they were or how 'noteworthy' or 'important' they are to attend in order to keep up with a certain taste. While we usually think about criticism as a reviewing practice offering judgement (even though criticism rarely pronounces negative judgements and is not just exhibition reviews), it is criticism's very production and dissemination that plays a role in naming and authorizing certain art works alongside certain manners of reading and agenda-setting. If you consider the number of exhibitions versus the few that are subject to any selective reading or in-depth criticism, reviewing is a poor practice in scope for what is happening: not all exhibitions receive reviews or even the rehash of their publicity notice as copy in a newspaper. It is not possible for a critic in a major city to see every show that is produced in a year. Selectivity is everywhere: art critics, like all audiences, follow certain trends, tendencies, and pay attention to certain galleries, venues or artists.

What has more impact (and for which audience, and in what sense): a selective reading of an installation that 500 people saw in a non-commercial space which is circulated in an academic article, or a review of a biennale which 250,000-500,000 attended in a daily newspaper? Online there is a certain flattening of these two types of criticism into 'the same' – particularly if the academic article is retrieved through a university library. The reality for those outside the university system is different: a scant attention to a popular newspaper and no access to the specialist academic article: access to this knowledge here is for a specialized few, it is not widely circulated. What is art criticism outside the review? I made a decision early on that *n.paradoxa* should not contain the collection of standard exhibition reviews that dominate art magazines. This is because I wanted to publish different models for writing feminist critique, more in-depth and without this need to be 'topical' in a journalistic sense. As a consequence, some people believe criticism should be a sharing of their own subjective discovery: an adventure or a travelogue and not an intellectual path or trajectory. This is why critics regularly anthologize their work, not only to demonstrate moments in their writing lives but also to present them as 'intellectual' endeavours. Carla Lonzi, however, makes a distinction between encounter and mediation in this respect and it is worth considering this.[8] Mediation would be the perfect reading: something digested or finished. An encounter would be a meeting on which you would reflect but it would be necessarily incomplete and temporary: another encounter would or could change your relationship. Critics change their views over time: think about Lippard's essay 'Changing since *Changing*'.[9] But it is also necessary to think about the forms in which we encounter art criticism. There are many other forms of art writing: the catalogue essay, the monographic essay, the art magazine/journal article or the artist's/critic's/curator's interview and these are the ones *n.paradoxa* specializes in publishing. Again, these have smaller, fragmented circulation. These, for me, are the priorities in art criticism: even when anthologized into books or published in journal volumes. However, all these forms, including the exhibition review, create the discourse or rather plurality of discourses that are the conversations which make up art criticism.

Notes

1 Robert Lane Kauffmann, 'Post-Criticism, or the Limits of Avant-Garde Theory', in: *Telos* 67 (Spring 1986), pp. 186–195.
2 Ibid., p. 186.
3 Suzana Milevska, 'Capital and Gender: Wild Being and Tamed Being', in *Capital and Gender*. ed. by Suzana Milevska, Skopje, 2001, pp. 16–20; Gayatri Chakravorty Spivak, *A Critique of Postcolonial Reason: Toward a History of the Vanishing Present*. Cambridge MA: Harvard University Press.
4 See: Silvia Federici, *Revolution at Point Zero: Housework, Reproduction, and Feminist Struggle,* Oakland: PM Press/ Common Notions, 2012, p. 208; Nira Yuval-Davis: 'What is Transversal Politics', in: *Soundings – A Journal of Politics and Culture,* Issue 12, Summer 1999, p. 94; Chandra T. Mohanty, *Feminism without Borders: Decolonizing theory, practicing solidarity*. Durham NC: Duke University Press, 2003.
5 Katy Deepwell, 'Equal but different: questions about rights, statistics and feminist strategies for change' in: *Frauenkunstwissenschaft* (Germany) (August 2009) English, pp. 9–27.
6 Katy Deepwell, '"Other" and "Not-All", Rethinking the Place of the woman artist in "Contemporary Art"', in: *Revista de Estudios Globales y Arte Contemporáneo: Art Global Age* Vol 2, No 1 (2014) online journal, University of Barcelona: http://revistes.ub.edu/index.php/REGAC/article/view/10253
7 This concept of 'Agora' comes from Chantal Mouffe's work, e.g. 'Deliberative Democracy or Agonistic Pluralism', in: *Reihe Politikwissenschaft Political Science Series*, December 2000: www.ihs.ac.at/publications/pol/pw_72.pdf
8 Carla Lonzi *Autoritratto* [1969] (Italian, Italy: et al, 2010) *Autoportrait*. ed. by Giovanna Zapperi) (French, JRP Ringier, 2012). This point about Lonzi's writing is made by Giulia Lamoni 'Ti darei un bacio': Notes on utopia and conviviality in *Autoritratto* by Carla Lonzi', in: *n.paradoxa* vol. 5 (January 2015), pp. 76–83.
9 Lucy Lippard 'Introduction: Changing since *Changing*', in; *From the Center: Feminist Essays on Women's Art*. New York: EP Dutton, 1976.

Information as a Site of Conflict and a Site of Critique

Jorinde Seijdel

The days when publicly voicing criticism was the prerogative of a select company of authorities, experts and professionals have long since gone. In our digital and globalized culture, criticism, in the basic sense of passing judgement, has become a daily routine practiced by all and sundry in almost all domains of life. In social networks people are continuously liking and disliking each other and commenting upon each other's activities, products and content. On Twitter, people constantly give their opinions about current topics; blogs and forums publish critical observations and web sites that sell or trade goods or services survive by the grace of ratings and reviews of products and traders.

This seemingly enthusiastic culture of participation appears to be absolutely democratic and open – everyone is encouraged to participate – but might also be regarded as a communication and information machine fuelled by all of us in a continuing process of capitalization and commodification of social relationships, knowledge, and ourselves. Within the current 'attention economies' this abundance of informal and public criticism then mainly functions as a marketing and promotional instrument for the continuous production of material and immaterial goods and affects and, not in the last place, of information. Within the collective production process of post-Fordist culture, criticism is first and foremost part of information and it is precisely the production, consumption, distribution and management of information that have become important economic, political and cultural activities that keep the capitalist system afloat.

Inevitably, this also puts pressure on the more academic and theoretical forms of cultural critique and art critique, the positions of which had already considerably weakened following the alleged end of the great ideologies. Regardless of whether these critical discourses join or oppose the latest developments, they will have to decide how to address them. Presuming that genuine critique questions power and seeks to be not only reflective but also socially effective and perceptible, the question here is: how can critique and critical thinking still have meaning in the digital information culture and how can they create new spaces for publicness, i.e. spaces that offer perspectives for acting? And what instruments of power must be defied in the process? This essay aims to address these questions by exploring a number of alternative concepts of critique in relation to information seen as a 'site of conflict'. Informations as a concept is interpreted here as derived from the Latin verb *informare* (to inform) in the sense of 'to give form to the mind', 'to discipline', instruct', 'teach'.[1] This is to say, information is a network of relations and involves power.

Criticality, Tactics of Irritating and Radical Affirmation

In a 2003 text,[2] Irit Rogoff introduced the distinction between criticism, critique and criticality: criticism simply means judging a clearly defined object, whether this is an artwork, a sports game or a meal, whereas critique consists of the study and analysis of the premises, values and ways of thinking that underpin the truth claims and paradigms of an era or knowledge domain. Observing that 'the old boundaries between making and theorizing, historicizing and displaying, criticizing and affirming have long been eroded' she then argues for an attitude of 'criticality', which means '... an emphasis on the present, of living out a situation, of understanding culture as a series of effects rather than of causes, of the possibilities of actualising some of its potential rather than revealing its faults'. Rogoff links criticality to risk and involvement that come from within. She is concerned with '... a cultural inhabitation that performatively acknowledges what it is risking without yet fully being able to articulate it'. Crucial in this is the position that the 'critic' occupies in the social or cultural field which he or she studies and their active participation in it.

More than a decade later, Rogoff's insights and propositions still seem relevant and criticality still seems to be an attitude towards culture and social reality that offers more perspectives to act than the superficial criticism or the purely detached academic critique. Having said that, the reality in which we act, work and live has substantially changed over that same decade by the advent of the Web 2.0 and social media – the contours of which were barely visible in 2003[3] – which enabled users to not only download information from the Internet but also upload information to it. There has probably never been a time in history when so much both formal and informal information and data were being produced, consumed and exchanged. And probably never before has information been so subject to inflation by the sheer overload of it while remaining so valuable in economic and political respect. Information bastions such as secret and semi-secret government agencies and the likes of Facebook and Google cannot be seen as separate from hackers, WikiLeaks and whistle-blowers such as Edward Snowden. 'Information wants to be free', that famous slogan of the pioneering technology activist Stewart Brand, proves to be still relevant as an important critical and activist issue. At the same time Brand himself complicated and problematized this issue by also stating that 'information wants to be expensive' and that the tension between 'free' and 'expensive' would never go away. Obviously Google Inc., a company that makes profit by distributing information apparently for free, is the actual embodiment of this tension, as is also illustrated by its mission statement: 'to organize the world's information and make it universally accessible and useful'. In addition, in the form of 'data bodies', we ourselves have become information as well. The data body is a virtual body that consists of all the files linked to an individual. In its book *Flesh Machine*, the Critical Art Ensemble collective calls the data body the 'fascist sibling' of the virtual body; it is 'a much more highly developed virtual form, and one that exists in complete service to the corporate and police state'.[4]

Our everyday living environments are increasingly digitized, globalized and privatized – the latter meaning not owned by the community or the state but primarily by private companies. As a result, publicness is steadily losing its critical function (cf. Jürgen Habermas' notion of the idealized public space in which rational discussions can be held, free of coercive forces, self-interest or competition.[5]) In the public domain numerous 'information wars' are waged in which hiding information and keeping it secret is faced with visibility and transparency and where access to and ownership of information are bones of contention.[6] It begs the increasingly urgent question of whether information has become nothing but a commodity and whether it can still function as a public good.

In terms of criticism, critique and criticality it is obvious that contemporary information societies are mainly characterized by forms of criticism, on approving or disapproving of material and immaterial goods and promoting the self. Social networks primarily prompt us to approve and affirm: Facebook's 'Like' button sets the trend in the production of an increasingly affirmative culture. In the *Unlike Us Reader*[7] Mercedes Bunz argues that the absence of an 'Unlike' or 'Hate' button is an efficient trick of the social network to shape and control the actions of its users:

> When its basic design avoids the dialectic order of the modern discourse, for or against, to replace it with the

> affirmative proposition 'I like', it unfolds a discursive style that is about to become more and more dominant in our societies: the rise of an affirmative discourse. Can critique be saved? (*Unlike Us Reader*, p. 138)

Bunz' observation that 'the order of the social discourse has embraced affirmation' (2013: 140) leads to her following, equally important question: 'How does power operate in the governance of affirmation?' (2013: 140) She states that the power rests with large media companies such as Facebook, which are capable of either dismissing criticism and opposition or appropriating them, by always blaming others for any exposed wrongs, thereby dodging any and all responsibility. Any negative or dialectical critique runs aground against this fatal pattern, says Bunz, and can no longer have an emancipating effect aimed at improvement and progress. When these tried and tested concepts of criticism and opposition no longer work, we should start to worry about the level of democracy of our societies, she concludes: 'If we let go of the concept of negation, we lose the tool of opposition' (2013: 142). Lastly, Bunz argues for a 'tactic of irritation' as an instrument of criticism. By causing irritation with an institute of power (such as Facebook) about a certain issue, the issue is at least brought to light and the fact that we don't want it is expressed. In spite of her clear analysis of the logic of the affirmative culture, in the end Bunz remains rather vague about the concrete effectiveness and applicability of irritation as a tool of critique and she does not fully develop the idea, making it not yet convincing as a possible alternative concept.

In her essay *In Critical Condition or Fully Out of Steam? Critical Thinking Today*,[8] philosopher Kathrin Thiele offers a quite different proposal for revitalising critique – to which Bunz also briefly refers[9] – by putting forward a notion of critical thinking as 'radical affirmative gesture':

> I claim that we need to re-conceptualize critique/criticality from being pictured as a dialectical process whose major task is 'to set apart' and 'divide', and transform it into a practice of com-passionate affirmation. Only by starting with such an affirmative ethos will critical engagement become again capable of negotiating appropriately the complex ecologico-socio-ethico-political conditions this world is made of today. (Thiele, 2012: 1)

She argues for a critical 'to think with' instead of a detached 'to think about', which is an immanent form of critique that takes place from a close involvement with the issues at stake. These issues can be mobilized and negotiated so they may possibly occur again and differently.[10]

Critique as an affirmative practice converges with Rogoff's notion of criticality. Like Bunz' tactic of irritating, both propositions attempt to recharge critical thinking for a present after the end of history and without binding ideologies, in which the dialectic, negative critique as a product or instrument of these ideologies would no longer suffice. Especially Bunz and Thiele link their concept of critique directly to the question of the operating of power, and refer to Foucault. In his lecture 'What is Critique?' (1971), Foucault traces the origins of the critical attitude back to the context of the resistance against techniques of control over the individual from the domain of religion, which became more and more part of daily life since the fifteenth century.[11] Critical thinking is thus inextricably linked to challenging power and its structures and to 'not want to be governed like that', as Foucault phrased it.

If the issue of power resides mainly in the control and ownership of information nowadays, as I assume here, then once again the question arises as to how critique can be meaningful in the information culture and how it might create spaces for publicness in which political moments may occur.

Illegality of Information

In order to establish what space there might be for resistance, publicness and critique within the order of information and its power systems, reading Foucault's analysis of the classical public execution, which he made in *Discipline & Punish: The Birth of the Prison*,[12] can be enlightening. In this study of the relationship between sovereign and disciplining power in both classical and modern times, through an analysis of the prison and penal system, Foucault reflects upon the function of public executions in the eighteenth century, in the chapter 'The Spectacle of the Scaffold'. He attaches much importance to the public aspect of it and to what he calls the accompanying 'popular illegality'. The presence of a public (the people) as witnesses was a crucial element of these executions, which could be regarded as demonstrations of the power of the sovereign over his people. But these events were not always just a demonstration of power, as the people also often took advantage of these spectacular opportunities to make themselves heard and even take the initiative by, for instance, attacking the condemned or, as the case may be, to free them. These illegal interventions – to which Foucault also refers as 'illegality of rights' – have a destabilising effect on the powers that be. Public executions not only subject the people but also provide it with a space for public participation and rebellion. In the eighteenth century, according to Foucault, these expressions of popular illegality experienced a crisis: the illegality of rights shifted to an illegality of goods. 'As new forms of production and capital accumulation emerged, popular practices relating to an illegality of rights became transformed into an illegality of property' (Foucault, 1995: 73-103).

If we take the liberty of extrapolating Foucault's thinking to the present, it is conceivable that an illegality of property, typical of the early-capitalist, Fordist era, will now be replaced by an 'illegality of information' as a factor of a neo-capitalist and post-Fordist order of immaterial labour, communication and information. While the media and social networks seem to be all about revealing and sharing information and the public/users are persuaded to engage in this whenever they can, there is at the same time an increasing 'illegality of information'. There are powerful information keepers (governments, services, companies) that regulate and control what information is public and what is not, but at the same time, for instance, the practices of WikiLeaks and whistle-blowers such as Edward Snowden – branded as illegal – demonstrate that information can be liberated. Illegality of information is thus expressed in moments of unrest and resistance, or in counter- information, which makes public and accessible the information that is being claimed or kept hidden by corporations or governments. Illegality of information challenges the power practices with regard to information and enforces the publicness and freedom of information, which may lead to political acts. Besides WikiLeaks and the NSA scandal, the uprisings in the Middle East are also examples of how certain groups can temporarily claim the power of the information media on behalf of alternative issues or use that power in a different manner in order to call attention to certain interests or to express demands. However, it would be naive to assume that illegality of information or popular illegality will occur automatically as an effective correction of power practices. After all, the political or social issues that are revealed in the process are then not necessarily solved for all time. In her essay ‘Know It All. WikiLeaks, Democracy and the Information Age’ (SKOR/*Open* 22), Jodi Dean, for instance, points out: ‘... that power in communicative capitalism relies on abundance, overkill, and repetition, on the excess of information, on the way that too much information is more incapacitating than too little information (even as it enhances the feeling that there is never enough)’ (Dean, 2011: 51). Communicative capitalism is also characterized by a decrease in effectiveness of symbols, as they are no longer understood in the same way by everyone. ‘Because we can never be certain, we always need more information. ... [which] is accompanied by a decline in a sense of the capacity for action’ (Dean, 2011: 49). Also, Boris Groys, in ‘WikiLeaks. The Revolt of the Clerks, or Universality as Conspiracy’ (SKOR/*Open* 22) detects a fundamental paradox in WikiLeaks, which he sees expressed in Julian Assange’s thinking. In interviews, Assange takes pride in the fact that he was able to create an encryption code that made the information on WikiLeaks inaccessible to the authorities. Groys concludes: ‘... universal public access is possible only under the conditions of a complete inaccessibility of the means that guarantee this accessibility. ... Universal openness is based on the most perfect closure’ (Groys, 2011: 44). At the same time, Groys points to hacking as the replacement of philosophical critique. WikiLeaks seems to be a practice that liberates the signs that were captured and controlled by individual subjectivity or third parties. There is only one difference, according to Groys: ‘... In the case of Internet we have to do not with the metaphysical but with purely technical control over the signs. Accordingly, hacking is used here instead of philosophical critique’ (Groys, 2011: 41).[13]

In the information age, publicness and secrecy, abundance and scarcity of information, are intricately interwoven and it is in their interaction that they exercise power. Illegality of information occurs when the balance between these elements is disturbed and information either spills over or withdraws. It is precisely as a ‘site of conflict’ – WikiLeaks is an exemplary case – that information can then be either a place of repression or of public resistance and that is where the possibilities for critique lie.

Information as a Site of Critique

If the information is indeed an urgent site of conflict nowadays, a place where power is simultaneously produced and reproduced as well as undermined and eroded, then perhaps it is also a site of critique. From where, through manifestations of popular illegality, counter-information is being produced and made public. As an immanent critical process that takes place within the information itself, this is similar to Rogoff's criticality and Thiele's radical affirmation. Still, there are differences, and popular illegality in Foucault's sense is not only affirmative. It concerns unsolicited, illegal negations of power, made manifest by informal actors (the people), such as the rebellious civilians in the Arab Spring or anonymous hackers or whistle-blowers – who may only be named after they have acted: Bradley Manning, Julian Assange, Edward Snowden. In the case of illegality of information and popular illegality the critical subject seems to be truly dissolved in the object of criticism in an exchange of power positions. There is a strong emphasis on popular participation and the public aspect. With Rogoff and Thiele, there is in fact still a critical subject that consciously chooses an object to engage with, even though both strive to obtain a position of mutual equality in doing so. At the same time, however, the affirmative dimension of illegality of information lies specifically in the fact that information is an imperative primacy for all those engaged in the conflict. They all strongly believe in the power and importance of information, only the interests and positions from which they act are different.

The cultural theorist and sociologist Scott Lash emphatically pronounced information to be the most important field of power of the twenty-first century. In his *Critique of Information* (2002) he concludes, in relation to the question of a new critical theory and position, that in the contemporary societies that are dominated by super-fast information flows there is no longer a separate space for critical reflection and that critique therefore has to be reinvented. According to Lash, in information societies power no longer exclusively functions in a discursive manner, as in Foucault's thinking, but increasingly in an 'informational' manner. Power is no longer directly linked to material possessions, as in the manufacturing age, but to intellectual property (in the form of patents, copyrights and trademarks). According to Lash, informational critique should therefore be aimed at the new inequalities of power and at the power constellations that are produced by the new economies of signs and space. He has developed a 'critique of information', in which he explicitly states that in the information age critique and reflexivity take place outside the subject. Ideas circulate through networks that consist of technological forms of life (actor-networks of humans and of things/machines). Only here, within these information networks themselves, can critique take shape. With regard to information, says Lash, there is no longer an 'outside' and therefore no longer a transcendental space for critical theory.

> [But] perhaps most important is that in the age of general informationalization, critique itself must become informational. There must necessarily be an informationalization of critique. (Lash, 2002: 10)

Without a constituent outside, informational critique also has to take place within information itself, which is also its affirmative aspect.

This essay posed the question of how critique and critical thinking can still be meaningful in the information culture and how they can create new spaces for publicness and participation (be it in the form of revolt, civil disobedience or whistle-blowing) in order that established power can be openly questioned. It was argued that in our digital capitalist culture criticism as an evaluative or corrective praxis is being eroded because the default setting is 'like' and because commercial and cultural domains often use the same prefabricated instruments of criticism. In an affirmative culture in which the Big Narratives no longer work, critique in the sense of an analysis and assessment of social, cultural and philosophic discourse is also under pressure.

Assuming that critique is aimed at power (Foucault's 'not to want to be governed like that') I have argued that at present information can be regarded as an important locus of technological power, which makes it a 'site of conflict', a site for critique, opposition and popular illegality, and thereby for publicness and politics. If propositions to revitalize and reposition critique in the form of criticality (Rogoff), tactics of irritation (Bunz) or radical affirmation (Thiele) are to be successful and relevant, information must, in my opinion, be recognized and acknowledged as a site of conflict, as Lash does in his *Critique of Information*. Information as a site of conflict encompasses the most urgent subjects of current critical thinking, including globalization, privatization, publicness, the commons, intellectual property, information monopolies, the control and distribution of knowledge, censorship, surveillance, privacy, big data, et cetera. Contemporary critique can derive its effectiveness, urgency and subversion to a large extent from the measure in which it, being itself information, contains or generates 'illegality of information'.

Notes

1 Informations as a concept is interpreted here as derived from the Latin verb informare (to inform) in the sense of 'to give form to the mind', 'to discipline', instruct', 'teach'. This is to say, information is a network of relations and involves power.

2 Irit Rogoff, From *Criticism to Critique to Criticality*, published on EIPCP, http://eipcp.net/transversal/0806/rogoff1/en, last visited 25-07-2014.

3 Google was launched in 1998, Facebook, like twitter, only became fully public in 2006.

4 Critical Art Ensemble, *Flesh Machine Cyborgs, Designer Babies, & New Eugenic Consciousness*, 1998, www.critical-art.net/books/flesh/ last visited 25-07-2014. Numerous contemporary artists, such as Trevor Paglen, Sean Snyder, Metahaven, Jill Magid, Tiqqun and Susan Schuppli, to name just a few, aim their work at the issues at stake in this essay. I don't involve their practices, which also raise many other questions, in this particular text, for the benefit of the clarity of my arguments.

5 Habermas J.(1962) *Strukturwandel der Öffentlichkeit*, Munich: Luchterhand Verlag.

6 *Open. Cahier on Art and the Public Domain*, "Transparency. Publicity and Secrecy in the Age of WikiLeaks", Amsterdam/Rotterdam, SKOR/NAi Publishers, 2011, #22.

7 *Unlike Us Reader Social Media Monopolies and their Alternatives*, in: Geert Lovink and Miriam Rasch (eds.), INC Reader #8, Institute of Network Cultures, Amsterdam, 2014, pp. 137–46.

8 Kathrin Thiele, Position Paper for 'Terra Critica: Re-visioning the Critical Task of the Humanities in a Globalized World', December 7/8, 2012, Utrecht University, In Critical Condition or Fully Out of Steam? Critical Thinking 'Today', http://terracritica.net/wp-content/uploads/Thiele_positionpaper.pdf, last visited 25-07-2014.

9 Bunz, pp. 143–44.

10 This praxis of affirmation is also championed by the philosopher Rosi Braidotti. From a neo-humanistic perspective he emphasizes the effectiveness of affects and imagination and the creative possibilities of empowerment, sustainability and community building.

11 Michel Foucault, 'What is Critique?' in: Sylvère Lotringer and Lysa Hochroth (eds.) *The Politics of Truth*, New York: Semiotext(e), 1997.

12 Michel Foucault, *Discipline & Punish: The Birth of the Prison*, transl. by A. Sheridan, 1977, New York: Vintage Books.

13 Groys' polemic suggestion that the age of Internet produced its own critic embodied by the hacker is valid if Internet could indeed be understood as a purely technical space. However, as a site of information it is also a social and a political space. Therefore, it needs critical reflection; the hacker is the activist counterpart of the philosophical critic.

Queerness in a Situational Sense

Terre Thaemlitz in Conversation with Daniel Givens and Niels Van Tomme

'In which way can this interview be considered art criticism?' was an inquiry we received from the editors of this book after handing in our text. Much of it depends, of course, on how one interprets and understands the concept of 'art criticism', a broad issue that has been discussed rather exhaustively and more appropriately elsewhere. One could go as far as claim that there is an entire industry that feeds upon the ongoing debate of criticism. So let us answer the above question head on, as pragmatically as possible. The world of contemporary art doesn't merely involve the production of art works, an approach to the arts that by now has become a commonplace, rather than a novel insight. Alongside these developments, there is an incredible amount of discourse being produced surrounding the production of art. Why, then, should this discourse – a never-ending stream of publications, statements, performances, lectures, papers, etc. – not be equally subjected to criticism? If *Spaces for Criticism* belongs to this auxiliary realm of contemporary art, then an analysis concerning its theoretical premises, mode of production, and final materialization should fall under the category 'art criticism' as well. Viewed within this framework, Thaemlitz's forceful response at the start of this interview is a critical intervention into the structures supporting the world of contemporary art that this book also represents. Such a critique drives the interviewee's career-long analysis of, and close involvement with, the economic structures surrounding cultural production, as well as the often-presupposed progressive and thus frequently wholly un-self-critical nature of academic and critical discourse in general.

At the same time, this text also functions as an introduction to Terre Thaemlitz's singular mode of artistic production, which in itself designates a form of critique. It focuses on the broader cultural and economic context of her work as DJ Sprinkles, her celebrated yet underground deep house DJ moniker, which was nurtured in New York's queer and transgender sex worker clubs. A critically acclaimed but always controversial composer, producer, writer, and lecturer, Terre Thaemlitz has been an active participant in a number of seemingly disconnected but in reality deeply entwined politico-cultural contexts since the late 1980s. As she explained in an earlier interview, outwardly digressive thematic concerns such as queer and transgender identity politics, the disenfranchisement of migrant workers, and HIV activism are only separated when one experiences them as such.

Thaemlitz makes a convincing case for a material approach to persistent issues of domination, discrimination, and violence, which consistently emerge throughout the entire cultural spectrum. Her multifaceted interventions, performances, and interviews are often antagonistic in nature, as they involve a systematic deconstruction of the false mechanisms supporting various types of cultural production. She, for example, regularly performs as an electro-acoustic composer in concert halls, performances that are preceded by a lecture-format introduction and followed by a Q&A session, as a way to critique the silence and serenity surrounding electro-acoustic work. She also, significantly, considers the culturally determined 'passionate' act of DJ-ing as a form of labour that should be based exclusively upon a working agreement, a sobering approach that challenges the audience's expectation of a DJ-set as a means of experiencing entertainment and escapism.

'It's ignored, and yet it has the market behind it', James Elkins famously wrote about the pitiful state of 'art criticism'. Considering the work of Terre Thaemlitz, which offers a highly precise and consistent analysis of the market mechanisms supporting contemporary cultural production, we should shift this by now clichéd dictum into something more affirmative: 'It's ignored, and yet it confronts the market behind it.'

Niels Van Tomme/Daniel Givens – When we initially approached you for an interview in the framework of this book, you objected to its predominantly academic framing of the notion of criticism, as opposed to, what you called, 'pragmatic notions of anger and socially motivated critiques grown out of consequence'. Do you think these two modes of critique necessarily contradict one another?

Terre Thaemlitz – I was reacting to this publication's 'Concept' document you had forwarded me, which stated:

> This book does not want to go along with the pessimism that has dominated the recent debates on art criticism. Instead of adding another swan song of criticism...

I told you that this struck me as typical of academics, in that 'pessimism' is positioned in relation to a kind of romantic melancholy – the swan song – as opposed to pragmatic notions of anger, and socially motivated critiques born of consequence. As you know, I have written at length about the connections between Western Evangelicism and the cultural demand for 'optimism', 'hope', 'dreams', et cetera, even within Leftist critical discourses. I very strongly reject this systemic rejection of the 'negative' and marvel at how it always speaks of the world being 'dominated' by negativity. What a crock of ideological production that is!

I also pointed out that there was no mention of a writer's fee, which we all know usually means either we must submit to slave labour, or the budget is given secretly to certain people – both conditions demonstrating an institutionalized ethic of exclusion and elitism.

NVT – I take responsibility for not mentioning the writer's fee. My initial contact with the editors of the book happened many months before our communication, and I had simply forgotten about their initial offer, so I needed to double check this with them first.

TT – I see. Well, in any case, from my end it was still the typical initial contact with no mention of payment from the person extending a work invitation. Out of fairness to the editors, in this instance that person was you – although experience tells me it would be fairly unusual for editors of a book like this to mention fees in their first contact email. I have little doubt we can all relate to this as a shared experience. This exclusion of talk of economics is usually part of the editorial process itself. Who knows if the editors are getting paid, or how much? Making books is not unlike making records, where the only people who are absolutely guaranteed to be paid are the owners of the pressing plants.

So these two exclusions of the very things that are vital to me (an active incorporation of economics, and of consequences) already sets the tone as adversarial to my interests – but in utterly familiar and unsurprising ways. These are completely typical exclusions, right? And that typicality sets a tone for what we are saying here. It compromises much of what one might wish to say.

It also places tremendous limitations on the types of audience or readership for this text, which compromises much of how one is heard.

If talking about this quite depressing reality with any clarity or pragmatism is going to be dismissed as melancholy or pissing on someone's parade, then what's the point? This would clearly not be a safe place to hold certain discussions... in which case I'll take my cut of the fee and put the money to use elsewhere. That's what many of us are constantly doing, right?

NVT/DG – Your artistic output is incredibly diverse and ranges from house productions and remixes, to electro-acoustic composition, ambient and experimental music, and media interventions. How were you introduced to house music? What were your first experiences and thoughts as a listener?

TT – I grew up with roller disco in the 1970s (skating rinks with live DJ's, proper disco lights, et cetera), and moved to New York in 1986, which was right at the cusp of the emergence of house as a genre. At that time, 'house music' still simply referred to the collection of records owned by a club. They were the 'house records'. Of course, each club's record collection had its own stylistic leanings, and those sensibilities eventually became branded as genres in themselves (Paradise Garage gave rise to 'garage house', the Loft to 'loft house', and so on). But at that time, and for people of my generation or earlier, we didn't have this kind of consumer experience people would have today, where you go out to buy a 'house album' and get a stylistically consistent album from start to finish. Hell, I guess people don't even 'go out' to buy music anymore, right? But I mean, collecting tracks was more a matter of hunting down one-offs. Consider something as huge as Donna Summer's 'I Feel Love'. If you hear that track, you'd expect the album it came off to be similarly electronic, but it's not at all. It's nine rather forgettable and conventionally orchestrated soul/R&B cuts followed by the very electronic 'I Feel Love'. So all of these dynamics created a very specific entry to house music that is not only lost, but generally unimaginable to later generations. Of course, we're talking about classic Marxist processes of commodification and reification. It is through those alienations that the genre of house has emerged in the marketplace as a clearly identifiable and solid genre. And it's worth pointing out that this same chaos-turned-genre parallels the construction of heterosexual/homosexual identity constructs. If you read early sexology books from the late 1800s and early 1900s, they are utter chaos. The historic transition of sexuality from behaviour (sanctioned vs. sodomy) to identity was not a simple one. Western Modernity's construction of a body-based heterosexuality/homosexuality strikes me as the ideological production of a very particular process of cultural alienation and reification. And, importantly, contemporary sexual discourses which emphasize identity, genetics, predisposition, et cetera, rely upon our not unravelling that process of reification. It relies upon our collective amnesia. And I am constantly aware of the parallels between this sexual history and certain audio histories – particularly audio genres inflected with queer roots that are systematically forgotten. House music's queerness is not only about its relation to sexual cruising grounds, but also the queerness of its early incoherency as an audio (non-)genre, right? It was really much more about contexts and situations than sounds. And it revolved around openly referential production processes like sampling. So for me, this was a sonic language capable of speaking of non-essentialism and the decentralization of bodies from strategies of identity.

Sample-based electroacoustic and non-rhythmic digital synthesis did something similar, but with a more open relation to socio-political content. My interest in that genre is summarized by that famous quote from Jacques Attali's *Noise*, '[Music's] order simulates the social order, and its dissonances express marginalities' and Ultra-red founder and sound activist Dont Rhine's statement: 'While the development of Queer-positive imagery and graphics exploded with AIDS activism in the 1980s, sonically we have little more than, "Hey-hey, ho-ho, Homophobia's got to go!"' So, for all the sonic 'diversity' of my productions, the actual approach to sound as language – and what vocabularies are afforded us by certain genres – is actually quite the same. Between house and ambient music's connections to anti-materialist spirituality, and electroacoustic music's connection to conservative academia, teaching myself to speak through these 'languages' has clearly come with different challenges and limitations. But those limitations were identifiable from the start, and keeping them at the fore has always been an active strategy of mine. I mean, this kind of working with limitations that betray us is part of queer existence, right?

I started DJ-ing in the late 1980s because my record collection was growing exponentially since moving to New York, and my roommates were upset about it taking up more and more space in our shared living room. They told me I should either 'do something with the records' or sell them – thinking I would sell them, I'm sure. But instead, I was like, 'Great idea', and went out and bought a mixer and proper DJ turntables. One of those roommates – my partner at the time – was a founding member of the ACT-UP A/PI Caucus, and they asked me to make a mix tape for their contingent to use in the Lesbian and Gay Pride Parade. I guess that was in 1988? That was my first public performance.

NVT/DG – From what context did your DJ Sprinkles moniker originate?

TT – I DJ'ed at some A/PI Caucus benefits, and started doing one-off nights at some of those clubs where the benefits were held. But it was always a disaster, because I hated the mainstream club music of the time (Lisa Stansfield, Whitney Houston, Madonna, et cetera), and the club regulars hated the instrumental minor-label records from my private collection. I wasn't playing the house's records – which creates an interesting contradiction in that I was therefore not a proper 'house DJ' through my very act of only playing records from my private collection – even though the style of those records I played was 'house'... So there was this interesting gap between the 'house's music' and 'house music'. As a result of that gap, I kept getting fired – which was fine with me, since they weren't paying shit anyway. Often not paying anything at all. Then a friend told me they were looking for a new resident DJ at Sally's II, a transsexual sex worker club in the Carter Hotel on 43rd Street. It was an unquestionably queer context, as opposed to a more reconciled 'gay' environment. The clientele was a mix of Latina and African-American MTF transgender people (mostly transsexual or on a pre-op path), and generally heterosexual-identified middle age johns of various backgrounds (including an elderly Hasidic Jewish man with a habit of busting into occupied ladies bathroom stalls with his cock out, trying to force the queens to give him blowjobs – this at the time when the New Yorker was under fire for running an 'impossible and offensive' Valentine's Day cover illustration of an African-American woman and Hasidic Jewish man locked in a passionate kiss...). The current DJ was a homophobic Puerto Rican high school student whose only words to me were: 'I can't wait to get away from these fucking faggots.' And because the space was dominated by transsexuals who could be quite hostile towards non-transitioning transgendered people (such as myself), part of negotiating my own body within that space was to dress in male drag. So that is why I got in the habit of wearing male clothes when performing as DJ Sprinkles, which is a habit that continues to this day.

Coming from the rural Midwest, where there were no 'safe spaces' for queers, and negotiation of sexual and gender expression was inseparable from tensions of personal safety, I guess I was equipped to deal with the dynamics of that kind of space. It requires an awareness of the distinction between queerness in a situational sense, versus homosexuality as an identity around which one can Pridefully associate with others. In my experience, I think the latter is only possible through an ideological investment into that Marxist alienation and reification I mentioned earlier. And I suppose you might say my refusal to ignore the realities of endless violence and risk is also where my model of queerness differs from what has transformed into academic 'Queer Studies'. I think that academic model usually leaves room for 'pride', whereas my model of queerness does not. I am vehemently suspicious of all pride, if only because pride has always been a key tool of those who bashed me. I don't want it. I don't need it. Pride is ultimately about asking for respect and power. In terms of social organizing, I am only interested in working on divestments of power.

NVT/DG – In what way can such divestments of power start manifesting themselves, both on a cultural and political level?

TT – In terms of praxis, I think it usually involves strategic non-cooperation and an insistence upon relentless self-critique – particularly within what one might term Left politics. I do not imagine such divestments being recognizable as a 'movement', precisely because they are rooted in a complication of the very notion of movement. They are not about 'community building' or 'bringing people together' – more the opposite – yet I would say they are vital to understandings of 'community'. I am talking about working with and through hypocrisies, despite almost every 'movement' I can think of attempting to frame itself as a resolution of hypocrisies.

Let's take cross-dressing as a simple example of an action anyone can take, yet few do, simply because it would immediately interfere with their immediate social relations. It would immediately impact relationships with people close to them, as well as strangers. It would mean having to invest time and effort into explaining to others how that simple act of cross-dressing does or does not alter existing social relations, which can range from family and friends to employers to local shop keepers we rely on for groceries. Of course, in that process of explaining to others, one is also explaining to oneself, and these experiences result in different cultural and political views. They also result in different cultural and political alliances, even if only through the breakdown and loss of existing alliances.

A lot of people who have never cross-dressed or attempted to physically alter their appearance might assume they can imagine the implications of such actions, but I am utterly convinced that this is something one must experience first-hand. It will really open up new depths of understanding towards feminism and gender issues. It really forces pragmatic problems to the fore, starting with the act of how to buy clothes. How will the store staff treat you? Will you be allowed to try things on? Would you feel comfortable trying things on in public? If store staff prohibit you from trying things on, or if you are simply afraid to ask to do so, do you have the economic privilege to waste money on clothes that may not fit you? If you do have such privilege, will you be able to maintain it if your employers 'catch you' in drag or some other non-binary gender state? Or will you soon be unemployed? If you are a dependent, will you be thrown on the street by your family or spouse? I mean, that's the ridiculous yet dangerous starting point, and it takes us back to those two issues I said are important to me at the start of this interview: economics and consequences.

For better or worse, the end results of 'divesting' usually have more to do with an awareness of what one is culturally/socially/politically no longer willing to do – as opposed to conventional power-based models of organizing that emphasize identifying what one can or should do. That power-based model will always remain dominant, and never fade away. So this question of how to divest of power is always something that responds to the inescapable dominations of identification. It is about recognizing the connections between certain behaviours and violence, and placing oneself at risk – socially, economically, et cetera – in order to materially alter one's relationships to those things one finds harmful.

NVT/DG – For this publication we were also interested in considering your house music productions as critical discourse, as something that offers a hyper-specific, analytical reading of the socio-political context of the genres you explore. It has perhaps become somewhat commonplace in alternative dance circles to directly attach your name and music to a critical assessment of dance music culture, even though your music is rarely approached on an analytical level. Instead of assuming the criticality embedded within the work, and taking it for granted, we would like to ask you how the formulation of these critical gestures is actually mediated on a musical-discursive level?

TT – Yes, although it is never surprising, it is a personal frustration that my projects are rarely approached on what you call an 'analytical level' (I guess I would call it being approached with the same rigor with which I attempted to produce them), but what can you do...

For me there is an important distinction to be drawn between 'critical gestures' and 'actions' or 'organizing', because we know that the 'gesture' is such an important part of conservative musicology, as well as dominant rhetoric about musical authenticity, creative process, blah, blah, blah. And, of course, it is our cultural domination by that rhetoric which makes it so rare and difficult for others to approach audio productions – mine and others – on that more rigorous level. It's hopeless. Truly. But operating without hope is also a frequent part of queer experiences, right? So, again, no surprises there.

NVT/DG – How should one approach your music production then?

TT – As a producer, I am approaching audio as a linguistic medium, and seek processes and genres that offer both vocabulary and metaphorical associations that resonate with the themes I am discussing.

On a broader cultural level, and in terms of audience, that mediation requires the listenership to have a bit of a queer ear. And that is reliant upon our having certain experiences that lead to the opening of our ears. It's like with disco, the majority of songs have lyrics about love between a 'she' and a 'he', and in dominant heteronormative fashion most of the world accepts these as songs about a woman and a man. But from a queer perspective we know these are mostly songs about two men, and the gender pronouns relate to a performance of gender, not a body-identification with gender. And we also know this kind of performative gender affiliation is a dimension of closets and self-defence strategies amidst heterosexist dominations. It is a cloaking device of sorts, to allow us to speak of lovers without outing ourselves, right? So this is how a project's 'intended audience' will always only be a subset of the more general 'consumer audience' (i.e., anyone who possesses a copy). This poses a different, a queer, model of audience, in that it refutes the common consumerist belief that possession constitutes affiliation. Buying one of my projects does not inherently make a person part of the audience for which the project was produced. Similarly, somebody saying they are a 'fan' says nothing to me about their audience relationship. Just one or two words more with most 'fans' at a gig reveals they have no fucking clue. The majority of self-declared 'huge fans' will go on to say they just heard my tracks for the first time earlier that day, through some fucked up lo-fi links on SoundCloud or whatever. Seriously.

So all of these factors are why audio is a rather difficult and inept medium of communication. And as you know, this is why I choose to work with audio: because it is such patent shit, despite most peoples' embrace of the medium as an 'honest' form of expression... perhaps even 'universal'. That's a really difficult notion to unpack for people. It's doomed to fail on any mass scale. And that impossibility resonates with my desire to cultivate strategies that subvert dominant desires for mass appeal, reaching as many people as possible, or having the quite specialized conversations I wish to have reframed in overly broad terms that could be accepted on a larger cultural level as inherently relatable 'truths'. I am not interested in 'how to make more people understand'. I am interested in why understanding is impossible, and how communication occurs through/despite terminal misunderstandings and alienations.

And within the framework of this publication, with its pronounced aversion to 'pessimism', I would ask how it could at all be objectionable or surprising to be negative, nihilistic or pessimistic? That aversion to 'pessimism' enacts its own processes of alienation and reification. There is no doubt in my mind. As I have written and said several times elsewhere, that critical aversion to negativity is symptomatic of the dominant cultural dynamics that systematically stop us from cultivating language and other tools for speaking through our alienations. The relegation of 'pessimism' to the realm of affect and swan songs denies us vital strategies for engaging the material realities of countless forms of violence. All of these academic 'anti-pessimism campaigns' strike me as little different from 'anti-disco campaigns'.

NVT/DG – Are you suggesting that music – when approached as a linguistic medium, on an analytical level – could cultivate a language to understand these dynamics?

TT – I think other, more politically engaged and culturally critical approaches to the usage of sound absolutely do exist, and have already been cultivated by both the Left and Right. It's just that these are oftentimes not happening within the cultural territories of music/art/media. They require thinking about sound and listening in a much broader sense, as opposed to thinking about those very limited models of sound usage that qualify as 'music'.

We can all think of examples of how sound has been used as a form of torture, for centuries and by many cultures around the world. Of course, sound has also been simultaneously deployed by those same cultures as a source of relaxation. So the deliberate cultivation and deployment of those torture and relaxation techniques demonstrates a long-standing social recognition that sound is a powerful cultural tool. Our social relationships to sound – acceptable and unacceptable sounds – are interwoven with our cultural and political agendas.

Actually, to give a very recent and practical example of active investigations into relationships between sound, listening and organizing, the international collective Ultra-red have a new box set coming out, called *URXX Nos. 1-9. Nine Workbooks, 2010-2014*, to be published by Koenig in Germany. As the title describes, it contains a series of workbooks that resulted from their various inquiries into community organizing in recent years. It also contains a data DVD with hours of audio and video media intended to generate further research. If you know Ultra-red, then you know their use of the term 'research' is not academic. It is more about encouraging research among communal organizers (many of whom have social and class-based antagonisms with academia), to cultivate the use of sound and acts of listening as tools for social organizing. I think it is quite interesting how Ultra-red have become increasingly skilled at collectively developing tools through self-interrogation, and then attempt to share those tool building techniques with others.

NVT/DG – There is of course a rich tradition of protest music out there, which is connected to forms of voice, agency, and participation but should also be considered in relationship to the music industry that produced and commoditized it. In what way does the merging of music and critique in your work find connections to, or differs from, historical notions of protest in music?

TT – One major distinction would be my rejection of any notion of 'authentic voice'. Most protest music speaks of experience through constructs of authentic voices. And as you pointed out earlier, that dominant tendency also frames the reception of my projects and activities. I am very much interested in speaking of experiences, but without invoking the 'authentic'. This means actively rejecting and dismantling the authentic whenever possible, despite it often falling on deaf ears. Again, those with the tools to hear are a subset – and this is not about access acquired through academic learning, but material experiences and exposure to contexts.

Most political music is interested in reaching as many people as possible, even if that breadth of audience must occur via horrific deafness to colonialism and globalization, such as 'We Are The World' or 'Do They Know It's Christmas?', both of which strike me as grotesque not only in relation to their lyrics or studio production, but their all-too-Humanist and neoliberal administration of funds raised.

I would generally avoid labelling my projects as 'political music' or 'protest music', if only because it quietly implies the existence of 'non-political music'. The old feminist maxim 'the personal is political' applies quite directly to the challenges of trying to divest audio from its cultural mythology as something supra-social ('personal', 'from the soul', 'from the heart', 'universal', et cetera).

NVT/DG – On *Midtown 120 Blues* (2009), there is a particularly productive contradiction in the record's often harshly vocalized sociocultural critique in the spoken word sections and the smooth, richly detailed and mostly synthetic nature of the music. How do you consider these two distinct artistic strategies that seem to run dialectically through the music?

TT – Well, that's all convention, isn't it? I mean, there is nothing happening sonically on my album that doesn't happen in a track like Mr. Fingers' 'Can You Feel It?' The only difference is that I more deliberately set out to engage those contradictions, and exploit the social metaphors and tensions they imply. In a stylistic sense, the two operative contradictions seem to be, on the one hand, a parallel between 'organic' elements of voice and acoustic instruments (piano, certain percussion sounds, et cetera); and on the other hand, the simultaneous awareness that these are largely tape-based, sampled or synthetically generated. Like I said earlier, this is what appeals to me about the production techniques of house. It contains practices that crack open spaces to speak of inauthenticity, the construction of the 'organic', et cetera. Not that most house producers do that, but the cracks are there to be widened and eroded.

NVT/DG – The music possesses a clean and manicured feel, as if it were sculpted, creating a very beautiful version of something that can be looked at as maybe unsophisticated and crude. Do you feel that there is a connection between the search and presentation of a pure and clear sound in the music you create and the self-creation aspect of gender reassignment? Is there perhaps a common search for beauty out of hardship involved?

TT – I guess I would interpret that kind of reading ('a very beautiful version of something that can be looked at as maybe unsophisticated and crude') in relation to conventions of primitivism. I mean, you could be describing Picasso's *Les Demoiselles d'Avignon*, or something by Keith Haring, or an album by the Tom Tom Club – all of which are quite shit references for me. I can't really tell if you endorse that reading, but you clearly invoke it. That primitivism continues to frame a lot of dominant discussions on poverty, race, and 'urban media's relation to 'fine art'. I think it is a quite uninteresting and problematic reading.

And, for better or worse, I can see how you then get to a kind of conventional, mainstream cultural rhetoric around gender transitioning as the excavation of a 'true' inner self, which I also find uninteresting and problematic. Even though members of transitioning communities are force-fed language of telos/creation/becoming, and are socially required to adapt and embrace such language in order to maintain access to treatments in most countries (submitting to diagnoses of GID, attending mandatory counselling and support groups, et cetera), I am generally speaking to the unspoken reality of transitioning as a process of 'unbecoming'. I am overwhelmed by the urgent need for other language.

Beauty out of hardship, the rose budding forth from the thorns... cliché drivel. Damaging cliché drivel I personally feel is to be avoided at all costs.

NVT/DG – That description of a process of 'unbecoming' is a striking starting point to reframe notions of gender transitioning, but how can you implement such radical shift in language, without, again, essentializing it?

TT – Yes, surely this term 'unbecoming' could quickly become unhelpful. One has to be constantly clear that the 'unbecoming' at issue is about deprogramming essentialist cultural indoctrinations. It is not about unbecoming 'female' or 'male' on an essentialist level. It is not about 'unbecoming' one thing in order to arrive at another, such as an essentialist 'third gender'. It is about acknowledging that binary gender systems (and other identity systems) enact violent exclusions of very real and uncountable variations of bodies, and responding to that awareness involves a cultural dismantling of sorts within oneself.

The uncountability of body variations complicates conventional scientific methods that rely upon models of quantification and categorization, and this presents new political dangers, primarily: 1) the risk of essentialization, as you pointed out; and 2) the risk of critique of scientific method leading to reinvestments in longstanding 'anti-science' methodologies such as metaphysics, spiritualisms, and so on. But these both strike me as the common dangers of any organizational process. We know that most (I want to say all) systems of domination rely upon the ideological production of essentialisms and metaphysics that explain and justify their power models. So this question you are asking is absolutely the correct question, but it is also the very question we must always be asking about everything, forever. This problem will never go away. Never. In that sense, we are fucked. Any useful answer to that question of how to avoid essentialisms will never be a solution for overcoming the problem. It will simply be about how to act through a recognition of the hopelessness of the situation (as opposed to a denial of the hopelessness of the situation).

NVT/DG – We recently saw you DJ in New York. Throughout the night you used isolators and effects to shift what was heard and the way it was interpreted. In a sense you were 'dubbing' the tracks. What is your connection to dub music/aesthetics, if any? Do you approach it from a purely technological tool point of view? What are you attempting to create by using them?

TT – I appreciate a lot of the ideas around dub music, and I like a few tracks here and there, but I am not really a fan of the genre. Between the heterosexist misogyny of most reggae and dub lyrics, and the fucked colonial dynamics around the dominant reception and consumption of the genre, I have just never found myself to be in a social context where I was listening to dub and feeling comfortable, you know? Since the 1980s it's been the de facto soundtrack for petit bourgeois (or petit bourgeois reconciled) people wanting to feel 'rootsy', with utter disregard for the very issues of class and race that lay behind the genre's importance.

Between US frat boys, UK pop like UB40, and Japanese reggae tourists who get off on hanging out in really poor areas of Jamaica and then coming back talking about nothing but how happy the natives are, I find it very upsetting. It all strikes me as even more extreme than the commodification of jazz. So without any direct cultural or experiential connections to deeper dub movements, I have basically come to avoid the genre in the same way I avoid going to third world tourist resorts. Non-participation as a kind of boycott of the larger dynamics of its consumption within the Western and Japanese contexts I have inhabited. I feel like the act of boycotting those local processes expresses more solidarity with the vital socio-political underpinnings of dub than if I were to place an emphasis on the act of listening to the genre. Clearly the techniques of dub have had a tremendous impact on the techniques of US disco and house. I would say my entry into those dubbing techniques is much more through those US disco techniques.

Although I have always used effects in my studio productions, I only started using them in DJ sets during my Tokyo residency at Club Module from 2003–2006. And that was simply about having exposure to the gear. In Japanese clubs it is commonplace to have a three-band frequency isolator, and something like a Pioneer EFX-500 effector, so that's where I really got into the habit of using filters and delays during sets. Japanese clubs basically have this gear because of the influence of New York DJ's such as Joe Claussell and François K.

NVT/DG – Also in relationship to your event, we were curious about the venues you play and how they are arranged. Do you have particular standards for the sound? Is the type of venue important? How often do you play for an exclusively queer audience these days? Is that still important to you?

TT – I only DJ and perform out of economic necessity. It is really 'just a job'. I am really quite uninterested in performance, both socially and aesthetically, and I have spoken out many times about the ironies of most 'non-performative' or 'anti-performative' electronic audio production economically relying upon performance. Culturally, I believe this is also a by-product of the anti-sampling campaigns of the

1980s and 1990s, whereby the only cultural position for audio producers was crystalized as a 'musician' (i.e. forced to function within the world of authorship, ownership and copyright). Since the 1990s, electronic audio production has become increasingly focused on 'musician' production strategies, and live/real-time performance – Max MSP, Ableton, et cetera. In cultural terms, this means I am generally working in environments without allies – employers and audience alike.

I also come from a background of working in shit clubs, with no expectations of a budget or means to improve things. So I don't have standards for the sound other than working with what is provided. To be blunt, I would rather they spend the money on my fee, so I can cover more rent and food expenses. If my rent isn't covered during times without income, I don't have a place or time to produce new projects.

I do prefer playing in queer or trans environments, as it (sometimes) increases the chance of certain themes which are important to me resonating among the audience within those social contexts. However, I rarely get asked to do so, and I have little say in the matter. The main reason I don't get many such invites has to do with a combination of economics and the style of audio I play. Most well-funded queer parties or venues tend to play more high energy dance music that I would classify as more techno than house. You know, the cliché of walking the foam floor in Ibiza and shit like that. As queer as deep house's roots may be, it has never been the dominant sound of queer parties. It is more commonly heard in underground, less funded contexts. So the money to fly me from Japan to spin a set is generally not there.

As for my track selection, I am still basically spinning the same old records I collected back in the late 1980s and early 1990s, combined with my own tracks. Again, I see it as 'just a job', so I tend to come in, do my thing, take the money and run. I don't really care how the audience reacts. I mean, I take my work seriously and fulfil my end of the arrangement – the fear of not getting paid keeps me working hard. But unlike a lot of DJ's, I don't see it as my job to please the audience. I guess part of that comes from starting in environments that were at times hostile towards my track selection, so I learned to ignore a lot of shit from the audience during my 1991 residency at Sally's II spinning 6 hours a night, 3 days a week. That was really good training, actually. I have way more skills for dealing with audience complaints than excitement.

NVT/DG – Do you nevertheless still feel there is a way to communicate the socio-political contexts from which house music arose through DJ sets? As you seem to suggest, people show up to be entertained whereas you strictly perform your contractual duties as a performer. How can the act of DJ-ing become a critical statement as well?

TT – It's quite difficult. The club or festival contexts where most DJ-ing occurs is rarely conducive to actual listening, neither socially nor technically. Socially, most people are chemically altered in ways that decrease comprehension, not enhance it. On the technical side, clubs and festivals often have massive sound systems, but they are often poorly balanced, EQ'ed for only one type of music, putting everything through compressors and limiters, et cetera. All of these things end up eliminating frequencies, which means the speakers only broadcast a fragment of the original recordings. It was more as a producer that I became aware of these subtractions of sound, because I would find dif-ferent elements of my tracks missing during playback in different environments. So this is why I produce projects with more consideration for the consumer audience and home listening. That seems to be where messages are more likely to get across. As a public practice, it seems the days of seeing DJ-ing as something in opposition to conventional 'live performance' are over. But personally speaking, that is where my interest in DJ-ing lies. As a DJ I am playing tapes. I am making sound, but not performing as a 'musician' in the traditional sense. I am not engaging in a traditionally 'creative' praxis. Of course, we know that DJ-ing has gradually been transformed into a creative act. The DJ's skills, as well as taste in tracks, become testimony to their 'talent'. We have DJ superstars. A lot of people consider DJ's to be musicians. But not everyone.

Like, I doubt you would find many rock drummers who would be willing to call a DJ a musician. For those self-touted 'real musicians', it is an insult to them if you call a DJ a musician. For me, it's the opposite. It is an insult to call a DJ a musician because that very notion of musicianship stops any dialogue I want to have that is against musicology. It refuses us any social space in which one may openly position oneself as anti-music. And that anti-music analysis is critical to other vital discussions against authorship, creativity, individuality, uniqueness, universality, et cetera.

So, in answer to your question, it is not a matter of 'becoming' a critical practice. There already are very practical ways in which DJ-ing is a deliberate and critical rejection of musicianship and creative practices. However, the larger cultural framework through which most people are exposed to DJ-ing leaves them with little to no tools for comprehending those critiques, let alone responding and contributing to them. Yes, most people can understand the how and why of traditional musicians wishing to differentiate themselves from DJ's (even if they disagree), but very few people would have language to speak about the DJ's desire to differentiate herself from musicians. Most people would try to 'defend' DJ's as musicians, which is a radically conservative cultural mistake as far as I am concerned.

NVT/DG – You have spoken about coming to terms with the idea of losing creativity, that everything is regurgitation. DJ Sprinkles' music refers to Chicago house during the late 1980s into the 1990s, and of course to New York and New Jersey deep house from the same era. In your DJ set, as well as on *Midtown 120 Blues*, the music has the feel of a certain epoch, like a time capsule of the 1990s. How do you relate this aesthetic framework to some of the things we discussed? Is it a strategy to make its political and contextual lineage audible, or is it purely an outcome of the musical equipment you use?

TT – It is not about the equipment I use. It is about sampling and mimicry. And of course it is deliberate. I see audio sampling as the sonic equivalent to a writer quoting or paraphrasing another text. However, as I have stated countless times over the years, audio producers are denied this right to 'quote'. Through anti-sampling law suits in the 1990s, the audio industry managed to dupe the public into hearing all audio as 'creative property'. As a result, we have culturally come to define electronic audio producers and DJ's as 'musicians' (to the utter exclusion of other 'non-creative' possibilities), and acts of listening are limited to the consumption of entertainment. There are very few people who think of sound as 'critical discourse', even within academia. This is a cultural loss. And it did not emerge organically. It is the result of particular capitalist enterprises that have legally restricted and redefined the cultural functions of sound around the globe. I would argue that the rhetoric of music's 'universality' itself is an ideological production of this cultural hegemony. It appears 'universal' because its social applications have been so sweepingly homogenized throughout the world.

This is why it is not enough to simply sample, but one must constantly speak and contextualize one's act of sampling. Unfortunately, again, legal restrictions make it difficult to speak freely here about the impetus for using specific samples. But the act of sampling itself can be spoken of. And I tend to sample or mimic the house sounds of the late 1980s and early 1990s because that was a period of great transition in groups such as ACT-UP. It was the time when the practices of ACT-UP had been absorbed and reflected back in dominant media, as well as co-opted by organizers in the radical right. It was also when a lot of direct action organizers began transitioning to working in CBO's [Community Based Organizations] with formal connections to the HHS (U.S. Department of Health and Human Services) or other local/state/federal government funding. I think it was also the cultural climax of US identity politics, where a rather young movement of anti-essentialism lost out to newfound essentialisms of 'minority' (which was also part of the Left's increasing cultural embrace of CBO's, and the essentialisms laying behind many constructions of who was included or excluded from definitions of 'community'). That whole period had a very large impact upon me, and those experiences continue to influence my perception of social organizing and cultural activities. That includes experiences that have left me irreparably 'pessimistic', but I would say to the editors of this book, that pessimism has personally fuelled far more action than existential paralysis.

NVT/DG – What is your current connection to queer culture? Are you still involved with organizations, or has your experience to the culture changed since leaving New York and living in Japan?

TT – Well, my days of conventional 'direct action' pretty much ended in the 1990s, with those cultural shifts I just mentioned. I think they rendered most strategies ineffective. More performative than organizational.

I've always expressed solidarity with the political sound-organizing efforts of Ultra-red, and worked with them in various ways over the years. However, I have never been a formal member.

My anti-essentialist views on gender and sexuality have alienated me from most people I have met through lesbian/gay community organizations. Similarly, my wish to continue with a non-medically mediated relationship to my body has me on the outs with most people I have met through transgendered organizations. So my connection to 'queer culture' remains very queer – by which I mean it lacks self-identification with any specific communities. But this is also not to be confused with an absence of solidarity or chances for cooperation. It means that solidarity is always strategically negotiated rather than presumed, and cooperation is an act of labour rather than some shared 'personal understanding'. There may be truckloads of bitterness and pessimism, but its soundtrack is not a swan song... although it may sound like one to unqueered ears, much as a gay disco song sounds straight to many. Understanding and working with such preconditions is part of what leads to queer strategies capable of interfering with or dismantling power, rather than seizing it. It kind of reminds me of the words of recently passed UK labour organizer Tony Benn (who is sampled by Mark Fell and me in our upcoming collaborative house EP), 'There's no final victory, no final defeat'.

The Beautiful Risk of Criticality

Ingrid Commandeur

In 2010 the curator and art critic Marta Kuzma, taking part in a panel discussion called 'Beyond Criticality' (Symposium *Institutional Attitudes*, Brussels, 24-25 April), opened her talk with the following statement:

> The intellectual historically has always been somebody in dynamic contestation with the establishment, but the challenge between the authority and the intellectual is now gone because neither the public, nor the authorities any longer care about the intellectual. ... The year 1989 marks an important paradigmatic shift in this respect, it is the starting point of a gradual disintegration, in which a global economic system has co-opted positions of criticality.[1]

One of the latest 'co-option strategies', according to Kuzma, is the tendency of art fairs to develop a public programme, thereby appropriating critical discourse. A second example she mentioned was the so-called 'educational turn in art'. Regarding the latter as yet another disguise of the total marketization of art and education, Kuzma seems to position herself alongside the criticasters of the educational turn.[2] The grim conclusion of Kuzma's speech: 'Intelligence is a difficult position to take nowadays'. Although I don't entirely agree with Kuzma's dark pessimism, in hindsight listening to her talk was the starting point of a rather nagging self-doubt: is art criticism, seen within the fixed boundaries of its discipline, as relevant as it used to be? And indeed, does the year 1989 mark an important paradigmatic shift in this respect?

Roughly at the same time, I was asked to participate in a large research project called *Dutch Art Criticism in the Netherlands 1885-2015*.[3] Taking the year 1989 as starting point I looked at two decades of Dutch art criticism (1989-2009). I literally read hundreds of texts ranging from newspaper journalism,to professional art journals and Internet critique. My studio gradually filled itself with archive boxes and texts neatly tucked away in all kinds of classifications. My initial thoughts were: if there *is* a crisis in art criticism, surely it would be possible to *trace it down* in a gradual demise in quality? I would be able to detect, identify and describe it, and thus have my fair share in how to deal with the crisis and contribute to its solution. But the more I gathered and read, the less relevant the initial question appeared to be. Instead, I became much more interested in art criticism as reception history and in the information one could read 'between the lines'. How did art critics actually respond to the changes in the models of production and dissemination of art from the 1990s onwards, and how did this affect the nature and/or definition of art criticism itself? Isn't this the more difficult and complex question to answer, given the fact that art criticism over the course of years developed itself as a multi-headed monster appearing in different guises, practices and places, both inside and outside the traditional printed media?

Also: the more I read about the crisis in art criticism – including the more recent internationalized version of the debate[4] – the more it dawned on me that this was becoming a historically situated discussion, inherited from the 1990s, with its heydays in the 2000s, but perhaps less relevant in our time. As the editors of this volume rightfully state: the relevant question to ask at this moment seems to be; 'where is art criticism?' in stead of 'what is art criticism?' Arthur Danto's postmodern *The End of Art*-philosophy, which states that the art critic as well as the public are in a state of limbo because of the lack of a common set of evaluative references, has become inadequate to explain the different positions of art criticism in a post-1989 society. But often this philosophy, in combination with the frequently mentioned influence of digital media and the impact of the global cultural industry on the total body of critical mass, is used as a valid argument to describe the 'crisis in art criticism'.[5] And although this certainly is part and parcel of the 'patient's diagnosis' – because yes, we have witnessed a demise in quality in the newspapers art sections; and yes there is uncertainty about the troubled question of 'judgment' and a general lack of contextualized and well-informed criticism; and yes art journals have suffered under a general neoliberal tendency, and yes the reader/consumer has become its own producer of content – still there is more than meets the eye.

While the above arguments rightly point out the influence of economic and societal developments and a changing media landscape on art criticism, the discussion about the dialectical relationship between art and art criticism remains frozen somewhere in the late 1980s. Trying to find articles that theorize this subject from a current perspective is like trying to find a needle in a haystack. Up until now it has hardly been theorized. Irit Rogoff's contribution to the debate stands out positively in this respect. She clearly addressed the fact that the practice of art criticism and art are intrinsically bound together. Therefore, in order to understand the complex nature of 'the crisis in art criticism', it is necessary to study the changes in the production and dissemination of art and criticism from the 1990s, as well.

Since this is quite a complex field of study, the modest intention of this article therefore is only to speculatively open up this field by providing a first glimpse into it. First, by counter-positioning two critics who have tried to theorize the position of art criticism in a post-1989 society: the German critic Peter Bürger and English theorist and curator Irit Rogoff. And second, by disclosing a small part of my research into the immediate history of Dutch art criticism. The point of focus therein is the reception of the experimental exhibition models of the 1990s in Dutch art criticism.

The Path for a Future Critique?

In 2010 the German critic Peter Bürger sketched a rather gloomy perspective in his article 'Definitions and Limitations of Art Criticism'. In his text he contrasts the strong spirit of social critique of the Student Movement of 1969 with our current age, in which 'the voice of critique has become strangely numb':

> The nations of the West responded to the new situation of global capitalism by reducing welfare structures and pursuing a robust 'policy of reform'. It no longer seemed scandalous that the gap between poor and rich widened, instead this became regarded as the ineluctable course of things. In this situation the will to critique became as lame as the confidence in its efficacy. Now, one cannot infer that the state of social critique implies a similar state in art criticism, but an, as it were osmotic effect of the general political climate can probably not be denied, I at any rate feel that somehow global capitalism has in general infected critique with paralyzing self-doubt.[6]

In line with Marta Kuzma, Bürger marks the beginning of the 1990s as the starting point of a gradual disintegration in which a global economic system co-opted positions of criticality. According to Bürger, the concept of critique needs to be rejuvenated and in order to do so we have to look at art itself. But Bürger then makes a strange turn in his argument by granting the centre stage of his considerations to the eighteenth-century concept of critique of the German cultural philosopher Friedrich Schlegel. In line with Schlegel, Bürger asserts that without a theoretical, normative vision of the future development of art, the critic is not capable of forming an engaged and in-depth opinion of art. The problem is though that in the course of history this very normative vision of art became a snake that bit its own tail. In their artistic and political utopian ideas of progress, the avant-garde movements left the public lagging far behind them, resulting in a gap between the artist and the public. According to Bürger, the neo-avant-gardes even developed to a point were all the possibilities to effectively voice any normative judgment about art was washed away:

> ... the neo-avant-gardes betrayed the historical project of the historical avant-gardes, but at the same time opened art up to a creative space in a domain from which it had hitherto been excluded. This space has since been filled. Sooner, or later, the dynamics of reduction and renunciation had to eliminate everything in the art work that could form the basis for aesthetic experience.[7]

With considerable sardonic pleasure Bürger recounts the pseudo-intellectualism that arose out of the lack of an aesthetic experience; even the most uninspired art could spark off critics to discover endless aesthetic qualities and art historical references, hence the necessity of critique 'to find a different agency'. But if an affirmative style of writing becomes too detached from placing the art work in a larger art-historical and theoretical framework, and art criticism framed by the normative vision of the art critic doesn't provide the solution of finding a new agency for critique either, what would? At the end of his text Bürger does try to formulate a new path for a future critique. He returns to Schlegel's eighteenth-century definition of 'immanent critique' and makes a remarkable turn by suggesting to restore the intuitive pre-judgement of the art critic, 'understanding the work on his own terms' without the aid of art and science, only to couple this in a second instance with a more theoretical, normative vision of the future development of art. The path of future art criticism, according to Bürger, thus would be: 'dovetailing theory and critique'.[8]

Although on first sight this may sound plausible, it goes without saying that Bürger's theory is not without inconsistencies itself. While he states at the beginning of his article to take the 'immanent qualities of art' as his guiding principle, his research is mainly based on the modernistic development of art, frozen in time and put to a standstill around the 1980s. He doesn't make any connections with recent developments in art, and in that sense he seems to fall prey to the dogma of his own theory. If we agree that positions of criticality are constantly being co-opted by a global, neoliberal economy, as stated before, the only way out of this dilemma is to try to develop new forms of agency and subjectivity outside this realm, *one way or another*. By dovetailing intuition and theory in art criticism, Bürger tries to do just that, but at the same time he falls back on an essentialist model of spectatorship in which the immanent qualities of an art work are hidden inside, to be discovered and disclosed by the critic. This prevents him from really being able to theorize new positions.

Criticality as a Form of Risk-taking

Another theorist, who did start theorizing new possible positions, is Irit Rogoff. According to Rogoff, instead of thinking of the earlier separation into creativity and criticism, production and application, we now have to think of all these practices, linked together in a complex process of knowledge production. In her article 'What is a Theorist?' she stated the following:

> The old boundaries between making and theorizing, historicizing and displaying, criticizing and affirming have long been eroded. Artistic practice is now being acknowledged as the production of knowledge and theoretical and curatorial endeavours have taken on a far more experimental and inventive dimension, both existing in the realm of potentiality and possibility rather than that of exclusively material production. The former pragmatic links, in which one area 'serviced' another have given way to an understanding that we face cultural issues in common and produce cultural insights in common. Instead of 'criticism' being an act of judgement addressed to a clear-cut object of criticism, we now recognize not just our own imbrication in the object or the cultural moment, but also the performative nature of any action or stance we might be taking in relation to it.[9]

Before elaborating further on what the actual consequences of this line of thought are, it is essential to first explain the distinction

Rogoff has made between art criticism, critique and criticality. Rogoff, who started her career as a visual culture-theorist, acknowledges to be influenced by, but at the same time renounces some of the consequences of the heritage of critical theory and cultural analysis of the 1990s. What is essential for the actualization of contemporary cultural practices is what she calls 'a shift away from a critique to criticality'. Rogoff:

> Briefly, this is a shift away from a model that says that the manifest of culture must yield up some latent values and intentions through endless processes of investigation and uncovering. ... Critical Analysis attempts to turn the latent of hidden conditions and unacknowledged desires and power relations into a cultural manifest. Using the vast range of structuralist, post and post post-structuralist tools and models of analysis we have at our disposal, we have been able to unveil, unravel, expose and lay bare the hidden meanings of cultural circulation and the overt and covert interests that they serve. But there is a serious problem here, as there is an assumption that meaning is immanent, that it is always already there and precedes its uncovering.[10]

Unlike Bürger, Rogoff strongly believes we have moved away from notions of immanent meanings that can be investigated, exposed and made obvious. Within the current performative nature of culture, meaning *takes place* as events unfold. In other words: meaning is never produced in isolation, but rather through intricate webs of connectedness and participants: audiences, students or researchers.

As Rogoff said: artistic practices are now being acknowledged as the production of knowledge in their own right and curatorial endeavours have taken on a far more experimental and 'critical' dimension. Criticism itself is migrating as well: to the internet and social media; to self-published magazines by artists; to the spectator, as witnessed by the blurring of the boundaries between the professional and the amateur; and last but not least to the proliferation of symposia, publications, reading groups and discussion forums in the art world. What this proves is that new subjectivities that try to resist the forced marriage between art, criticism and the cultural industry *are already being* and *will be* constantly formed. And this of course sheds a totally different light on the diagnosis of the crisis of art criticism. If you look at this 'problem' from a different angle, suddenly it seems there is a lot of potential, but this does require the ability to look beyond the 'traditional' boundaries of professional disciplines. Because if we effectively understand art criticism as generating a public platform of debate where notions of criticality around art can be shared and discussed, then of course this is by no means confined to the boundaries of art criticism in the printed media.

The importance Rogoff grants to the notion of the event, of meaning as something unfolding, and of learning as a process of risk-taking has also been taken up recently by education philosophers such as Gert Biesta (*The Beautiful Risk of Education*) and Dennis Atkinsons (*Art, Equality and Learning. Pedagogies Against the State*).[11] In line with Rogoff, they point to the fact that learning students how to be 'critical' (in the sense of analysing or deconstructing a problem) is different from teaching them how to analyse and at the same time *inhabit a problem*. Similar processes that force us to view art criticism as part of a complex process of knowledge production are also at hand in education. It can be found in the current interest in the relation between art, science and technology, which manifests itself in the renewed attention for its historical points of intersection, and in the revival of a different kind of interdisciplinarity; an interdisciplinarity that is not concerned which crossing boundaries between cultural (art, design, fashion, architecture) and/or academic disciplines (anthropology, social sciences, critical studies, philosophy), but one that is geared towards producing hybrid forms of knowledge production in between art, science and technology. On the one hand, science is invested with a notion of risk-taking, of crossing borders of disciplines, of experiment and exploration rather than measurable outcome. And on the other hand, the arts are being saturated with the notion of research and knowledge production. In other words: cultural practitioners themselves are resisting the dichotomy between art and science.

However, to return to my initial line of thought: are the blurring boundaries between creativity and criticism, production and application not in fact created by the curatorial and intellectual classes themselves, instead of having evolved out of (artistic) practice, one might ask? Rogoff has been accused of leading the life of a typical lecture-circuit theorist, far removed from the less self-aware masses of audiences and art critics, who are lost to the corruption of the market and the culture industry.[12] So, are Rogoff's ideas in fact abstract, intellectual theories devoid of everyday reality, not grounded in everyday (artistic) practice? I don't think this is the case, and it is interesting to point out in this respect that the notion of participation, performativity and *meaning taking place as events unfold* is very much inherited from, and put into action by developments in the art scene of the 1990s itself. And it is worthwhile to conclude this article with a short journey into our immediate history of art, to both substantiate these arguments and come to a balanced critical perception of recent developments such as the educational turn in art, and how this relates to the discussion about the crisis in art criticism.

Meaning Taking Place as Events Unfold

In order to do so, I will briefly focus on the reception in Dutch art criticism of experimental exhibition models of the early 1990s in Europe. After the art boom of the 1980s, artists and curators felt the need to critically re-evaluate the function of art within society. The museum as institutional frame was once again scrutinized, and codes and frameworks of exhibition models deliberately altered. Especially the year 1993 marked the consolidation of a new type of site-specific exhibition, which in the course of time would become an important reference point for present day exhibition models.[13] Some remarkable examples of the time include: *Project Unité*, *Sonsbeek 93* and *On taking a normal situation and retranslating it into overlapping and multiple reading of conditions in past and present.*[14] These exhibition directly addressed the site as a socially constituted phenomenon, rather than as a formal entity and were conceptualized as open-ended, process-based, convivial 'projects', in which – certainly in the case of *Project Unité* and *Sonsbeek 93* – collaboration was defined as a good in itself.

Although of course all different and unique in their own respect, for the sake of this article I would like to summarize the most important common features of these exhibitions. First, there was a strong awareness of the instrumentalization of art by institutional frameworks and the art market, which resulted in a strong urge to bridge the gap between art and life and situate art within the social domain. Second, there was a preference for exploratory, experimental and multi-disciplinary approaches and site-specific, contextualized works. Artists were invited to respond to and engage with the local, architectural, historical and social context, which involved confronting the public with the private, and extending the exhibition format to become a part of the social domain. Third, there was a strong tendency towards process-based versus object-based production, co-participation and an exhibition format of an open and public nature. Finally, the notion of collaborative production became very important: the exhibitions were regarded as a *Gesamtkunstwerk* initiated by the curators, who set the parameters for the exhibition as a social and critical medium. The new exhibition formats were a clear response to the critical debate rising around the cultural and political implications of the international 'group' exhibition. But curators also responded to the practice of artists in the 1990s weaving scientific, sociological and anthropological methods into their art practices, engaging themselves in a cultural investigation of the real, daily experience of individuals and communities, laying bare the interactive structuring and layering of culture.

In her thought-provoking book *Artificial Hells. Participatory Art and the Politics of Spectatorship* (2012) the American art historian Claire Bishop rightfully pointed out that the socially engaged art of the 1990s can be seen as the historical counterpart of the educational turn in art. The current popularity of educational models among artists and curators seems to be a next step in involving the public as participants in art projects: informal learning, de-/un-schooling and the exhibition as educational model: 'today's education is figured as art's potential ally in an age of ever-decreasing public space, rampant privatisation and instrumentalized bureaucracy'.[15] Bishop also argues that the renewed social awareness of artists in the 1990s marks a shift that is 'yet to be fully theorized by art historians and critics'.[16] Because of this far-reaching influence that the experimental exhibition formats of the 1990s would prove to have on the cultural scene, it is interesting to have a brief look into how they were received by art critics at the time. Unlike what one would expect, the exhibitions were quite heavily criticized, not only by the general public, but particularly also by progressive art critics. What can we learn from the reception of these exhibitions in Dutch art criticism and how does this relate to the educational turn as its contemporary counterpart?

Towards a Post-hierarchical Learning Environment

In 1993, the Dutch curator and art critic Mark Kremer wrote a provocative text called 'The Meagre Harvest of a Cultural Migrant Worker' ('De schrale oogst van culturele gastarbeid'), responding to the exhibition *On taking a normal situation...*[17] He opened his article by stating that exhibition concepts that take the social relevance of art as a starting point provide artists with a rigid framework to which they tend to respond in a mechanical way. Artistic practices are being 'institutionalized' by a political correct framework set by the curator, while still being in a stage of development. Artists responding in their practices to societal issues and contexts, should display their work at locations that are inherently connected to this very context. The public space of a city (in the case of *Sonsbeek 93*) or an architectural monument and apartment block (in the case of *Project Unité*) is a too constructed and fictional environment for this purpose. For Kremer this pointed to an even more fundamental problematic. While artists are increasingly invited to respond to the local context of larger-scale exhibitions and biennials, they are not able to stay for a long period of time. As a result, their research or understanding of the local context is often limited: a tendency, which Kremer ironically called 'the artist as the cultural migrant worker'. While this problematic nature of the exhibition asks for a critical approach, the discourse generated by the curators often lacked this nuance or criticality. As a consequence, according to Kremer, the exhibitions run the risk of becoming just as much part of the cultural machinery they claim to break away from.

The Dutch media theorist and cultural critic Jorinde Seijdel formulated an equally critical response in her 1997 article: 'On the Integration of the Everyday. The Crisis of the Exhibition'.[18] In her article, Seijdel more or less continued Kremer's line of thought by stating that trying to escape the exhibition as institution and context is problematic, because its surrounding structures (press release, catalogue, visitor guidance) always work towards protecting the nature of the event as an exhibition. According to Seijdel, despite their experimental nature and deviating character, exhibitions such as *Sonsbeek 93* and *Project Unité* didn't change the fundamental characteristics of the exhibition format. According to her, the crucial question to ask therefore is whether the preoccupation of art with reality or the social domain doesn't get stuck in 'directing, simulating and framing reality, rendering it aesthetic and giving it museum-like qualities, thereby exhibiting or parasitizing on reality and the social domain'? Seijdel also directed her attention to the growing imbalance between the artist and curator, the latter holding an increasingly dominant position within the cultural industry. If the work of an artist is supposed to correspond to a larger social context on its own accord, how is that possible within a cultural context in which curators are the dominant, global mediators between art and its public context? In other words: the conditions that make these exhibitions possible – showing cultural goods outside the realm of capitalism – are at the same time the preconditions for their constant crisis.

If we summarize the conclusion of the criticism opinionated above, the exhibitions, despite their claims, failed to construct an in-depth relationship between art and its social context, and as result of this failed to generate the intended meaningful relationship with the visitor as participant, as opposed to the visitor as consumer of art. Obviously, it remains a subject of debate and further research, whether one can fully agree to this kind of criticism, and how it would apply to each of the exhibitions individually. What we can safely conclude though, is that the effort to bridge the gap between art and life, or between exhibition and social reality has remained an unresolved and a highly problematic issue to this very day, while on the other hand exhibition formats that go back to the history of the experimental exhibition formats of the 1990s have become a dominant part of the artistic discourse. It is by no means a coincidence that one of the main curators of *On taking a normal situation...*, Carolyn Christov-Bakargiev, would become the head of the prestigious *dOCUMENTA (13).*

It therefore comes as no surprise either that a recent tendency like the educational turn in art can be seen as a response to the ideals and strategies of the experimental exhibition models of the 1990s, albeit of course on very different grounds: how do they try to overcome their contested claims? Let me first shortly state that by referring to the educational turn I adhere to the definition of it as given by O'Neill and Wilson in *Curating and the Educational Turn*.[19] They have described the educational turn as a tendency in which curating increasingly operates as an expanded educational praxis: educational formats, methods, programmes, processes and procedures have become pervasive in the praxis of both curating and the production of contemporary art and in their attendant critical frameworks. And discussions, talks, symposia, educational programmes and discursive practices not only play a supporting role to the exhibition, but have become central to contemporary practice. Also, again for the sake of and within the boundaries of this article, I consciously take on a rather generalizing approach, in order to focus on the main points.

First, within the educational turn, the exhibitions and projects show a preference for adopting a participatory structure or educational model, which operates as a social medium. But noticeably different: instead of inviting artists to respond to local and social circumstances, curators create micro-social domains through the formation of particular communities in which a meaningful exchange can take place. At the core of all this stands the principle of a post-hierarchical learning environment where the visitors are co-participants. The supposed authorial primacy of the curator is countered by the open-ended nature of the cultural encounter and exchange. Second, there is a preference for the exploratory, experimental and multi-disciplinary approaches to knowledge production. But noticeably different: an emphasis is placed on the framing and mediation of art and the circulation of ideas around art, rather than on its production and display.

The parameters clearly have changed, but has this resolved the problematic opposition between the viewer as consumer and the desired position of the viewer as participant? Not entirely. After all, the issue of cultural authority and power could still be at hand, because the discursive models appeal primarily to certain publics while they exclude others. There is still a risk that the educational turn is being mobilized at a rhetorical level, without altering business-as-usual, jostling for symbolic capital in the economy of cultural entrepreneurship and being dressed up as emancipatory, or open-ended practice.

The Beautiful Risk of Criticality

So does this bring us back to the beginning of this article and to Kuzma's pessimistic conclusion? Not quite: Rogoff, in her attempt to pinpoint the most important features of contemporary developments in art, also described the far-reaching influence the experimental exhibition formats of the 1990s would have on our current cultural climate and critical discourse. Namely, the fact that we are now able to relate to the idea of *producing meaning through the temporality of the event* of an exhibition or display, the idea of art works or thematic exhibitions functioning as *fields of possibilities for different audiences in different cultural circumstances*, and the reality of our current, *performative nature of cultural displays*. And therefore one might wonder whether the cultural changes that the socially engaged art of the 1990s brought into play, are perhaps more deeply imbedded than we currently realize.

The reciprocal relation between art and criticism, or notions of criticality, is not a superficial cultural phenomenon driven by the curatorial class, but the result of this deeper, cultural shift. One way or another, this confronts us with the reality of looking at art criticism as being part of a larger field of knowledge production, and this should prompt us to radically change the parameters of the debate of the 'crisis in art criticism'. We should now accept the contextualization of art criticism within a larger and complex field of knowledge production as a given; a reality that surrounds us, whether we like it or not. A reality also, that is defined by cultural practitioners themselves in the course of history and can be seen as a consequence of the apparent process of searching for new kinds of positions of criticality and new subjectivities within the context of global capitalism.

The current magnitude of the political and ecological problems we are faced with, not only seem to render the claims of the art of the 1990s to bridge 'art' and 'life' pointless, it also threatens to make art criticism an obsolete activity. After all, who would be in need of reflection on a seemingly bourgeois notion as art in the face of much more urgent problems to tackle, which will no doubt take centre stage in the coming decades? Just acknowledging art criticism as being part of a wider landscape of media, as well as of a larger field of knowledge production and a micro climate of different media and social and intellectual modalities of resistance, already requires us to examine assumptions about the different fields of operation and to ponder the productive overlaps and incompatibilities that might arise from their conjunction, with the consequence of reinventing both.

In the Netherlands, every two years the 'Jonge Prijs voor de Kunstkritiek' is awarded to a few talented young art critics. For the 2014 edition, a new category was included, called: 'visual art criticism', posing the question: how can the format of a review become stronger, more light-hearted and attractive by integrating graphics, cinematic, musical media? The visual criticism was supposed to last between 4 and 7 minutes, should not be a reportage or a interview, but a clearly opinionated piece of visual art criticism. Apart from these preconditions, a whole set of other criteria, set for criticism in printed media-categories, also applied to the visual art criticism. Although this idea for innovation should be much applauded,[20] it seems a very timid way of doing it: a new category is introduced but already rendered numb before it is in place by a set of boundaries and criteria that are ultimately derived from art criticism in printed media. It therefore comes as no surprise that there was no winner in this particular category, and the prize for visual art criticism was not awarded. Perhaps we have to conclude that it is not possible to invent a new category within the boundaries of art criticism in printed media, but also that it is extremely difficult to shape the conditions under which one could stimulate alternative forms of criticism – on line, visual, staged or displayed – that are a result of experimentation with media and formats in the true sense of the word. The truth is we don't know what direction it will exactly take, but it will certainly not be a neatly paved path into one or the other direction; we are talking here about the notion of criticism as a multi-headed monster that crawls its way into every direction it can take.

In that sense, the idea of newspaper journalism or art journals holding the exclusive right to notions of criticality or independent journalism is a claim that no longer holds. We now live in a world in which neither criticism nor cultural productions can escape the influence of neoliberal capitalism. Our reality is shaped by a scattered landscape of printed, visual and social media, democratizing citizens as participants, but just as strongly capitalizing on their subjectivity as well. This new reality of the information society challenges us to a debate about what the potentials of art criticism or criticality truly can be, how this relates to notions of commonality and accessibility and the conditions under which different publics and the so-called 'prosumer', can have access to different kinds of informed debates through different media (newspapers, magazines, local, international, cultural institutions, large-scale exhibitions, et cetera). In this situation it is no longer possible to hold on to fixed positions between printed or online criticism, or between criticism, display and cultural production as such. And rather than seeing this as a threat to the traditional art critic or journalist, it is to be regarded as a reciprocal process of keeping each other sharp.

Also, the boundaries between art, science and technology are being contested. Perhaps the biggest threat that we are facing now is the fact that the arts are being marginalized by the notion of the creative practitioner in the service of the digitalized, neoliberal economy. Capitalism renders us numb, it will not be geared towards finding solutions that are effectively in the service of the common good of our planet, but will increase the amount of wealth in the hands of global companies. What alternatives are there to be invented and what factions, partnerships, co-operations, interdisciplinarities and modes of criticality can be formed between art, science and technology to counter this dominant discourse? What remains the same for critics, cultural practitioners and art educators alike is to take up the challenge of the beautiful risk of criticality.

Notes

1 Marta Kuzma's thoughts were inspired by Franco Berardi's book: *The Soul at Work. From Alienation to Autonomy*, Cambridge MA:MIT Press, 2009.

2 Critical voices like Dieter Roelstraete ironically stated that while the wealth of seminars, workshops, exhibitions and literature dedicated to the educational turn has multiplied, art criticism is in crisis. See: Dieter Roelstraete, "Critical Mess: On the Ruins of the Museum's Research Departments", in: *Mousse Magazine,* Issue #26, November 2010. Others have pointed out to the fact that while we are witnessing the burgeoning of new academic degrees in the arts, this also coincides with budget cuts, increasing bureaucratization, the rise of student fees, and the merge of departments in the Humanities.

3 The research project *Dutch Art Criticism in the Netherlands 1885-2015* will result in a series of 11 publications, three of which have already been released: Peter de Ruiter, *De Terugkeer van het schilderen. Kunstkritische opvattingen over een ijzersterk medium 1975-1989,* Rotterdam: NAi Publishers, 2014, Jonneke Fritz Jobse, *De schilderkunst in een kritiek stadium? Critici in debat over realism en abstractie in een tijd van wederopbouw en Koude Oorlog 1945-1960,* Rotterdam: NAi Publishers, 2014 and Rogier Schumacher, *Kunstkritiek als exact vak? De kunsthistoricus als criticus 1960-2005,* Rotterdam: NAi Publishers, 2015.

4 See for instance: 'Where do you stand, Collegue?', in: *Texte zur Kunst*, No. 81, March 2011. To mark its 20th anniversary, the Berlin-based journal *Texte Zur Kunst* put on a conference (published in its March 2011 issue) to address 'the fundamental question of the relationship between art criticism and social critique'. The Vancouver-based magazine *Fillip* published the results of a 2009 forum about art criticism, in: Jeff Khonsary; Melanie O'Brian, *Judgment and Contemporary Art Criticism,* Vancounver: Artspeak/Fillip Editions, 2010. At Tate Britain in December 2010, for the newly established annual lecture of the International Association of Art Critics (AICA) James Elkins reasserted his argument that there is currently no clear definition or common understanding what art criticism is or does, no canon of art critical writing, and no coherent methodology that might define it as a discipline.

5 See: James Elkins, 'On the Absence of Judgement in Art Criticism', in: James Elkins and Michael Newman (eds.), *The State of Art Criticism*, London/New York: Routledge, 2008.

6 Peter Bürger, 'Definitions and Limitations of Art Criticism', in: *Oase Journal for Architecture*, No. 81: *Constructing Criticism*, 2010, p. 14. First published in: *Werkur, Deutsche Zeitschrift fur Europaïschen Denken*, No. 11, November 2009.

7 Ibid., p. 26.

8 Ibid., p. 32.

9 Irit Rogoff, 'What is a Theorist?, in: James Elkins and Michael Newman (eds.), *The State of Art Criticism*, London/New York: Routledge, 2008, p. 97.

10 Irit Rogoff, 'Smuggling – An Embodied Criticality', published at the website of European Institute for Progressive Cultural Policies, august, 2006. See http://transform.eipcp.net.

11 See Gert J.J. Biesta, *The Beautiful Risk of Education*, Boulder: Paradigm Publishers, 2014; and Dennis Atkinsons, *Art, Equality and Learning. Pedagogies Against the State,* Rotterdam: Sense Publishers, 2011.

12 See J.J. Charlesworth, 'Criticism versus Critique', in: *Art Monthly*, No. 346, May 2011.

13 Claire Bishop made a similar same argument in: 'Chapter 7: Former West: Art as Project in the Early 1990s', in: *Participatory Art and the Politics of Spectatorship*, London/New York: Verso, 2010. She signalled out *Project Unité*, *Sonsbeek 93* and *Culture in Action* as examples. The examples I looked are situated in a European context, besides *Project Unité*, *Sonsbeek 93* also *On taking a normal situation* (see below); *Kontext Kunst* (Neue Galerie im Künsterhaus, Graz, 1993); *This is the show and the show is many things* (MuKHA, Antwerp, 1994); *Crap Shoot* (De Appel, Amsterdam, 1996), et cetera.

14 The exhibition *Project Unité* (1992–1993) was located in Le Corbusier's Unité d'Habitation, a monumental block of low-income apartments in Firminy, central France. Unité d'Habitation consisted of 414 apartments along with public spaces, a preschool, and a roof area with a combined playground and open-air theatre. Curator Yves Aupetitallot handed over the 28 empty apartments to an invited selection of around 40 artists, artists' groups, designers and architects. Their works explored present-day

socio-economic and cultural aspects that contributed to the failed utopia of modernist city planning in Firminy. *Sonsbeek 93* (June 5-September 26, 1993) was located at various locations in the city of Arnhem (the Netherlands) the Sonsbeek Park and several remote locations outside the city centre. Curator Valerie Smith pictured the city of Arnhem as a target with three circles that symbolized Park Sonsbeek, the city and its immediate surroundings. She invited 38 artists to take root in one of the three 'areas' and respond to the specific social, historical, architectural and rural conditions. She encouraged the artist to rethink their methodologies in relation to 'actual' social environments. In doing so, she advanced the idea that art, released from its institutional cage, could be an agent for social commentary. *On taking a normal situation and translating it into overlapping and multiple readings of conditions in past and present* (September 19–November 28, 1993) was located in MuHKA in Antwerp and curated by Carolyn Christov-Bakargiev, Iwona Blazwick and Yves Aupetitallot. The title of the exhibition was derived from a text by Gordon Matta-Clark. In 1993 Antwerp was European Capital of the World, the curators of the exhibition wanted to critically reflect on the notion of an international exhibition in the light of these circumstances. According to Carolyn Christov-Bakargiev the relation between Antwerp 93, the MuHKA and Antwerp's history as a centre for contemporary art was central to the exhibition, a context in which to discuss 'questions regarding the local/international and centre/periphery paradigm'. 16 artists were invited to respond to this theme with research and newly conceived works for, what Christov-Bakargiev called, a 'culturally-specific' exhibition. Carolyn Christov-Bakargiev, Iwona Blazwick and Yves Aupetitallot (eds.), *On taking a normal situation and translating it into overlapping and multiple readings of conditions in past and present.Texts,* ex. cat. MuKHA, Antwerp, 1993.

15 Claire Bishop, *Participatory Art and the Politics of Spectatorship*, London/New York: Verso Books, 2010, p. 242.

16 Ibid., p. 215. Bishop also wrote in this respect: '... during the early 1990s the exhibition itself becomes conceptualised as an open-ended, process-based, convivial "project", without a definable goal beyond collaboration as a good in itself.' See also p. 217: 'The reason why it is *exhibitions* (rather than individual works) that frame this discussion of art's renewed interest in the social in the early 1990s becomes clearer in this light. ... In paying attention to relationships, rather than to individual objects, it is the conceptualisation of the ensemble that seems to gain strength while the individual works recede.'

17 Mark Kremer, 'De schrale oogst van culturele gastarbeid', in: *De Witte Raaf,* No. 46, 1993.

18 Jorinde Seijdel, 'Over het inburgeren van alledaagsheid. De crisis van de tentoonstelling', in: *HTV de IJsberg,* 1997.

19 Paul O' Neill and Mick Wilson (eds.), *Curating and the Educational Turn*, London: Open Editions/de Appel, 2010.

20 See also: Wouter Hillaert, 'De Toekomst van de kritiek ligt in de vorm', in: *De Groene Amsterdammer,* 18-06-2014. He advocates a shift from a paper to an on line form of thinking, and points out to the democratizing and communal strength of online media inn opposition to the established media. His idea of renewal in mainly based on the opposition of on line and paper media, while this paper obviously tries to argue the situation is even more complex than that.

Contributors

Luc Boltanski is Professor at the École des hautes études en sciences sociales, Paris, and one of the leading figures of the pragmatic turn in contemporary social theory. His books *On Justification* (2006 [1991]), *The New Spirit of Capitalism* (2005 [1999]) and *On Critique* (2011 [2009]) have shaped the current debate about the possibilities of critique. His most recent book is *Mysteries and Conspiracies. Detective Stories, Spy Novels and the Making of Modern Societies* (2014 [2012]).

Sabeth Buchmann, art historian/ art critic, Professor of Modern and Postmodern Art at the Academy of Fine Arts Vienna, co-editor with Helmut Draxler, Clemens Krümmel and Susanne Leeb of *Polypen* – a publication series on art criticism and political theory. Publications (selection): with Max Jorge Hinderer Cruz (co-author): *Hélio Oiticica, Neville D'Almeida and others. Block-Experiments in Cosmococa*, London: 2013, co-editor with Helmut Draxler and Stephan Geene of *Film, Avantgarde und Biopolitik*, Vienna: 2009; *Denken gegen das Denken. Produktion – Technologie – Subjektivität bei Sol LeWitt, Hélio Oiticica und Yvonne Rainer*, Berlin: 2007, co-editor with Alexander Alberro of *Art After Conceptual Art*. Cambridge, MA/ Cologne: 2006.

Robin Celikates is Associate Professor of Political and Social Philosophy at the University of Amsterdam. He is the author of *Kritik als soziale Praxis* (2009) and the co-author of *Politische Philosophie* (2013). Most recently, he has co-edited *Transformations of Democracy. Crisis, Protest, and Legitimation* and *The Irregularization of Migration in Contemporary Europe. Detention, Deportation, Drowning* (both 2015).

Hans D. Christ (*1963) studied art and literary studies at the University of Dortmund. In 1993 he was chief coordinator of the project *Standorte: Akademie auf Zeit (Sites: Temporary Academy)* with Magdalena Jetelová, Fabrizio Plessi, and students of various art academies in North Rhine-Westphalia. In 1996, he founded the Hartware MedienKunstVerein in Dortmund together with Iris Dressler, which they co-directed until 2004. Additionally, from 2002 to 2004, he worked as curator at the Museum am Ostwall in Dortmund. In 2004 he was co-curator of the biennial Media City Seoul. Since 2005, he and Iris Dressler have shared directorship of the Württembergischer Kunstverein in Stuttgart. In 2013 Christ was co-curator of the Werkleitz-Festival in Halle. Since the nineties he has been teaching regularly at various academies throughout Europe, Asia, and the United States. He has published articles on artists such as Stan Douglas, Peggy Buth, Bettina Lockemann, or Noh Suntag, as well as on subjects such as curatorial and institutional practices or the politics of space.

Ingrid Commandeur is course director of the Master Education in Arts at the Piet Zwart Institute for post-graduate studies and research in Rotterdam, art critic and researcher. Recently she curated the lecture series *Critical Pedagogies of the 21th Century* (2014). She holds an MA in Art History from the VU University in Amsterdam. Prior to working at the Piet Zwart Institute, Commandeur was senior editor of *METROPOLIS M, Magazine of Contemporary Art* (2004–2010) and theory tutor at the Gerrit Rietveld Academie in Amsterdam (2010–2014). Ingrid Commandeur has published extensively on contemporary art. Among her publications are: *Now Is the Time. Art & Theory in the 21st Century* (Rotterdam, 2010), *Museutopia. A Photographic Research Project by Ilya Rabinovich* (Amsterdam, 2012) and *Robert Smithson. Art in Continual Movement* (Amsterdam, 2012). Her current research interests revolve around the recent developments in higher art education (the function of the arts and humanities in a period of utilitarian educational regimes under the influence of post-Fordism), research methodologies in/through art and education philosophy.

Katy Deepwell is Professor of Contemporary Art, Theory and Criticism at Middlesex University. She is an art critic and writes art history and art criticism about twentieth- and twenty-first-century art with a specialism in feminist art criticism and theory about contemporary women artists. She has been teaching in higher education since 1986, including academic posts, as: Head of Research Training and Reader in Contemporary Art, Theory and Criticism, University of the Arts, London (2004–2010); Research Fellow in Art and Design Department at University of Ulster, Belfast (1999–2002); In addition, she has taught at many other colleges and Universities including: Goldsmiths College, University of London; University of Copenhagen; Farnham (now UCCA); Canterbury and Maidstone (once KIAD, now UCCA).

She was a Leverhulme Research Fellow in 2008–2009. She is the founder and editor of *n.paradoxa*: international feminist art journal (started in 1998). She has a PhD in Art History from Birkbeck College, University of London.

Iris Dressler (*1966) studied art history, philosophy, and literary studies in Marburg and Bochum. In 1996 she founded the Hartware MedienKunstVerein in Dortmund together with Hans D. Christ, which they codirected until 2004. Additionally, from 2002 to 2004, she worked as curator at the Museum am Ostwall in Dortmund. Since 2005, she and Hans D. Christ have shared directorship of the Württembergischer Kunstverein in Stuttgart. Since 2013, she has been a lecturer at the Stuttgart State Academy of Art and Design. In 2013 Dressler was co-curator of the Werkleitz-Festival in Halle. She has published articles on artists such as Stan Douglas, Antoni Muntadas, Daniel García Andújar, Teresa Hubbard and Alexander Birchler, Marco Poloni, José Perez Ocaña, and Jenny Holzer, as well as on a range of other subjects, including: curatorial and institutional practices; the conceptualisms of the South and the East; body politics; the politics and poetics of the voice; or museum and musealization.

Sonja Eismann (*1973) is a writer and cultural critic living in Berlin. She is one of the founders of *Missy Magazine* and the author and editor of several books, including *Hot Topic. Popfeminismus heute* (2007), *absolute Fashion* (2012) and *ShePOP. Frauen.Macht. Musik* (2013). She teaches and researches in the fields of contemporary feminist discourses and activism, the representations of gender in popular culture and fashion theory.

John Ellingsworth is a writer and editor with a heavy contemporary circus specialism. He founded the website Sideshow as a platform for writing and research on circus art and as a space to experiment with multimedia and data journalism. Through another organization, CRKO, he is also designing an online course teaching contemporary circus aesthetics. Somewhere in 2015, all being well, he will publish *Enough Rope*, a book of avant-garde strategies for corde lisse creation.

Pascal Gielen (*1970) is director of the research centre Arts in Society at Groningen University where he is full Professor for Sociology of Art. Gielen is editor-in-chief of the book series 'Arts in Society' (Fontys School of Fine and Performing Arts,

Tilburg & Groningen University) and has written several books on contemporary art, cultural heritage and cultural politics, including *Being an Artist in Post-Fordist Times* (2009, NAi Publishers), *The Murmuring of the Artistic Multitude. Global Art, Memory and Post-Fordism* (2009, 2010 and 2015, Valiz), *Teaching Art in the Neoliberal Realm. Realism versus Cynicism* (2013, Valiz), *Creativity and other Fundamentalisms* (2013, Mondriaan Fund), *Institutional Attitudes. Instituting Art in a Flat World* (2013, Valiz), *The Ethics of Art* (2014, Valiz), and *Aesthetic Justice* (2014, Valiz). His books have been tranlated into English, Korean, Russian, Spanish and Turkish. His research focuses on cultural politics and the institutional contexts of the arts.

Daniel Marcellus Givens is a Chicago-born, New York-based sound/visual artist, writer, poet, DJ, performer and record/book buyer for Other Music. His subject matter comments on the cross section of race, gender, sexuality, and class in the African diaspora and its interaction with the world at large. He has released several albums for the Aesthetics label, including his debut, *Age*, which won best album of 2000 from Italy's *Blow Up* magazine. He has toured Europe several times, most recently performing with Danish band Efterklang and the Sonderjyllands Symfoniorkester and has collaborated with members of the A.A.C.M. & Black Rock Coalition, various choreo-graphers, and artists. He wrote, directed, and starred in the full-length musical play *First Dark Drama* which premiered at Richard Foreman's Ontological Theater. He currently lives in Harlem.

Max Jorge Hinderer Cruz is a writer and editor based in São Paulo. He is the author of the book *Hélio Oiticica and Neville D'Almeida. Block-Experiments in Cosmococa – Program in Process* (Afterall Books, London/MIT Press, Cambridge MA, 2013 – in co-authorship with Sabeth Buchmann). His recent work as an editor or co-editor includes the posthumous edition of Tim Stüttgen's *IN A QU*A*RE TIME AND PLACE. Post-Slavery Temporalities, Blaxploitation, and Sun Ra's Afrofuturism between Intersectionality and Heterogeneity* (B_Books Berlin / Autonomedia New York, 2014 – with the Tim Stüttgen Archiv); and the essay collection *Art and the Critique of Ideology After 1989* (Verlag der Buchhandlung Walther König, Cologne/Kunsthaus Bregenz, 2014 – co-edited with Eva Birkenstock, Jens Kastner, and Ruth

Sonderegger). From 2008–2011, together with Alice Creischer and Andreas Siekmann, he was curator and editor of the publication and exhibition project *The Potosí Principle/Principio Potosí*, presented at Museo Nacional Centro de Arte Reina Sofia Madrid, Haus der Kulturen der Welt in Berlin, and Museo Nacional de Arte and MUSEF in La Paz, Bolivia. Since 2014, together with Suely Rolnik, Amilcar Packer and Pedro Cesarino, he is programme coordinator of P.A.C.A. (Programme for Autonomous Cultural Action, São Paulo).

Christian Höller is editor of *springerin – Hefte für Gegenwartskunst* (www.springerin.at) and has written extensively on art and cultural theory. Between 2002 and 2007, he was Visiting Professor at the École supérieure des beaux-arts in Geneva. He curated the film programmes *Pop Unlimited?* (2000) and *No Wave New York 1976–84* (2010) at the International Short Film Festival Oberhausen; co-curator of the exhibition *Hauntings – Ghost Box Media* (Medienturm Graz) and the accompanying concert series *Sonic Spectres*; most recently, curator of the film series *Scan Scroll Surf – Digital Film Aesthetics Today* (mumok, Vienna, 2014). He edited the anthologies *Pop Unlimited?* (Turia + Kant, Vienna, 2001), *Techno-Visionen* (Folio, Vienna/Bolzano, 2005; co-editor), the catalogue *Hans Weigand* (Walther König, Cologne, 2005), and *L'Internationale. Post-War Avant-Gardes Between 1957 and 1986* (JRP | Ringier, Zurich, 2012). His volume of interviews *Time Action Vision. Conversations in Cultural Studies, Theory, and Activism* was published by JRP | Ringier, Zurich/Les presses du réel, Dijon in 2010.

Ines Kleesattel studied philosophy and fine arts and is currently finishing her PhD at the Academy of Fine Arts Vienna with a comparative thesis on Theodor W. Adorno and Jacques Rancière. She teaches art theory in Vienna and Zurich. As an art critic she writes in *Texte zur Kunst* and *springerin*. In 2011 she received the Austrian 'Junior Art Critics Award'.

Vida Knežević (*1980) is an art historian, curator, cultural worker, and member of Kontekst Collective. Currently she is taking a doctoral studies course at the Department of Art and Media Theory of the University of Arts in Belgrade. She was co-founder of the Kontekst Gallery in Belgrade 2006–2010, and is a member of AICA (Association

Internationale des Critiques d'Art) section in Serbia. In her research, she is dealing with the relations between cultural production, politics and activism. www.kontekst.rs

Thijs Lijster (*1981) studied philosophy at the University of Groningen and the New School for Social Research in New York. In 2012 he received his PhD in philosophy (*cum laude*) at the University of Groningen, for a dissertation on Walter Benjamin's and Theodor W. Adorno's concepts of art criticism. Currently he is a researcher and coordinator of the research centre Arts in Society at the same university. He lectured on philosophy of art and culture at the Faculties of Philosophy and Arts of the University of Groningen, and the Faculty of Humanities of the University of Amsterdam. In 2009, he received the ABG/VN Essay prize and in 2010 the Dutch/Flemish Prize for Young Art Criticism and in 2015 the Boekman dissertation award. He contributed to books such as *Conceptions of Critique in Modern and Contemporary Philosophy* (eds. De Boer and Sonderegger), *Institutional Attitudes* and *No Culture, No Europe* (ed. Gielen) and was co-editor of *De Nieuwe Duitse Filosofie* (The New German Philosophy, 2013) and *De Kunst van Kritiek* (The Art of Critique, 2015).

Ivana Marjanović (*1979) is an art historian, cultural studies researcher, author, curator and cultural producer in the field of contemporary arts and theory; co-founder of the Kontekst Gallery in Belgrade, member of Kontekst Collective and AICA (Association Internationale des Critiques d'Art) section in Serbia. Since 2006, she lives in Vienna. Currently she is working on collective performance project *Pfusch Baustelle* http://pfuschbaustelleproject.wordpress.com/.

Suzana Milevska is a theorist and curator of visual art and culture from Macedonia. Currently she is Endowed Professor for Central and South European Art Histories at the Academy of Fine Arts in Vienna. Her theoretical and curatorial interests include postcolonial critique of hegemonic regimes of representation, feminist art and gender theory, participatory and collaborative art practices. She has a PhD in visual cultures from Goldsmiths College London where she also taught from 2002–2004. In 2004 Milevska was a Fulbright Senior Research Scholar at the Library of Congress. In 2010 Milevska published the book *Gender Difference in the Balkans*

(Saarbrücken: VDM Verlag, 2010). She was a researcher for the project *Call the Witness – Roma Pavilion* at the 54 International Art Exhibition (Venice Biennale) Collateral Event (2011) and curated the exhibition *Call the Witness,* BAK, Utrecht, and the *Roma Protocol* at the Austrian Parliament. In 2012 Milevska was awarded the Igor Zabel Award for Culture and Theory.

Dan Perjovschi is an artist from Romania. He was born in Sibiu, Romania, in 1961 and he lives and works in Bucharest. He first introduced his unique critical drawings as commentaries on contemporary politics in daily newspapers in Romania as a cartoonist. Later he transformed the walls of many international museums and galleries into spaces for criticism with his humorous but critical comments on the art world. His solo exhibitions include *What Happened to US?*, Museum of Modern Art, New York (2007); *I Am Not Exotic I Am Exhausted*, Kunsthalle, Basel (2007); *The Room Drawing*, Tate Modern, London (2006); and *Naked Drawings*, Ludwig Museum, Cologne (2005). He has exhibited in such group shows as the Sydney Biennial (2008); *The Magellanic Cloud*, Centre Georges Pompidou, Paris (2007); and the 52nd Venice Biennial (2007). He was awarded the George Maciunas Prize in 2004.

Jorinde Seijdel is an independent writer, editor, lecturer and art theorist on subjects that are concerned with the topic of art and media in the developing society and its public sphere. She is editor-in-chief of Open! Platform for Art, Culture & the Public Domain (www.onlineopen.org) and teaches at Gerrit Rietveld Academie in Amsterdam and the Dutch Art Institute (MFA ArtEZ) in Arnhem.

Ruth Sonderegger (*1967) is Professor of Philosophy and Aesthetic Theory at the Academy of Fine Arts Vienna. Publications include: *Für eine Ästhetik des Spiels. Hermeneutik, Dekonstruktion und der Eigensinn der Kunst*, Frankfurt am Main 2000; co-editor (with Diedrich Diederichsen et al.) of *Golden Years: Queere Subkultur zwischen 1959 und 1974*, Graz 2006; co-editor (with Karin de Boer) of *Conceptions of Critique in Modern and Contemporary Philosophy*, Houndmills Basingstoke 2011; co-editor (with Eva Birkenstock, Max Jorge Hinderer Cruz, Jens Kastner) of *Art and the Critique of Ideology. After 1989*, Bregenz/ Cologne 2013; co-editor (with Jens Kastner) of *Pierre*

Bourdieu und Jacques Rancière. Emanzipatorische Praxis denken, Wien 2014.

Terre Thaemlitz (*1968) is an award-winning multi-media producer, writer, public speaker, educator, audio remixer, DJ and owner of the Comatonse Recordings record label. Her work combines a critical look at identity politics – including gender, sexuality, class, linguistics, ethnicity and race – with an ongoing analysis of the socio-economics of commercial media production. He has released over 15 solo albums, as well as numerous 12-inch singles and video works. Her writings on music and culture have been published internationally in a number of books, academic journals and magazines.
As a speaker and educator on issues of non-essentialist Transgenderism and Queerness, Thaemlitz has lectured and participated in panel discussions throughout Europe and Japan. As of January, 2001, he resides in Kawasaki, Japan.
www.comatonse.com/thaemlitz/

Niels Van Tomme (*1977) is a New York-based curator, researcher, and critic working on the intersections of contemporary culture, politics, and aesthetics. Currently associated with the Center for Art, Design and Visual Culture at UMBC in Baltimore, he is the appointed curator of the 7th Bucharest Biennale, 2016. His exhibitions and public programmes are shown at venues such as The Kitchen (New York), National Gallery of Art (Washington, DC), Contemporary Arts Center (New Orleans), Gallery 400 (Chicago), and Akademie der Künste (Berlin). A Contributing Editor of Art Papers, Van Tomme publishes internationally in journals, magazines, and exhibition catalogues. His books include *Where Do We Migrate To?* (2011), *Visibility Machines: Harun Farocki and Trevor Paglen* (2014), and, most recently, *Aesthetic Justice* (2015), co-edited with Pascal Gielen.

Index

A

Adorno, Theodor W. 30, 36, 153, 155, 156, 177
Agamben, Giorgio 135, 138, 149
Althusser, Louis 57
Andújar, Daniel G. 143
Assange, Julian 200, 201
Atkinsons, Dennis 238
Attali, Jacques 212
Auer, Elke 72
Augé, Marc 29
Aupetitallot, Yves 247, 248

B

Badiou, Alain 157
Baratta, Karl 149
Baudelaire, Charles 26, 38
Baudrillard, Jean 30
Bauman, Zygmunt 16, 28, 29, 100
Belić, Goca 72
Benjamin, Walter 12, 19, 26–28, 32, 36, 38, 58, 61, 63, 153, 155, 177
Bergen Triennial 130
Berger, John 38
Biesta, Gert 238
Biscotti, Rossella 166
Bishop, Claire 240, 247, 248
Blazwick, Iwona 248
Boltanski, Luc 16, 112–115, 134, 157, 162, 166
Bourdieu, Pierre 112, 113, 115
Bourriaud, Nicolas 33, 36
Bovenschen, Silvia 166
Braidotti, Rosi 204
Brand, Stewart 196
Brandenburger, Elfe 153
Buchloh, Benjamin 34
Buchmann, Sabeth 17, 152
Bunz, Mercedes 196–198, 202
Burchill, Julie 152
Bürger, Peter 234–237
Butler, Judith 162

C

Cameron, David 97
Carp, Stefanie 149
Carter Hotel, New York 214
Centar za Kulturu, Stari grad 55
Centre Pompidou, Paris 122
Certeau, Michel de 39, 40
Chiapello, Ève 113, 114, 134, 166
Christ, Hans D. 16, 17
Christov-Bakargiev, Carolyn 242, 248
City Shopping Mall (GTC), Skopje 179
Clair, Jean 124
Clement, Hal 108
Club Module, Tokyo 224
Collins, Wilkie 122
Columbus, Christopher 46
Commandeur, Ingrid 18
Copernicus, Nicolaus 46
Critical Art Ensemble collective 196
Cvejić, Bojana 68

D

Damian, Diana 89
Danto, Arthur 233
Dath, Dietmar 161
Dean, Jodi 200
Deepwell, Katy 17, 172
Degot, Ekaterina 149
Diederichsen, Diedrich 152
Doderer, Yvonne P. 143
Draxler, Helmut 157, 158, 162
Drechsler, Clara 152
Dressler, Iris 16, 17

E

Egermann, Eva 72
Eiblmayr, Silvia 178
Eismann, Sonja 17
Eliot, T.S. 41
Elkins, James 209, 247
Ellingsworth, John 15
Enwezor, Okwui 69, 70
Esquerre, Arnaud 114, 122

F

Federici, Silvia 71, 166, 180
Fell, Mark 229
Fire Department Museum, Stuttgart 140
Fisher, Mark 36, 37
Foucault, Michel 38, 130–133, 135, 137, 146, 164, 198, 199, 201, 202
Fraser, Andrea 158
Freudmann, Eduard 72

G

Garcés, Marina 64
Geene, Stephan 153
Germer, Stephan 159
Giacometti, Alberto 119
Giacometti Foundation, Paris 122
Gielen, Pascal 14
Gilbert, Jeremy 16, 100-102, 105
Givens, David 18
Goethe, Johann Wolfgang von 26
Gramsci, Antonio 16, 63, 64, 68, 97–99, 102
Graw, Isabella 159
Grenier, Catherine 122

Grlja, Dušan 59
Groys, Boris 32, 117, 200, 204
Guys, Constantin 38

H
Habermas, Jürgen 27, 34, 196
Hall, Stuart 16, 96–98, 101, 102, 107
Haring, Keith 221
Harvard University, Cambridge MA 89
Harvey, David 27–29
Hillaert, Wouter 248
Hinderer Cruz, Max Jorge 15
Hirst, Damien 37
Hobbes, Thomas 101
Holert, Tom 157, 158, 161
Höller, Christian 16
Hoskoté, Ranjit 137
Houston, Whitney 213
Huysmans, Joris-Karl 26
Huyssen, Andreas 30

I
In Between Time festival 89

J
Jameson, Fredric 30, 37, 38

K
Kauffmann, Robert Lane 177
Khan Academy 84, 89
Kleesattel, Ines 17
Klein, Yves 125
Knežević, Vida 15, 66, 67, 71, 72
Koether, Jutta 152
Kontekst, Belgrade 15, 54–56, 59, 61, 65–67
Koolhaas, Rem 29, 30
Koons, Jeff 37
Köperl, Stephan 143
Kremer, Mark 241
Kujačić, Mirko 61, 62
Kuzma, Marta 232, 234, 243, 247

L
Lash, Scott 201, 202
Levine, David 33, 35
Lewis, Ben 37
Lijster, Thijs 14, 27
Lind, Maria 178
Lippard, Lucy 178, 189
Lonzi, Carla 189, 190
Lyotard, Jean-François 157

M
Madonna 213
Madžoski, Vesna 71
Magid, Jill 204
Manning, Bradley 201
Marchart, Oliver 66
Marcuse, Herbert 58, 59
Marjanović, Ivana 15, 67, 72
Marx, Karl 57, 71, 125
Matta-Clark, Gordon 248
Mau, Bruce 29
McLuhan, Marshall 27, 28, 31
Melián, Michaela 166
Metahaven 204
Michaux, Henri 120
Middlesex University, London 183
Milevska, Suzana 17
Minh-ha, Trinh T. 131, 146
Minimal Club 153
MIT, Cambridge MA 89
Munder, Heike 33
Muntadas, Antoni 138
Museum of Contemporary Art (MuHKA), Antwerp 248
Museum of Contemporary Art Vojvodina, Novi Sad 65
Museum of Modern Art (MoMA), New York 184
Museum of the City, Skopje 180

N
Nicklin, Hannah 89
Noack, Ruth 178

O
O'Neill, Paul 242
O'Shea, Alan 16, 96–98, 101, 102, 107
October Salon, Belgrade 56, 60
Opera, Stuttgart 140
Oppermann, Anna 138, 145–147
Osborne, Peter 164

P
Paglen, Trevor 204
Parobrod, Ustanoa kultur, Belgrade 56
Paterson, Mary 89
Pees, Matthias 149
Pejic, Bojana 178
Perjovschi, Dan 17, 143
Picasso, Pablo 221
Piškur, Bojana 62, 68
Plato 165
Popovski, Živko 179
Prelom Collective 58, 68
Proust, Marcel 123
Pureber, Tjaša 62

R

Radić, Jelena 72
Radical Education Collective, Ljubljana 62, 73
Rancière, Jacques 134–136, 146, 149, 155
Raunig, Gerald 63, 64
Reed, Lou 94
Renoir, Pierre-Auguste 120
Resler, Oliver 70
Riff, David 149
Roelstraete, Dieter 247
Rogoff, Irit 18, 33, 195, 198, 201, 202, 233, 234, 236–239, 243
Romero, Pedro G. 132
Rosa, Hartmut 28
Roundhouse, London 81
RUK group 66
Rule, Alix 33, 35
Ruskin, John 26
Ružičić, Milica 72

S

Sally's II 214, 226
Sartre, Jean-Paul 116
Savić, Maja 72
Saxenhuber, Hewdig 149
Schlegel, Friedrich 153, 156, 235
Schöllhammer, Georg 149
Schulman, Sarah 166
Schuppli, Susan 204
Sei, Keiko 143
Seijdel, Jorinde 18, 241, 242
Shedhalle, Zürich 166
Sheikh, Simon 133
Smith, Valerie 248
Snowden, Edward 196, 199, 201
Snyder, Sean 204
Sonderegger, Ruth 17
Sontag, Susan 38
Soulages Museum, Rodez 122
SPILL Festival 89
Spivak, Gaytri Chakravorty 180
Staël, Madame de 26
Stansfield, Lisa 213
State School of the Arts, Stuttgart 140
Stendhal (Marie-Henri Beyle) 26
Straganz, Esther 72
Student Cultural Center (SKC), Belgrade 71
Summer, Donna 211
Suntag, Noh 143
Susen, Simon 115
Šuvaković, Miško 54, 71

T

Thaemlitz, Terre 18, 208, 209
Thévenot, Laurent 113, 115, 117
Thiele, Kathrin 197, 198, 201, 202
Tom Tom Club 221
Tucker, Marcia 178

U

UB40 223
Ultra-red collective 212, 219, 220, 229

V

Van Tomme, Niels 18
Vesić, Jelena 59
Virilio, Paul 28
Vogl, Joseph 146
Vorkoeper, Ute 146, 148
Vuković, Steven 61, 67

W

White, Cynthia 118
White, Harrison 118
Wieger, Julia 72
Wiener Festwochen festival 130
Wilson, Mick 242
Winkler, Sylvia 143
Wittmann, Mano 153
Wuggenig, Ulf 33
Württembergischer Kunstverein, Stuttgart 16, 130, 133, 135, 141

Y

Yuval-Davis, Nira 180

Z

Zegher, Catherine de 178

Colophon

Colophon

Spaces for Criticism
Shifts in Contemporary Art Discourses

Editors
Thijs Lijster
Suzana Milevska
Pascal Gielen
Ruth Sonderegger

Contributors
Luc Boltanski
Sabeth Buchmann
Robin Celikates
Hans D. Christ
Ingrid Commandeur
Katy Deepwell
Iris Dressler
Sonja Eismann
John Ellingsworth
Pascal Gielen
Daniel Givens
Max Jorge Hinderer Cruz
Christian Höller
Ines Kleesattel
Vida Knežević
Thijs Lijster
Ivana Marjanović
Suzana Milevska
Dan Perjovschi
Jorinde Seijdel
Ruth Sonderegger
Terre Thaemlitz
Niels Van Tomme

Antennae Series N° 19
by Valiz, Amsterdam

Part of the Series
'Arts *in* Society"

Translation Dutch-English
Leo Reijnen

Copy editing
Leo Reijnen

Literature and Proof Check
Els Brinkman

Index
Elke Stevens

Design
Metahaven

Paper inside
Munken Print 100 gr 1.5
Paper cover
Bioset 240 gr

Printing and binding
Ten Brink, Meppel

Publisher
Valiz, Amsterdam, 2015
www.valiz.nl

ISBN 978-90-78088-75-2

This publication was made possible through the generous support of

Mondriaan Fund
www.mondriaanfonds.nl

University of Groningen
www.rug.nl

Distribution:
USA /Canada/Latin America: D.A.P., www.artbook.com
GB/IE: Anagram Books, www.anagrambooks.com
NL/BE/LU: Coen Sligting, www.coensligtingbookimport.nl
Europe/Asia/Australia: Idea Books, www.ideabooks.nl

ISBN 978-90-78088-75-2
NUR 651

Printed and bound in the Netherlands

Antennae

Antennae Series

Antennae N° 1
The Fall of the Studio
Artists at Work
edited by Wouter Davidts & Kim Paice
Amsterdam: Valiz, 2009 (2nd ed.: 2010),
ISBN 978-90-78088-29-5

Antennae N° 2
Take Place
Photography and Place from Multiple Perspectives
edited by Helen Westgeest
Amsterdam: Valiz, 2009,
ISBN 978-90-78088-35-6

Antennae N° 3
The Murmuring of the Artistic Multitude
Global Art, Memory and Post-Fordism
Pascal Gielen (author)
Arts *in* Society
Amsterdam: Valiz, 2009 (2nd ed.: 2011),
ISBN 978-90-78088-34-9

Antennae N° 4
Locating the Producers
Durational Approaches to Public Art
edited by Paul O'Neill & Claire Doherty
Amsterdam: Valiz, 2011,
ISBN 978-90-78088-51-6

Antennae N° 5
Community Art
The Politics of Trespassing
edited by Paul De Bruyne & Pascal Gielen
Arts *in* Society
Amsterdam: Valiz, 2011 (2nd ed.: 2013),
ISBN 978-90-78088-50-9

Antennae N° 6
See it Again, Say it Again
The Artist as Researcher
edited by Janneke Wesseling
Amsterdam: Valiz, 2011,
ISBN 978-90-78088-53-0

Antennae N° 7
Teaching Art in the Neoliberal Realm
Realism versus Cynicism
edited by Pascal Gielen & Paul De Bruyne
Arts *in* Society
Amsterdam: Valiz, 2012 (2nd ed.: 2013),
ISBN 978-90-78088-57-8

Antennae N° 8
Institutional Attitudes
Instituting Art in a Flat World
edited by Pascal Gielen
Arts *in* Society
Amsterdam: Valiz, 2013,
ISBN 978-90-78088-68-4

Antennae N° 9
Dread
The Dizziness of Freedom
edited by Juha van 't Zelfde
Amsterdam: Valiz, 2013,
ISBN 978-90-78088-81-3

Antennae N° 10
Participation Is Risky
Approaches to Joint Creative Processes
edited by Liesbeth Huybrechts
Amsterdam: Valiz, 2014,
ISBN 978-90-78088-77-6

Antennae N° 11
The Ethics of Art
Ecological Turns in the Performing Arts
edited by Guy Cools & Pascal Gielen
Arts *in* Society
Amsterdam: Valiz, 2014,
ISBN 978-90-78088-87-5

Antennae N° 12
Alternative Mainstream
Making Choices in Pop Music
Gert Keunen (author)
Arts *in* Society
Amsterdam: Valiz, 2014,
ISBN 978-90-78088-95-0

Antennae N° 13
The Murmuring of the Artistic Multitude
Global Art, Politics and Post-Fordism
Pascal Gielen (author)
Completely revised and enlarged edition of Antennae N° 3
Arts *in* Society
Amsterdam: Valiz, 2015,
ISBN 978-94-92095-04-6

Antennae N° 14
Aesthetic Justice
Intersecting Artistic and Moral Perspectives
edited by Pascal Gielen & Niels Van Tomme
Arts *in* Society
Amsterdam: Valiz, 2015,
ISBN 978-90-78088-86-8

Antennae N° 15
No Culture, No Europe
On the Foundation of Politics
edited by Pascal Gielen
Arts *in* Society
Amsterdam: Valiz, 2015,
ISBN 978-94-92095-03-9

Antennae N° 16
Arts Education Beyond Art
Teaching Art in Times of Change
edited by Pascal Gielen &
Barend van Heusden
Arts *in* Society
Amsterdam: Valiz, 2015,
ISBN 978-90-78088-85-1

Antennae N° 17
Mobile Autonomy
Exercises in Artists' Self-Organization
edited by Nico Dockx &
Pascal Gielen
Arts *in* Society
Amsterdam: Valiz, 2015,
ISBN 978-94-92095-10-7

Antennae N° 18
Moving Together
Theorizing and Making
Contemporary Dance
Rudi Laermans (author)
Arts *in* Society
Amsterdam: Valiz, 2015.
ISBN 978-90-78088-52-3